Building Mobile Applications with Python

A Step-by-Step Guide with Coding Examples

PART I

By

Dr. Hesham Mohamed Elsherif

Dr. Salwa Elmeawad

ABOUT THE AUTHOR

Dr. Hesham Mohamed Elsherif stands at the forefront of library management, research, and technology, with an outstanding 25-year career in the programming field, working with multiple programming languages, including AI languages like Natural Language Processing (NLP). Boasting an impressive 22-year tenure in library management and research, Dr. Elsherif holds dual doctoral degrees in Management and Organizational Leadership, and Information Systems and Technology. This unique blend of expertise equips him with a comprehensive understanding of both the managerial and technical aspects of his work.

An expert in Empirical research methodology, particularly in the Qualitative approach and Action research, Dr. Elsherif has not only advanced his research endeavors but has also contributed invaluable insights and innovations in these areas. His extensive experience in programming further enhances his ability to approach problems with a robust, multifaceted perspective.

Over the years, Dr. Elsherif has made significant contributions to academia, not only as a professional researcher but also as an Adjunct Professor. His dual role in education has solidified his reputation as a thought leader and pioneer. His expertise extends globally, serving as a consultant to numerous educational institutions, where he shares best practices, innovative strategies, and deep insights into the ever-evolving fields of management, technology, and programming.

Combining a passion for education with unparalleled depth in programming and AI, Dr. Elsherif continues to inspire, educate, and lead in the library, technology, and academic communities.

ABOUT THE CONTRIBUTOR

Dr. Salwa Elmeawad stands out as a luminary in both the academic and community service spheres. With an illustrious career at the helm of adult services manager at Queens Library, she has profoundly impacted the field of information access and literacy. Dr. Elmeawad's educational journey is marked by not one, but two doctoral degrees, showcasing her dedication to lifelong learning and expertise in both organizational leadership and information systems and technology.

Her commitment extends beyond the academic realm into spirited community service. As the Distinguished Lieutenant Governor for the Kiwanis Queens East Division, Dr. Elmeawad plays a pivotal role in steering community-focused initiatives and fostering a spirit of service. Her role as a board member of the KPTC further exemplifies her dedication to impactful community work, particularly in areas of pediatric care and trauma prevention.

Dr. Elmeawad's passion for mentorship and youth development is evident through her involvement with the Benjamin Cardozo High School Key Club. As a lead mentor, coach, and advisor, she guides young minds in their personal and professional development, instilling in them the values of leadership and community service.

Her multifaceted expertise and unwavering commitment to both academic excellence and community service make Dr. Salwa Elmeawad a distinguished figure in her field and an inspiration to many.

PREFACE

Purpose and Objectives

"Building Mobile Applications with Python: A Step-by-Step Guide with Coding Examples" is designed to serve as a comprehensive resource for anyone looking to venture into mobile application development using Python. Whether you're an experienced Python developer eager to expand your skill set into mobile platforms or a novice developer seeking a structured guide to building your first mobile app, this book offers a clear, methodical approach to learning and mastering the necessary tools, concepts, and best practices.

Purpose: The primary purpose of this book is to bridge the gap between Python programming and mobile app development, making it accessible and manageable for developers of all skill levels. The book aims to:

1. **Demystify Mobile Development:** For many Python developers, the world of mobile development can seem daunting due to the complexities of native programming languages like Swift for iOS and Kotlin for Android. This book simplifies the process by focusing on Python-based frameworks that allow you to build mobile apps without needing to learn these platform-specific languages.

2. **Provide a Practical, Hands-On Learning Experience:** The book is structured around practical examples and step-by-step tutorials that guide you through the process of building functional mobile applications. Each chapter is designed to incrementally build your knowledge, ensuring you gain hands-on

experience as you progress from basic concepts to more advanced topics.

3. **Offer a Comprehensive Understanding of Python Mobile Frameworks:** Python offers several frameworks for mobile development, each with its strengths and use cases. This book explores these frameworks, with a focus on Kivy and BeeWare, helping you understand their features, advantages, and limitations so you can choose the right tool for your project.

4. **Equip You with the Skills to Build Real-World Applications:** By the end of this book, you will have the skills to design, develop, and deploy complete mobile applications. The projects in the latter part of the book are designed to simulate real-world scenarios, providing you with practical experience that can be directly applied to your own projects or professional work.

5. **Instill Best Practices and Industry Standards:** Beyond just coding, this book emphasizes the importance of following best practices in mobile app development. From UI/UX design principles to performance optimization, security considerations, and testing, you'll learn how to build applications that are not only functional but also efficient, secure, and user-friendly.

Objectives: To achieve its purpose, this book is structured around several key objectives:

1. **Comprehensive Introduction to Mobile Development with Python:** The book begins with an overview of the mobile app development landscape and

the role Python can play in it. It introduces you to the basic concepts, tools, and frameworks you'll need to get started.

2. **Step-by-Step Instructional Approach:** Each chapter is carefully crafted to build upon the previous one, guiding you from setting up your development environment to deploying your app in the app store. The instructional approach ensures that even complex topics are broken down into manageable steps, with clear explanations and illustrative examples.

3. **In-Depth Coverage of Core Concepts:** The book delves into essential mobile development topics such as UI design, state management, database integration, and navigation. These core concepts are crucial for building robust applications, and the book ensures you have a solid understanding of each.

4. **Practical Application Through Projects:** The inclusion of real-world projects is a key objective of the book. These projects are designed to reinforce the concepts you've learned by applying them in practical, hands-on scenarios. By working through these projects, you'll gain confidence in your ability to develop full-fledged mobile applications.

5. **Advanced Topics for Continued Learning:** For those looking to go beyond the basics, the book covers advanced topics such as performance optimization, security, machine learning integration, and augmented reality. These chapters are intended to push your skills further and expose you to cutting-edge technologies and techniques.

6. **Resources for Ongoing Development:** The book concludes with guidance on how to stay current with the ever-evolving field of mobile development. It provides recommendations for further reading, community engagement, and ways to continue honing your skills beyond the content of the book.

In summary, "Building Mobile Applications with Python" is not just a technical manual, but a comprehensive learning journey. It aims to equip you with the knowledge, skills, and confidence to create mobile applications from scratch using Python, while also providing the foundation for further exploration and professional growth in the field of mobile development.

Who Should Read This Book

"Building Mobile Applications with Python: A Step-by-Step Guide with Coding Examples" is crafted to cater to a wide audience, ranging from beginners in programming to seasoned developers looking to expand their expertise into mobile application development. The book is structured to ensure that readers at various skill levels can follow along, grasp the concepts, and apply the knowledge to build functional mobile apps. Below is an outline of the primary audiences who will benefit from this book:

1. Aspiring Mobile App Developers:

- **Beginners with Little to No Programming Experience:** If you're new to programming and interested in mobile app development, this book provides a gentle introduction to both Python and mobile development concepts. The step-by-step tutorials and clear explanations are designed to help you build your first mobile app from the ground up, with no prior experience required.

- **Intermediate Programmers:** If you have some experience in programming, particularly in Python or another language, this book will help you transition into mobile development. It covers the essentials and gradually introduces more complex topics, enabling you to leverage your existing knowledge while learning the nuances of mobile app creation.

2. Python Developers Seeking to Expand into Mobile Development:

- **Experienced Python Programmers:** If you are already proficient in Python and want to expand your skill set to include mobile application development, this book is an ideal resource. It focuses on using Python-specific frameworks like Kivy and BeeWare, allowing you to apply your Python knowledge in the mobile development domain without having to learn new languages like Swift or Kotlin.

- **Web Developers Interested in Mobile:** Python web developers who want to diversify their portfolio by adding mobile apps to their skill set will find this book particularly useful. The transition from web to mobile development is made easier by the book's focus on Python, a language you're already familiar with.

3. Cross-Platform Developers:

- **Developers Seeking a Cross-Platform Solution:** If you're interested in developing mobile apps that work across multiple platforms (Android, iOS, etc.) without having to write separate code for each platform, this book will be invaluable. It explores Python frameworks that support cross-platform development, enabling you to write once and deploy your app on multiple platforms with minimal changes.

4. Students and Educators:

- **Students Learning Mobile Development:** This book is an excellent resource for students in computer science or software engineering programs who are learning about mobile development. It provides a practical, hands-on approach to building mobile apps, making it a great supplement to theoretical coursework.

- **Educators Looking for a Teaching Resource:** Instructors teaching courses in mobile development or Python programming will find this book a comprehensive resource. The structured approach, clear examples, and real-world projects make it an ideal textbook or reference material for classroom use.

5. Hobbyists and Independent Developers:

- **Tech Enthusiasts and Hobbyists:** If you're a tech enthusiast or hobbyist with an interest in creating your own mobile applications, this book is perfect for you. Its practical focus allows you to quickly get up to speed with mobile development and start building your own apps, whether for personal use, to share with friends, or to publish on app stores.

- **Independent Developers and Freelancers:** For independent developers and freelancers looking to offer mobile development services to clients, this book serves as a practical guide to mastering Python-based mobile development. It covers the full lifecycle of mobile app creation, from design and development to deployment and optimization, providing you with the skills needed to deliver high-quality mobile solutions.

6. Professional Developers Transitioning to Mobile:

- **Developers from Other Domains:** If you're a developer with experience in other areas, such as desktop software or backend services, and are looking to move into mobile development, this book will help you make the transition. The book bridges the gap between traditional software development and mobile app creation, focusing on the unique challenges and opportunities presented by mobile platforms.

- **Mobile Developers Exploring Python:** If you're already a mobile developer familiar with languages like Java, Swift, or Kotlin but want to explore Python as a development tool, this book offers a comprehensive introduction. It demonstrates how Python can be effectively used to build mobile apps, offering an alternative approach that might align better with your development style or project requirements.

7. Technical Managers and Team Leads:

- **Technical Leads Overseeing Mobile Development Projects:** For technical managers or team leads who oversee mobile app development teams, this book provides a solid understanding of the tools and frameworks your team might be using. It can help you make informed decisions about technology stacks, understand the challenges your developers face, and contribute more effectively to project planning and execution.

- **Project Managers and Product Owners:** While this book is primarily technical, project managers and product owners involved in mobile app projects may also benefit from understanding the development process outlined here. It will give you a better grasp of what's involved in building mobile apps with Python, helping you to better manage timelines, resources, and expectations.

8. Entrepreneurs and Startups:

- **Entrepreneurs Building Mobile Solutions:** If you're an entrepreneur with an idea for a mobile app but don't have a technical background, this book can serve as a starting point. It will guide you through the basics of app development, allowing you to prototype your ideas and understand the development process, even if you ultimately hire a team to build the final product.

- **Startups Looking for Cost-Effective Development:** Startups often need to deliver mobile solutions quickly and efficiently. This book teaches you how to use Python to develop mobile apps with a faster learning curve and lower costs, making it ideal for small teams and limited budgets.

9. Anyone Interested in Learning Mobile Development with Python:

- **Curious Learners:** Finally, this book is for anyone with a curiosity about mobile development and a willingness to learn. Whether you want to explore a new hobby, develop an app idea, or simply expand your technical skills, this book is designed to make mobile development accessible and enjoyable.

In summary, "Building Mobile Applications with Python" is a versatile and comprehensive resource that caters to a broad audience, from complete beginners to seasoned developers. No matter your background or motivation, if you're interested in mobile app development using Python, this book will provide you with the knowledge and skills you need to succeed.

How to Use This Book

"Building Mobile Applications with Python: A Step-by-Step Guide with Coding Examples" is designed to be a flexible resource that you can tailor to your individual learning style, experience level, and project needs. Whether you are a complete beginner or a seasoned developer, the book is structured in a way that allows you to progress sequentially or skip to specific sections as needed. Here's a guide on how to make the most out of this book:

1. Sequential Reading for Comprehensive Learning:

- **Start from the Beginning:** If you are new to mobile development or Python, it is recommended that you start from Chapter 1 and work your way through the book in order. Each chapter builds on the previous one, gradually introducing you to more advanced concepts and techniques. This approach ensures that you develop a solid foundation before tackling more complex topics.

- **Complete the Exercises:** At the end of each chapter, you'll find exercises designed to reinforce what you've learned. These exercises vary from simple coding tasks to more comprehensive projects. Completing these exercises will help solidify your understanding and give you practical experience in applying the concepts discussed.

- **Review Key Takeaways:** Each chapter concludes with a summary of key points. Reviewing these takeaways is an excellent way to reinforce your learning and ensure that you have grasped the essential concepts before moving on to the next chapter.

2. Selective Reading for Targeted Learning:

- **Focus on Specific Frameworks:** If you are already familiar with Python and mobile development but are new to a particular framework like Kivy or BeeWare, you can jump directly to the chapters dedicated to those frameworks. This allows you to dive into the specifics of the tools you're most interested in without going through the entire book.

- **Use as a Reference Guide:** This book is designed to be a valuable reference even after you've completed the initial reading. If you encounter specific challenges or need to revisit certain concepts during your development process, you can refer back to the relevant chapters. The detailed Table of Contents and Index make it easy to locate the information you need.

- **Skip Non-Essential Chapters:** Depending on your background and goals, some chapters may be less relevant to you. For example, if you're not interested in advanced topics like machine learning or augmented reality, you can skip those sections and focus on the core material that aligns with your immediate needs.

3. Practical Application Through Projects:

- **Build Along with the Book:** The book includes several real-world projects that guide you through the process of building complete mobile applications. These projects are designed to apply the concepts and techniques discussed in earlier chapters in a practical, hands-on way. You can choose to build these projects as you progress through the book or revisit them after completing the foundational chapters.

- **Adapt Projects to Your Own Ideas:** As you work through the projects, consider how you can adapt the examples to your own app ideas. The code examples are meant to be flexible and modular, allowing you to modify and expand upon them to suit your specific goals.

4. Utilize Supplemental Resources:

- **Access the Sample Code Repository:** The book provides access to a repository where all code examples and project files are stored. Make sure to download and explore these resources as you work through the book. They serve as a valuable reference and can save you time by providing working code that you can modify and experiment with.

- **Engage with the Community:** The book encourages you to engage with the broader Python and mobile development communities. Whether through forums, online groups, or conferences, participating in discussions and sharing your progress can greatly enhance your learning experience. The book may also recommend specific communities or resources where you can connect with others who are following the same path.

5. Continuous Learning and Development:

- **Revisit Advanced Topics:** Once you've gained confidence in the basics, revisit the advanced chapters on topics like performance optimization, security, and integration of machine learning models. These chapters are designed to push your skills further and introduce you to cutting-edge techniques that can enhance your mobile applications.

- **Stay Updated:** Mobile development and Python are constantly evolving fields. Use the final chapters of the book, which provide guidance on staying updated with the latest trends, tools, and best practices. Regularly revisiting these sections will help you stay current and continue growing as a developer.

6. Collaborative Learning and Teaching:

- **Work with Peers or Study Groups:** If you're part of a study group or a team, consider using this book as a collective learning tool. Each member can focus on different sections or projects, and then share insights and challenges with the group. This collaborative approach can lead to deeper understanding and innovative solutions.

- **Use as a Teaching Resource:** For educators and mentors, this book can serve as a comprehensive teaching guide. The structured chapters, exercises, and projects are ideal for classroom settings or coding bootcamps. You can assign chapters as reading material, use the exercises as homework, and guide students through the projects in a hands-on lab setting.

7. Tailoring Your Learning Experience:

- **Set Your Own Pace:** Everyone learns at a different pace. This book is designed to accommodate that by allowing you to move through the material at a speed that suits you. Whether you're looking to quickly acquire a specific skill or take a more leisurely approach to mastering mobile development, the book's structure supports both fast and slow learning styles.

- **Customize Your Learning Path:** Based on your goals, you can customize your learning journey. For example, if you're primarily interested in building Android apps, focus on the sections most relevant to Android development. If your goal is to develop a cross-platform app, concentrate on the chapters that address cross-platform tools and techniques.

8. Preparing for Real-World Application:

- **Apply What You Learn to Real Projects:** As you progress through the book, start thinking about how you can apply what you've learned to real-world projects. Whether it's a personal project, a freelance job, or a contribution to an open-source initiative, applying your skills in real scenarios will reinforce your learning and help you build a portfolio.

- **Use the Book as a Career Resource:** Beyond just teaching you how to build mobile apps, this book can serve as a resource for career development. The knowledge and skills you gain here can open doors to new job opportunities, freelance work, or entrepreneurial ventures in the mobile app industry.

In summary, "Building Mobile Applications with Python" is more than just a textbook—it's a versatile guide designed to meet you where you are in your learning journey and help you reach your mobile development goals. Whether you choose to follow the book sequentially or dive into specific sections based on your needs, this resource is structured to support your growth as a Python developer and mobile app creator.

Conventions Used in This Book

To ensure clarity and consistency throughout "Building Mobile Applications with Python: A Step-by-Step Guide with Coding Examples," several conventions are employed to help you navigate the content, understand the examples, and implement the techniques effectively. These conventions cover everything from code formatting to the way information is presented in the text. Familiarizing yourself with these conventions will enhance your reading experience and help you get the most out of this book.

1. Text Formatting Conventions:

- **Bold Text:** Key terms, important concepts, and chapter titles are highlighted in **bold** to draw your attention to them. For instance, terms like **framework**, **API**, and **deployment** will be bolded when they are first introduced or when they are crucial to the understanding of the content.

- **Italicized Text:** Italics are used for emphasis and to denote book titles, URLs, or other sources. For example, references to external documentation or further reading might be presented as *Python Official Documentation*.

- **Monospaced Text:** Code-related elements, such as variable names, function names, file paths, and code snippets, are presented in a monospaced font to differentiate them from the regular text. For example, my_function() or /path/to/file will appear in a monospaced font.

2. Code Conventions:

- **Code Blocks:** All code examples in the book are presented in clearly delineated code blocks. These blocks are formatted to resemble actual code editors, making it easier for you to distinguish between regular text and code. Each block is intended to be copy-paste friendly, so you can easily try out the examples in your development environment.

```
def hello_world():
```

```
print("Hello, World!")
```

- **Syntax Highlighting:** Within code blocks, syntax highlighting is used to differentiate between various elements of the code, such as keywords, variables, strings, and comments. This helps you quickly identify different parts of the code and understand their roles.
- **Inline Code:** Short pieces of code or commands that are mentioned within the text are displayed in a monospaced font and are typically enclosed in backticks (). For example, pip install kivy` represents a command you would run in your terminal.
- **Comments in Code:** Comments within code examples are used to explain what the code does. These comments are prefixed by a # symbol and are intended to clarify complex sections or provide additional context.

```
def add_numbers(a, b):
    # This function adds two numbers and returns the result
    return a + b
```

3. Icons and Sidebars:

- **Notes:** Important information, tips, or additional context that can aid your understanding are placed in sidebars labeled as **Notes**. These are set apart from the main text to highlight useful insights or reminders that might not fit within the flow of the main discussion.

Note: Remember to always keep your Python and framework versions up to date to avoid compatibility issues.

- **Warnings:** Potential pitfalls, common errors, or important cautions are marked with a **Warning** icon. These are crucial to pay attention to, as they can help you avoid mistakes that could lead to bugs or other issues in your development process.

Warning: Be careful when handling user input to avoid security vulnerabilities such as SQL injection or cross-site scripting (XSS).

- **Tips:** Practical advice, shortcuts, or best practices that can make your development process smoother are presented as **Tips**. These are designed to enhance your efficiency and help you apply industry standards to your work.

Tip: Use virtual environments to manage dependencies for different projects. This prevents conflicts and keeps your development environment clean.

- **Exercises:** At the end of each chapter, you'll find **Exercises** designed to reinforce the concepts discussed. These exercises are formatted to clearly distinguish them from the main text and typically include a brief description of the task along with any necessary instructions.

4. Numbering and Bullet Points:

- **Numbered Lists:** When steps need to be followed in a specific order, they are presented in a numbered list. This is particularly useful for installation guides, configuration steps, or sequences in coding projects.

- **Bullet Points:** For lists that do not require a specific order, bullet points are used. These are often used to enumerate options, features, or components that can be addressed in any order.

5. Cross-References:

- **Internal References:** Throughout the book, you'll find references to other chapters or sections that are relevant to the current discussion. These are provided to help you deepen your understanding or revisit related concepts. For example, you might see a note like "For more details on setting up your development environment, see Chapter 2."

- **External References:** When external resources are mentioned, such as documentation, tools, or further reading, URLs are provided either directly in the text or in a footnote. These references are intended to complement the book's content and provide avenues for further exploration.

6. Examples and Real-World Projects:

- **Progressive Examples:** The book often builds upon earlier examples in later chapters. This progressive approach allows you to see how a simple application can be expanded with more features and complexity as you learn new concepts.

- **Project-Based Learning:** Real-world projects are presented in dedicated chapters, with clear objectives, step-by-step instructions, and comprehensive walkthroughs. Each project chapter is designed to be a mini-guide that you can follow from start to finish, resulting in a fully functional mobile application.

7. Language and Tone:

- **Clear and Concise:** The language used in this book is clear and concise, avoiding unnecessary jargon or overly complex explanations. The goal is to make even the most complex concepts accessible and easy to understand, regardless of your experience level.

- **Friendly and Encouraging:** The tone of the book is friendly and encouraging, aiming to support your learning journey. Whether you're tackling a challenging concept or working through an exercise, the book's tone is meant to motivate you to keep going and build your confidence as a developer.

By adhering to these conventions, "Building Mobile Applications with Python" ensures that the information is presented in a way that is easy to understand and apply. These conventions are intended to make the book not only a learning resource but also a practical guide that you can refer to again and again as you develop your mobile applications.

Happy Reading!

Dr. Hesham Mohamed Elsherif

Dr. Salwa Elmeawad

Table of Contents

Part I: Introduction to Mobile Development with Python

Chapter 1: Getting Started with Mobile App Development

Mobile app development has become an essential skill in today's technology-driven world, where smartphones and tablets are ubiquitous and apps play a crucial role in our daily lives. From social networking and gaming to productivity tools and e-commerce platforms, mobile applications are at the forefront of digital innovation.

What is Mobile App Development?

Mobile app development refers to the process of creating software applications that run on mobile devices such as smartphones, tablets, and wearable devices. These apps can be pre-installed on the device, downloaded from app stores, or accessed through a web browser.

Mobile apps are typically developed for specific platforms, the most popular being:

- **iOS (Apple's operating system for iPhone and iPad)**

- **Android (Google's operating system for smartphones and tablets)**

These platforms provide their own software development kits (SDKs), tools, and guidelines for app creation, which are usually based on specific programming languages like Swift for iOS and Kotlin for Android.

However, mobile development has evolved to support cross-platform solutions, where a single codebase can be used to create apps for multiple platforms. This is where Python comes into play, offering a way to develop mobile applications using a language that many developers are already familiar with.

The Evolution of Mobile App Development

The mobile development landscape has evolved significantly over the past decade. Initially, mobile apps were simple, single-purpose tools, often created by individual developers or small teams. Today, mobile applications are complex, feature-rich software solutions developed by large teams using advanced tools and frameworks.

This evolution has been driven by several factors:

- **Increased Processing Power:** Modern smartphones have become incredibly powerful, enabling the development of more sophisticated applications.

- **Advanced Operating Systems:** Both iOS and Android have introduced a wealth of features and APIs that developers can leverage to create rich user experiences.

- **User Expectations:** As mobile devices have become more integrated into everyday life, user expectations for app performance, design, and functionality have increased.

- **Cross-Platform Development:** The demand for apps that work seamlessly across multiple platforms has led to the rise of cross-platform development tools and frameworks.

Python, traditionally known for its simplicity and readability, has adapted to these trends, offering frameworks that enable developers to create mobile apps that meet modern standards.

Native vs. Cross-Platform Development

When starting with mobile app development, one of the first decisions you'll need to make is whether to develop your app natively for a specific platform or use a cross-platform approach.

Native Development:

- **Platform-Specific:** Native apps are developed for a particular operating system—either iOS or Android—using platform-specific programming languages (Swift for iOS, Kotlin for Android).

- **Optimized Performance:** Since native apps are built specifically for one platform, they can fully leverage the device's hardware and operating system features, resulting in optimized performance.

- **Rich User Experience:** Native development allows for the creation of user interfaces that adhere closely to the platform's design guidelines, providing a more integrated and seamless user experience.

Cross-Platform Development:

- **Single Codebase:** Cross-platform development allows you to write code once and deploy it across multiple platforms, saving time and effort.

- **Lower Development Costs:** By using a single codebase, you reduce the need for separate development teams for iOS and Android, leading to lower development costs.

- **Consistent User Experience:** Cross-platform tools strive to deliver a consistent user experience across different devices and operating systems.

Python excels in the cross-platform development space, allowing developers to build mobile applications that can run on both iOS and Android using frameworks like Kivy and BeeWare. This approach is particularly beneficial for developers who want to maximize their reach with a single app without compromising on quality.

Why Choose Python for Mobile Development?

Python is a powerful, high-level programming language known for its simplicity and readability. It has gained popularity across various domains, including web development, data science, machine learning, and, more recently, mobile development. Here are several reasons why Python is an excellent choice for mobile app development:

1. Readability and Simplicity:

- Python's syntax is clean and easy to understand, making it an ideal language for beginners and experienced developers alike. This simplicity reduces the learning curve and allows you to focus on the app's functionality rather than the intricacies of the language.

2. Versatility:

- Python is a versatile language that can be used for various aspects of app development, from backend server-side scripting to frontend user interfaces. This versatility makes it possible to build comprehensive applications using Python alone or in combination with other languages and tools.

3. Strong Community Support:

- Python has a vast and active community of developers who contribute to an extensive ecosystem of libraries, frameworks, and tools. This community-driven support ensures that you have access to the resources and help you need as you develop your mobile app.

4. Cross-Platform Frameworks:

- Python's cross-platform frameworks like Kivy and BeeWare enable you to write code that runs on multiple platforms, including iOS, Android, Windows, macOS, and Linux. These frameworks are designed to provide the necessary tools and libraries for building feature-rich, responsive mobile apps.

5. Integration with Other Technologies:

- Python integrates well with other technologies and languages, making it easy to incorporate web services, APIs, databases, and even machine learning models into your mobile app. This integration capability allows you to build sophisticated, data-driven applications.

6. Rapid Prototyping:

- Python's simplicity and the availability of powerful frameworks enable rapid prototyping, allowing you to quickly create and test app concepts. This agility is particularly useful in environments where time-to-market is crucial.

Introduction to Python-Based Mobile Frameworks

Python offers several frameworks specifically designed for mobile app development. In this book, we'll explore two of the most popular ones—Kivy and BeeWare—along with a brief overview of other notable frameworks.

Kivy:

- **Cross-Platform Compatibility:** Kivy is an open-source Python framework that supports the development of applications for iOS, Android, Windows, macOS, and Linux. It is particularly well-suited for creating multi-touch applications and offers a rich set of widgets for building custom user interfaces.

- **Focus on User Experience:** Kivy is designed with user experience in mind, offering tools for creating intuitive, responsive, and visually appealing applications. It uses its own graphics engine, which ensures that your app performs consistently across different devices.

- **Kv Language:** Kivy includes a declarative language called Kv, which simplifies the process of designing user interfaces by allowing you to separate the UI code from the application logic.

BeeWare:

- **Native User Interfaces:** BeeWare enables you to build native applications for multiple platforms using Python. It allows you to write your app in Python and deploy it as a native app on each platform, leveraging the platform's native UI toolkit.

- **Toga Framework:** BeeWare's core project is Toga, a widget toolkit that provides a native interface for building cross-platform applications. With Toga, you can create apps that look and feel native on each platform.

- **Briefcase:** BeeWare also offers Briefcase, a tool that packages your Python code into standalone applications that can be distributed to end-users.

Other Notable Frameworks:

- **PyQt/PySide:** These are Python bindings for the Qt application framework, which can be used to create cross-platform applications with native-looking interfaces.

- **PyMob:** A lightweight framework for mobile development with Python, particularly useful for building simple apps with basic functionality.

- **SL4A (Scripting Layer for Android):** An older but still useful tool for running Python scripts on Android devices.

Overview of Mobile App Development:

Mobile app development involves creating software applications that are designed to run on mobile devices such as smartphones and tablets. This field has rapidly evolved, with mobile apps becoming a cornerstone of digital interaction in various sectors, including social media, entertainment, productivity, and commerce.

1. Understanding the Mobile App Development Lifecycle

The mobile app development process typically follows a series of stages, each crucial to the successful deployment of an application. Understanding this lifecycle is essential, as it guides the development process from concept to launch and beyond.

Stages of Mobile App Development:

1. **Planning and Conceptualization:**

   - **Define the App Idea:** This involves identifying the purpose of the app, its target audience, and the core features it will offer.

   - **Market Research:** Analyze the market to understand the competition, user needs, and potential gaps your app can fill.

   - **Technical Feasibility:** Determine whether your app idea is technically feasible given your resources, including development tools, time, and budget.

2. **Design:**

   - **User Interface (UI) Design:** Focus on creating an intuitive and aesthetically pleasing interface that enhances user experience.

   - **User Experience (UX) Design:** Consider the flow of the app, ensuring it's easy to navigate and interacts with users smoothly.

- o **Wireframing:** Develop wireframes or mockups of the app's screens to visualize its layout and functionality.

3. **Development:**

    - o **Front-End Development:** Implement the app's UI, focusing on elements that users interact with directly.

    - o **Back-End Development:** Develop the server-side logic, database management, and integration with external services.

    - o **API Integration:** Connect your app to external services or backends through APIs, ensuring seamless data exchange.

4. **Testing:**

    - o **Unit Testing:** Test individual components or modules of the app to ensure they function correctly.

    - o **Integration Testing:** Verify that different parts of the app work together as expected.

    - o **User Acceptance Testing (UAT):** Gather feedback from actual users to ensure the app meets their needs and expectations.

5. **Deployment:**

    - o **App Store Submission:** Prepare your app for submission to platforms like the Apple App Store or Google Play Store.

- o **Version Control and Updates:** Manage versions of the app, addressing bugs, and releasing new features through updates.

6. **Maintenance and Support:**

- o **Monitoring:** Continuously monitor the app's performance using analytics and user feedback.

- o **Bug Fixes and Updates:** Regularly update the app to fix bugs, improve performance, and introduce new features.

- o **User Support:** Provide ongoing support to address user issues and inquiries.

2. Platforms for Mobile App Development

Mobile apps are typically developed for two primary platforms: **iOS** and **Android**. Each platform has its own set of tools, guidelines, and programming languages:

- **iOS:** The operating system for Apple devices (iPhone, iPad). Apps are traditionally developed using Swift or Objective-C and are distributed through the Apple App Store.

- **Android:** The operating system for a wide range of devices by various manufacturers. Apps are primarily developed using Kotlin or Java and are distributed through the Google Play Store.

Python, while not a native language for either platform, offers cross-platform frameworks that allow developers to create apps for both iOS and Android using a single codebase.

3. Introduction to Python in Mobile Development

Python is known for its simplicity, readability, and broad application across various domains, including web development, data science, and automation. In mobile app development, Python offers powerful frameworks that allow developers to build applications that can run on multiple platforms without needing to write separate code for each.

Popular Python Mobile Frameworks:

- **Kivy:** A popular open-source Python framework for developing multi-touch applications. Kivy supports iOS, Android, Windows, macOS, and Linux, making it an excellent choice for cross-platform development.

- **BeeWare:** Another Python framework that allows you to write apps in Python and deploy them across multiple platforms, including iOS, Android, and desktop environments. BeeWare provides a native look and feel on each platform, making your app seamless across devices.

Let's look at a basic example to illustrate how Python can be used for mobile development with Kivy.

4. Basic Example: A Simple "Hello, World!" App Using Kivy

To give you a taste of mobile development with Python, we'll create a simple "Hello, World!" application using Kivy. This example will introduce you to the basics of setting up a Python project for mobile development and give you a glimpse of how Kivy works.

Step 1: Set Up Your Development Environment

First, ensure you have Python installed on your system. You can download Python from the official Python website. Once Python is installed, you can install Kivy using pip, the Python package manager.

pip install kivy

Step 2: Write the Code for Your First App

Create a new Python file named main.py and add the following code:

import kivy

from kivy.app import App

from kivy.uix.label import Label

Define the main application class

class HelloWorldApp(App):

   def build(self):

      # Create a simple label widget with the text "Hello, World!"

      return Label(text="Hello, World!")

Run the app

if __name__ == '__main__':

   HelloWorldApp().run()

Explanation:

- **Import Kivy and its Modules:** We begin by importing Kivy and the necessary modules. App is the base class for creating Kivy applications, and Label is a widget used to display text.

- **Define the Main Application Class:** The HelloWorldApp class inherits from App. The build() method is where we define the UI elements of the app. In this case, it returns a Label widget with the text "Hello, World!".

- **Run the App:** The if __name__ == '__main__': block ensures that the app runs when the script is executed.

Step 3: Run the App

To run the app, simply execute the Python file:

python main.py

When you run this code, Kivy will open a window (on your desktop) displaying the text "Hello, World!" in the center. If you're developing on a mobile device, the same code would display "Hello, World!" on your phone's screen.

Step 4: Deploying to Mobile Devices

Once your app is ready, you can package it for mobile platforms:

- **For Android:** Use buildozer to compile your Kivy app into an APK, which can be installed on Android devices.

pip install buildozer

buildozer init

buildozer -v android debug

- **For iOS:** You would typically use Xcode along with a tool like PyBee (BeeWare's toolchain) to deploy your Kivy app to an iOS device.

5. Beyond "Hello, World!": Expanding Your App

Once you've successfully created a basic app, the next steps involve adding more functionality. This could include:

- **User Input:** Handling user input through text fields, buttons, or other interactive widgets.

- **Navigation:** Implementing navigation between different screens or views in your app.

- **Data Handling:** Storing and retrieving data locally or from a remote server.

As you progress through this book, you'll learn how to implement these and many more features, gradually building your skills in mobile app development with Python.

This overview has provided a foundational understanding of what mobile app development entails, the typical lifecycle of a mobile app, and how Python can be leveraged to create cross-platform applications. The "Hello, World!" example using Kivy serves as your first step into the world of Python mobile development. As you move forward, you'll build on this knowledge to create more complex and feature-rich applications, mastering the art of mobile development with Python.

Native vs. Cross-Platform Development:

When embarking on mobile app development, one of the fundamental decisions you'll need to make is whether to develop your app natively for a specific platform (such as iOS or Android) or to use a cross-platform approach that allows your app to run on multiple platforms with a single codebase. Each approach has its own set of advantages and trade-offs, and understanding these is crucial in determining the best path for your project.

1. Native Development

What is Native Development?

Native development involves building mobile applications using the programming languages and tools that are specific to a particular platform. For iOS, this typically means using **Swift** or **Objective-C** with **Xcode**, while for Android, it involves using **Kotlin** or **Java** with **Android Studio**.

Advantages of Native Development:

- **Performance:** Native apps are optimized for their respective platforms, providing the best possible performance. They can take full advantage of the device's hardware and operating system features.

- **Access to Platform-Specific Features:** Native development allows developers to utilize platform-specific APIs, which means you can access all the latest features offered by iOS or Android.

- **User Experience:** Native apps adhere to the platform's design guidelines, ensuring a consistent and familiar user esxperience. This can be crucial for user adoption and satisfaction.

Drawbacks of Native Development:

- **Multiple Codebases:** Developing for multiple platforms requires maintaining separate codebases for each, which increases development time, cost, and complexity.

- **Learning Curve:** Native development requires knowledge of platform-specific languages and tools, which may require additional learning for developers who are not familiar with them.

Example of Native Development:

Below is a basic example of a native "Hello, World!" app for both iOS and Android.

iOS Example in Swift:

This is a simple iOS app written in Swift that displays "Hello, World!" on the screen.

```swift
import UIKit


class ViewController: UIViewController {


    override func viewDidLoad() {
        super.viewDidLoad()


        // Create a label
        let label = UILabel()
```

```
        label.text = "Hello, World!"

        label.textAlignment = .center

        label.frame = view.bounds


        // Add the label to the view

        view.addSubview(label)

    }

}
```

In this example, UILabel is used to create a text label that displays "Hello, World!" in the center of the screen. The viewDidLoad() method is part of the UIViewController lifecycle and is called when the view is loaded into memory, making it the perfect place to set up your UI components.

Android Example in Kotlin:

This is a basic Android app written in Kotlin that displays "Hello, World!" on the screen.

```kotlin
package com.example.helloworld


import android.os.Bundle

import androidx.appcompat.app.AppCompatActivity

import android.widget.TextView
```

```kotlin
class MainActivity : AppCompatActivity() {

    override fun onCreate(savedInstanceState: Bundle?) {
        super.onCreate(savedInstanceState)
        setContentView(R.layout.activity_main)

        // Find the TextView by its ID and set the text
        val textView: TextView = findViewById(R.id.text_view)
        textView.text = "Hello, World!"

    }
}
```

In this Kotlin example, the TextView is used to display "Hello, World!" on the screen. The onCreate() method is where you typically initialize your activity and set up your UI components. The setContentView() method sets the layout resource, which contains the UI elements defined in XML.

2. Cross-Platform Development

What is Cross-Platform Development?

Cross-platform development allows you to create applications that run on multiple platforms (such as iOS and Android) from a single codebase. This is achieved through frameworks that provide the tools and libraries necessary to develop apps that work on various platforms with minimal platform-specific code.

Popular Cross-Platform Frameworks:

- **React Native:** Developed by Facebook, React Native allows you to build mobile apps using JavaScript and React. It provides near-native performance and a rich set of components for building UIs.

- **Flutter:** Developed by Google, Flutter uses the Dart language to create natively compiled applications for mobile, web, and desktop from a single codebase.

- **Xamarin:** Supported by Microsoft, Xamarin uses C# and .NET to build apps for Android, iOS, and Windows with a single codebase.

- **Python-Based Frameworks:** Kivy and BeeWare are popular Python frameworks that enable cross-platform development using Python.

Advantages of Cross-Platform Development:

- **Single Codebase:** Write your code once and deploy it across multiple platforms, significantly reducing development time and costs.

- **Faster Time to Market:** With a unified codebase, you can develop and deploy your app more quickly across different platforms.

- **Consistent User Experience:** Cross-platform frameworks aim to provide a consistent user experience across platforms, although there may be some limitations compared to native development.

Drawbacks of Cross-Platform Development:

- **Performance Limitations:** While cross-platform frameworks have made significant strides in performance, they may still fall short of the performance of native apps, especially in complex or resource-intensive applications.

- **Limited Access to Native Features:** Cross-platform frameworks may not always have immediate access to the latest platform-specific features, and integrating these features may require writing additional native code.

- **UI/UX Differences:** Achieving a perfectly native look and feel across different platforms can be challenging, as each platform has its own design guidelines and user expectations.

Example of Cross-Platform Development with Python (Using Kivy):

Let's look at how you can create a cross-platform "Hello, World!" app using Kivy, a popular Python framework for mobile development.

```python
import kivy

from kivy.app import App

from kivy.uix.label import Label


class HelloWorldApp(App):
    def build(self):
        # Create a label widget with the text "Hello, World!"
```

```python
    return Label(text="Hello, World!")


if __name__ == '__main__':

  HelloWorldApp().run()
```

Explanation:

- **Single Codebase:** This code is written once in Python and can be deployed on multiple platforms, including iOS and Android.

- **Kivy Framework:** Kivy handles the rendering and interaction, ensuring the app looks and behaves consistently across different platforms.

Deploying the Kivy App:

- **For Android:** Use Buildozer to package your Kivy app into an APK file.

- **For iOS:** Use BeeWare's Briefcase tool or Xcode to deploy your Kivy app on iOS devices.

Step-by-Step for Android:

1. Install Buildozer:

```
pip install buildozer
```

2. Initialize Buildozer in your project directory:

buildozer init

3. Build the APK:

buildozer -v android debug

This will generate an APK that you can install on any Android device.

Step-by-Step for iOS (Using BeeWare's Toga):

BeeWare's Toga allows you to build native applications using Python. Below is a simple example:

```python
import toga

from toga.style import Pack

from toga.style.pack import COLUMN, CENTER


def build(app):
    # Create a label with "Hello, World!"

    label = toga.Label('Hello, World!',
style=Pack(text_align=CENTER))


    # Create a box container

    box = toga.Box(children=[label],
style=Pack(direction=COLUMN, alignment=CENTER))


    # Return the main window with the box as its content

    return toga.MainWindow(title='Hello World App',
content=box)


def main():
```

```python
    return toga.App('Hello World', 'org.beeware.helloworld',
startup=build)


if __name__ == '__main__':

    main().main_loop()
```

Explanation:

- **Toga Framework:** Toga is a part of the BeeWare suite and provides native widgets that render using the native UI toolkit on each platform.

- **Cross-Platform Compatibility:** This code can be deployed on macOS, iOS, Android, Windows, and more, all from a single Python codebase.

Deploying the Toga App:

1. Install Briefcase:

```
pip install briefcase
```

2. Create a new project:

briefcase new

3. **Build and run the app:**

briefcase run

This will create a native app that you can run on your target platform.

3. Choosing Between Native and Cross-Platform Development

The choice between native and cross-platform development depends on several factors, including:

- **Project Requirements:** If your app requires access to platform-specific features or needs the highest possible performance, native development may be the better choice. However, if you need to reach a broad audience across multiple platforms quickly, cross-platform development is often more efficient.

- **Team Expertise:** Consider the expertise of your development team. If your team is already skilled in a specific native language, it might be more efficient to develop natively. On the other hand, if your team is proficient in Python or another cross-platform language, using a cross-platform framework could save time and resources.

- **Budget and Timeline:** Cross-platform development typically requires less time and money since you maintain only one codebase. If you have a limited budget or need to launch quickly, cross-platform development might be the way to go.

Native and cross-platform development each have their own strengths and weaknesses. Native development provides the best performance and access to platform-specific features, while cross-platform development offers the advantage of a single codebase that can run on multiple platforms. Python's cross-platform frameworks, like Kivy and BeeWare, allow developers to leverage Python's simplicity and power to build mobile apps that work across different devices and operating systems. By understanding the trade-offs and benefits of each approach, you can make an informed decision that best suits your project's goals and constraints.

Why Choose Python for Mobile Development?

Python has long been celebrated for its simplicity, readability, and versatility, making it one of the most popular programming languages in the world. While Python is often associated with web development, data science, and automation, its application in mobile development is growing, thanks to the emergence of powerful frameworks and tools.

1. Simplicity and Readability

One of Python's greatest strengths is its simplicity and readability. The language's clean syntax allows developers to focus on solving problems rather than getting bogged down by complex language rules. This is particularly beneficial in mobile development, where the complexity of building user interfaces, managing state, and handling platform-specific quirks can already be challenging.

Example: Simple Python Code vs. Complex Java/Kotlin Code

Consider the simplicity of defining a function in Python compared to doing the same in Java/Kotlin:

Python:

```python
def greet(name):
    return f"Hello, {name}!"
```

Java:

```java
public String greet(String name) {
```

```
    return "Hello, " + name + "!";
}
```

Kotlin:

```
fun greet(name: String): String {
    return "Hello, $name!"
}
```

Python's syntax is straightforward and requires less boilerplate code, making it easier to read, write, and maintain.

2. Cross-Platform Compatibility

Python excels in cross-platform development, allowing developers to write a single codebase that can be deployed across multiple platforms, such as iOS, Android, Windows, macOS, and Linux. This is made possible by frameworks like Kivy and BeeWare, which abstract away platform-specific details and provide a consistent API for building mobile applications.

Example: Cross-Platform "Hello, World!" Using Kivy

With Kivy, you can write a "Hello, World!" app that runs on both iOS and Android with the same code.

```python
from kivy.app import App

from kivy.uix.label import Label


class HelloWorldApp(App):
    def build(self):
```

```
        return Label(text="Hello, World!")


if __name__ == '__main__':

    HelloWorldApp().run()
```

Explanation:

- **Single Codebase:** This single Python script can be deployed on both Android and iOS devices.

- **Kivy's Role:** Kivy handles the underlying platform-specific details, such as rendering the UI and responding to user interactions, allowing you to focus on the app's logic and design.

3. Extensive Libraries and Frameworks

Python boasts a vast ecosystem of libraries and frameworks that can be leveraged in mobile development. These tools allow developers to integrate a wide range of functionalities into their apps, from web services and data management to machine learning and multimedia processing.

Example: Integrating a REST API with Python's requests Library

Suppose you want to fetch data from a REST API and display it in your mobile app. Python's requests library makes this easy:

```
import requests

from kivy.app import App

from kivy.uix.boxlayout import BoxLayout

from kivy.uix.label import Label
```

```python
class WeatherApp(App):

    def build(self):

        layout = BoxLayout(orientation='vertical')

        weather_data = self.get_weather()

        layout.add_widget(Label(text=f"Temperature:
{weather_data['temp']}°C"))

        layout.add_widget(Label(text=f"Condition:
{weather_data['weather']}"))

        return layout


    def get_weather(self):

        response =
requests.get("https://api.openweathermap.org/data/2.5/weat
her",

                        params={"q": "London", "appid":
"your_api_key", "units": "metric"})

        return response.json()["main"]


if __name__ == '__main__':

    WeatherApp().run()
```

Explanation:

- **Fetching Data:** The requests library is used to send an HTTP GET request to the OpenWeatherMap API to fetch weather data.

- **Displaying Data:** The data is then displayed in the app using Kivy's Label widget.

This example illustrates how Python's rich ecosystem can simplify the integration of external services into your mobile app.

4. Rapid Prototyping and Development

Python's simplicity and the availability of powerful frameworks make it ideal for rapid prototyping. Developers can quickly create and iterate on app ideas, testing concepts and features without the overhead associated with more complex languages.

Example: Prototyping a Simple Calculator App with Kivy

Let's say you want to prototype a basic calculator app. With Python and Kivy, you can quickly put together a working prototype:

```python
from kivy.app import App

from kivy.uix.gridlayout import GridLayout

from kivy.uix.button import Button

from kivy.uix.textinput import TextInput


class CalculatorApp(App):

    def build(self):
```

```python
        self.operand = ""

        layout = GridLayout(cols=4)


        self.display = TextInput(multiline=False,
readonly=True, halign="right", font_size=32)
        layout.add_widget(self.display)


        buttons = [
            '7', '8', '9', '/',
            '4', '5', '6', '*',
            '1', '2', '3', '-',
            'C', '0', '=', '+'
        ]


        for button in buttons:
            layout.add_widget(Button(text=button,
on_press=self.on_button_press))


        return layout


    def on_button_press(self, instance):
        text = instance.text
```

```python
        if text == "C":
            self.operand = ""
            self.display.text = ""
        elif text == "=":
            try:
                self.display.text = str(eval(self.operand))
            except Exception:
                self.display.text = "Error"
            self.operand = ""
        else:
            self.operand += text
            self.display.text = self.operand


if __name__ == '__main__':
    CalculatorApp().run()
```

Explanation:

- **GridLayout:** The calculator interface is created using a grid layout, with buttons arranged in a 4x4 grid.

- **TextInput:** The TextInput widget serves as the display, showing the current input and result.

- **Button Handling:** The on_button_press() method handles button presses, updating the display or calculating the result as appropriate.

This prototype can be developed further into a full-fledged app, but even at this stage, it demonstrates how quickly you can move from concept to a working prototype using Python.

5. Strong Community and Support

Python has a large and active community of developers who contribute to a wealth of resources, including documentation, tutorials, libraries, and forums. This community support is invaluable, particularly when you encounter challenges or need guidance during the development process.

Example: Leveraging Community Resources

Suppose you're building an app that requires geolocation features. Instead of writing everything from scratch, you can leverage Python libraries like geopy or explore community-contributed Kivy extensions that offer geolocation capabilities.

```python
from geopy.geocoders import Nominatim

from kivy.app import App

from kivy.uix.label import Label


class LocationApp(App):
    def build(self):
        geolocator =
Nominatim(user_agent="geoapiExercises")
        location = geolocator.geocode("Eiffel Tower, Paris")
```

```
        return Label(text=f"Coordinates: {location.latitude},
{location.longitude}")


if __name__ == '__main__':

    LocationApp().run()
```

Explanation:

- **Using geopy:** The geopy library is used to convert an address into geographic coordinates (latitude and longitude).

- **Community Contributions:** By leveraging community-contributed tools and libraries, you can significantly speed up your development process.

6. Integration with Emerging Technologies

Python's versatility extends to emerging technologies like machine learning, artificial intelligence, and IoT. By integrating these technologies into your mobile app, you can create innovative and intelligent applications that stand out in the market.

Example: Integrating Machine Learning with TensorFlow and Kivy

Imagine you want to integrate a machine learning model into your app to perform image classification. With Python, you can use TensorFlow to load a pre-trained model and classify images captured by the user.

```
import tensorflow as tf

from kivy.app import App
```

```python
from kivy.uix.boxlayout import BoxLayout

from kivy.uix.button import Button

from kivy.uix.image import Image

from kivy.uix.label import Label

from kivy.core.window import Window


class ImageClassifierApp(App):
    def build(self):
        self.model =
tf.keras.models.load_model('path/to/your/model.h5')

        self.layout = BoxLayout(orientation='vertical')


        self.image = Image(size_hint=(1, 0.8))
        self.layout.add_widget(self.image)


        self.label = Label(text="Upload an image to classify",
size_hint=(1, 0.1))
        self.layout.add_widget(self.label)


        self.button = Button(text="Classify Image",
size_hint=(1, 0.1))
        self.button.bind(on_press=self.classify_image)
        self.layout.add_widget(self.button)
```

```python
        return self.layout

    def classify_image(self, instance):
        # Dummy image data (replace with actual image data)
        image_data = tf.random.uniform((1, 224, 224, 3))
        predictions = self.model.predict(image_data)
        self.label.text = f"Predicted Class: {predictions.argmax()}"


if __name__ == '__main__':
    ImageClassifierApp().run()
```

Explanation:

- **Loading a Model:** The TensorFlow model is loaded once the app starts.

- **Classifying Images:** The classify_image() method performs image classification and updates the label with the predicted class.

- **Integration with Kivy:** Kivy is used to create the app's UI, integrating seamlessly with TensorFlow for the machine learning tasks.

7. Python as a Gateway to Learning Mobile Development

For beginners, Python serves as an excellent entry point into mobile development. Its simplicity lowers the barrier to entry, allowing new developers to focus on understanding the core concepts of mobile development without being overwhelmed by complex syntax or language-specific intricacies.

Example: A Simple Mobile Game with Kivy

Here's a very basic example of how Python can be used to create a simple mobile game using Kivy:

```python
from kivy.app import App

from kivy.uix.widget import Widget

from kivy.properties import NumericProperty

from kivy.clock import Clock


class SimpleGame(Widget):
    score = NumericProperty(0)


    def on_touch_down(self, touch):
        self.score += 1


class GameApp(App):
    def build(self):
        game = SimpleGame()
        Clock.schedule_interval(game.update, 1.0 / 60.0)
        return game
```

```
if __name__ == '__main__':

    GameApp().run()
```

Explanation:

- **Touch Interaction:** The game increments the score each time the user touches the screen.

- **Real-Time Updates:** The Clock.schedule_interval() method is used to update the game at 60 frames per second.

- **Beginner-Friendly:** This simple game example demonstrates how easily beginners can start creating interactive mobile applications using Python.

Choosing Python for mobile development offers numerous advantages, especially for developers seeking simplicity, flexibility, and a strong ecosystem of tools and libraries. Python's readability and ease of use make it an ideal choice for rapid development and prototyping, while its extensive libraries and frameworks support the creation of sophisticated, cross-platform mobile applications. Moreover, Python's integration with emerging technologies, like machine learning, positions it as a future-proof language in the evolving landscape of mobile development.

Introduction to Python-Based Mobile Frameworks:

Python's versatility extends into the realm of mobile app development, offering developers a variety of frameworks that simplify the process of building applications for multiple platforms. These frameworks allow you to write code once and deploy it across different operating systems, including iOS, Android, Windows, macOS, and Linux.

1. Kivy: A Cross-Platform Framework

Overview: Kivy is one of the most popular Python frameworks for developing cross-platform applications. It is open-source and supports the creation of applications that run on iOS, Android, Windows, macOS, and Linux. Kivy is particularly well-suited for developing applications that require multi-touch interfaces, making it a powerful tool for creating interactive and visually appealing mobile apps.

Key Features:

- **Multi-Touch Support:** Kivy is designed from the ground up to support multi-touch gestures, making it ideal for mobile applications where touch interaction is paramount.

- **Customizable Widgets:** Kivy provides a rich set of widgets that you can customize extensively to create unique user interfaces.

- **Graphics Engine:** Kivy comes with its own graphics engine, enabling high-performance rendering of complex UIs and animations.

Basic Example: "Hello, World!" App Using Kivy

Let's start with a basic example to see how Kivy works. We'll create a simple "Hello, World!" application that displays a text label on the screen.

from kivy.app import App

from kivy.uix.label import Label

```python
class HelloWorldApp(App):

    def build(self):

        # Create a label widget with the text "Hello, World!"

        return Label(text="Hello, World!")


if __name__ == '__main__':

    HelloWorldApp().run()
```

Explanation:

- **App Class:** In Kivy, every application must inherit from the App class. The build() method is overridden to define the root widget of the application.

- **Label Widget:** The Label widget is used to display text on the screen. In this case, it shows "Hello, World!" in the center of the app's window.

- **Running the App:** The run() method starts the Kivy application, opening a window (or screen on a mobile device) with the specified UI.

Advanced Example: A Simple Calculator App Using Kivy

Now, let's extend our example to create a simple calculator app. This app will have a basic UI with buttons for digits and operations, and it will display the result on the screen.

```python
from kivy.app import App

from kivy.uix.gridlayout import GridLayout

from kivy.uix.button import Button

from kivy.uix.textinput import TextInput


class CalculatorApp(App):

    def build(self):

        # Create the main layout as a GridLayout with 4
columns

        self.operand = ""

        layout = GridLayout(cols=4)


        # Create the display widget

        self.display = TextInput(multiline=False,
readonly=True, halign="right", font_size=32)

        layout.add_widget(self.display, colspan=4)  # Span
across all columns


        # Define the calculator buttons

        buttons = [

            '7', '8', '9', '/',

            '4', '5', '6', '*',

            '1', '2', '3', '-',
```

```python
        'C', '0', '=', '+'
    ]

    # Create and add buttons to the layout
    for button in buttons:
        layout.add_widget(Button(text=button,
on_press=self.on_button_press))

    return layout

def on_button_press(self, instance):
    # Handle button press events
    text = instance.text

    if text == "C":
        self.operand = ""
        self.display.text = ""
    elif text == "=":
        try:
            self.display.text = str(eval(self.operand))
        except Exception:
            self.display.text = "Error"
```

```
        self.operand = ""

    else:

        self.operand += text

        self.display.text = self.operand


if __name__ == '__main__':

    CalculatorApp().run()
```

Explanation:

- **GridLayout:** The app uses a GridLayout to arrange the calculator buttons in a 4x4 grid. The TextInput widget serves as the display for input and results.

- **Button Handling:** Each button press updates the display or calculates the result based on the user's input using the eval() function.

- **Kivy Flexibility:** This example highlights Kivy's flexibility in building interactive UIs with custom behavior.

2. BeeWare: A Native UI Toolkit

Overview: BeeWare is a collection of tools and libraries that enables you to write Python applications with a native user interface for multiple platforms. BeeWare's core project, **Toga**, is a native, cross-platform GUI toolkit that provides a consistent API for building applications with a truly native look and feel on each platform. BeeWare supports iOS, Android, Windows, macOS, Linux, and even web applications.

Key Features:

- **Native Look and Feel:** Applications built with BeeWare use the native UI components of each platform, ensuring that your app looks and feels like it belongs on the device it's running on.

- **Multi-Platform Support:** With BeeWare, you can target multiple platforms from a single codebase, similar to Kivy, but with a focus on providing a native experience.

- **Open-Source and Extensible:** BeeWare is open-source, and its components are modular, allowing developers to extend and customize the toolkit to fit their needs.

Basic Example: "Hello, World!" App Using BeeWare (Toga)

Let's create a simple "Hello, World!" app using Toga, the GUI toolkit of BeeWare.

```python
import toga

from toga.style import Pack

from toga.style.pack import COLUMN, CENTER


def build(app):
    # Create a label widget with the text "Hello, World!"
    label = toga.Label('Hello, World!',
style=Pack(text_align=CENTER))
```

```python
# Create a box container for the label

box = toga.Box(children=[label],
style=Pack(direction=COLUMN, alignment=CENTER))


# Return the main window with the box as its content

return toga.MainWindow(title='Hello World App',
content=box)


def main():

    return toga.App('Hello World', 'org.beeware.helloworld',
startup=build)


if __name__ == '__main__':

    main().main_loop()
```

Explanation:

- **Toga Widgets:** Toga provides native widgets such as Label and Box, which render using the native UI toolkit on each platform.

- **Box Container:** The Box widget is used to arrange child widgets in a column with centered alignment.

- **Main Window:** The MainWindow is the primary window of the application, and it displays the Box containing the label.

Advanced Example: A To-Do List App Using BeeWare

We can create a simple To-Do List application using BeeWare's Toga framework. This app will allow users to add, view, and remove tasks.

```python
import toga

from toga.style import Pack

from toga.style.pack import COLUMN, ROW


class ToDoListApp(toga.App):
    def startup(self):
        # Set up the main window
        self.main_window = toga.MainWindow(title="To-Do List")


        # Create the input box for new tasks
        self.task_input = toga.TextInput(placeholder="Enter a new task", style=Pack(flex=1))


        # Create the list to hold tasks
        self.task_list = toga.Table(['Tasks'], style=Pack(flex=1))


        # Create buttons
        add_button = toga.Button('Add Task', on_press=self.add_task, style=Pack(width=100))
```

```python
        delete_button = toga.Button('Delete Task',
on_press=self.delete_task, style=Pack(width=100))


        # Arrange widgets in a vertical box layout

        input_box = toga.Box(children=[self.task_input,
add_button], style=Pack(direction=ROW, padding=5))

        button_box = toga.Box(children=[delete_button],
style=Pack(direction=ROW, padding=5))

        main_box = toga.Box(children=[input_box,
self.task_list, button_box],
style=Pack(direction=COLUMN, padding=10))


        self.main_window.content = main_box

        self.main_window.show()


    def add_task(self, widget):
        task = self.task_input.value
        if task:
            self.task_list.data.append([task])
            self.task_input.value = "


    def delete_task(self, widget):
        selection = self.task_list.selection
        if selection:
```

```python
    self.task_list.data.remove(selection[0])


def main():

  return ToDoListApp()


if __name__ == '__main__':

  main().main_loop()
```

Explanation:

- **Task Management:** The ToDoListApp class manages tasks, allowing users to add tasks through a TextInput and remove selected tasks from a Table.

- **Layout Management:** The app's UI is arranged using Box widgets with ROW and COLUMN layouts to position the input fields, buttons, and task list.

- **Native UI:** The Table widget displays tasks, and the entire UI adapts to the native look and feel of the platform it runs on.

3. Other Python-Based Mobile Frameworks

While Kivy and BeeWare are among the most popular, several other Python-based frameworks can be used for mobile development. Here's a brief overview:

a. PyQt/PySide:

- **Overview:** PyQt and PySide are Python bindings for the Qt application framework, which is widely used for building cross-platform desktop applications. While not primarily designed for mobile development, they can be used to create mobile apps with a native look and feel.

- **Use Case:** Ideal for developers who are familiar with Qt and need to create applications that can run on both desktop and mobile platforms.

b. Pyjnius:

- **Overview:** Pyjnius is a Python library that allows Python code to call Java classes. This is particularly useful for Android development when you need to access platform-specific Java APIs directly from Python.

- **Use Case:** Uscful for Python developers who need to implement platform-specific features on Android that are not supported by standard Python libraries.

c. Pybee (Predecessor to BeeWare):

- **Overview:** Pybee was an earlier attempt to bring Python to mobile devices, leading to the development of BeeWare. It focused on creating cross-platform applications, and many of its ideas were incorporated into BeeWare.

- **Use Case:** Historical interest or for understanding the evolution of Python mobile frameworks.

4. When to Use Each Framework

Choosing the right Python-based framework for mobile development depends on your project requirements and development goals:

- **Use Kivy:** If you need a powerful, cross-platform framework that supports multi-touch and rich user interfaces, Kivy is an excellent choice. It's particularly well-suited for applications that require custom graphics and interactive elements.

- **Use BeeWare:** If your priority is to build applications with a native look and feel on multiple platforms while using Python, BeeWare's Toga toolkit is the best option. It's ideal for projects where a consistent native user experience is crucial.

- **Use PyQt/PySide:** If you are already familiar with Qt or are developing an application that needs to run on both desktop and mobile platforms, PyQt or PySide might be appropriate.

- **Use Pyjnius:** When developing Android apps with Python and you need to directly interact with Java APIs to access platform-specific features, Pyjnius is a good choice.

Python's versatility and the availability of powerful frameworks like Kivy and BeeWare make it a strong contender for mobile app development. Whether you're looking to build cross-platform applications with rich, interactive UIs or native applications with a seamless user experience, Python-based frameworks provide the tools you need. By understanding the strengths and use cases of each framework, you can choose the right one for your project and start building mobile apps that are both functional and visually appealing.

Conclusion

This chapter has introduced you to the fundamentals of mobile app development, highlighting the differences between native and cross-platform approaches, and explaining why Python is an excellent choice for developing mobile applications. As you progress through this book, you'll delve deeper into the Python-based frameworks that make mobile development accessible and efficient, and you'll gain the skills needed to bring your app ideas to life.

Chapter 2: Setting Up Your Development Environment

<u>Installing Python:</u>

Python is the foundational language for your mobile app development environment. Before you start building applications, you need to install Python on your system. This section will walk you through the installation process, covering different operating systems, and ensuring that your Python installation is correctly configured for development.

Step 1: Download Python

The first step is to download the latest version of Python from the official website.

1. **Visit the Python Website:**

   o Go to the official <u>Python website</u>.

2. **Select the Latest Version:**

   o The homepage typically highlights the latest stable release of Python. Click the yellow "Download Python X.X.X" button (where X.X.X is the version number).

Step 2: Install Python on Your Operating System

The installation process varies slightly depending on your operating system. Below are detailed instructions for Windows, macOS, and Linux.

Installing Python on Windows:

1. **Run the Installer:**

   o Once the .exe file is downloaded, locate it in your downloads folder and double-click it to launch the installer.

2. **Customize Installation (Important!):**

   o On the first screen of the installer, **check the box that says "Add Python X.X to PATH"**. This step is crucial as it makes Python accessible from the command line.

3. **Choose Installation Type:**

   o Select "Customize installation" to access additional options, or click "Install Now" for a default installation.

   o If you choose "Customize installation," you can select optional features like documentation, pip (Python's package manager), and other utilities. Ensure "pip" is selected.

4. **Complete Installation:**

   o Once you've selected your options, click "Install" and wait for the process to complete. After installation, you may be prompted to disable the path length limit—a useful option for avoiding issues with file path lengths in Python.

5. **Verify Installation:**

    o   Open Command Prompt (search for cmd in the Start menu) and type python --version or python3 --version. You should see the installed Python version.

C:\> python --version

Python 3.X.X

Installing Python on macOS:

1. **Download the Installer:**

    o   After downloading the .pkg file, double-click it to launch the installer.

2. **Follow the Installer Prompts:**

    o   The installer will guide you through the installation steps. It's recommended to leave the default settings unchanged unless you have specific needs.

3. **Verify Installation:**

    o   Open Terminal (you can find it using Spotlight Search) and type python3 --version to confirm the installation.

$ python3 --version

Python 3.X.X

Installing Python on Linux (Ubuntu Example):

1. **Use the Package Manager:**

   o   On most Linux distributions, Python can be installed via the package manager. For Ubuntu, open Terminal and run:

sudo apt update

sudo apt install python3

2. **Verify Installation:**

   • After installation, confirm it by checking the version with:

python3 –version

Step 3: Install pip (Python's Package Manager)

pip is a package manager for Python that allows you to install and manage additional libraries and dependencies that are not included in the standard library.

1. **Check if pip is Installed:**

   o   After installing Python, pip is usually installed automatically. You can verify it by typing:

pip –version

2. **Installing pip (If Not Installed):**

   • If pip is not installed, you can install it using the following command:

sudo apt install python3-pip

Step 4: Setting Up a Virtual Environment (Optional but Recommended)

A virtual environment is an isolated environment where you can install libraries and dependencies without affecting the global Python installation. This is particularly useful for managing project-specific dependencies.

1. **Install venv Module:**

   o Python's standard library includes venv, a module that creates virtual environments. You can install it if it's not already available:

sudo apt install python3-venv

2. **Create a Virtual Environment:**

   • Navigate to your project directory and create a virtual environment by running:

python3 -m venv myenv

   • Replace myenv with the desired name for your virtual environment.

3. **Activate the Virtual Environment:**

   • Activate the virtual environment with the following command:

source myenv/bin/activate

   • On Windows, the command is:

myenv\Scripts\activate

   • When activated, your terminal prompt will change to show the name of the active environment.

4. **Install Dependencies:**

- Once the virtual environment is activated, you can use pip to install the necessary libraries. For example, to install Kivy:

pip install kivy

5. **Deactivating the Virtual Environment:**

- When you're done working in the virtual environment, deactivate it by running:

Deactivate

Step 5: Setting Up Your Integrated Development Environment (IDE)

While you can write Python code in any text editor, using an Integrated Development Environment (IDE) can greatly enhance your productivity by providing features like code completion, debugging, and project management.

Recommended IDEs:

1. **Visual Studio Code (VS Code):**

   - **Installation:** Download and install VS Code from the official website.

   - **Python Extension:** After installing VS Code, open it and install the Python extension by Microsoft from the Extensions marketplace.

2. **PyCharm:**

   - **Installation:** Download PyCharm from the JetBrains website.

- o **Setup:** Once installed, PyCharm automatically detects your Python installation. You can configure a virtual environment for your projects directly from the PyCharm interface.

3. **Configuring the IDE:**

   - o Set the Python interpreter in your IDE to point to the Python version or virtual environment you want to use for your project. This ensures that your code runs with the correct Python version and dependencies.

   - o For PyCharm, you can do this by going to **File > Settings > Project: [Project Name] > Python Interpreter**.

Step 6: Verifying the Setup

To ensure everything is set up correctly, create a new Python file (main.py) in your IDE and write a simple script to test your environment.

```
print("Hello, World!")
```

Run the Script: Execute the script using your IDE's run command or by running it from the terminal:

```
python main.py
```

Expected Output: You should see "Hello, World!" printed in the terminal or console output.

By following these steps, you've successfully installed Python, configured your development environment, and verified that everything is working correctly. Your environment is now ready for Python-based mobile app development. Whether you're using Kivy, BeeWare, or any other Python framework, this setup will serve as the foundation for all your development efforts.

Setting Up IDEs:

Integrated Development Environments (IDEs) are essential tools for developers, providing a suite of features that make coding easier, more efficient, and less error-prone. Popular IDEs like Visual Studio Code (VS Code) and PyCharm offer powerful functionalities such as code autocompletion, debugging, version control integration, and more.

1. Setting Up Visual Studio Code (VS Code)

Visual Studio Code is a free, open-source code editor developed by Microsoft. It is lightweight yet powerful, with a vast library of extensions that enhance its capabilities. Here's how to set it up for Python development.

Step 1: Install Visual Studio Code

1. **Download VS Code:**

    o Visit the Visual Studio Code website and download the installer for your operating system (Windows, macOS, or Linux).

2. **Run the Installer:**

    o For Windows, run the .exe file you downloaded. For macOS, open the .dmg file and drag VS Code into your Applications folder. On Linux, you may need to extract and run the package or use your package manager to install it.

3. **Complete the Installation:**

    o   Follow the prompts to complete the installation. On Windows, you might want to select the option to add VS Code to your PATH during installation for easier command-line access.

Step 2: Install Python Extension for VS Code

1. **Open VS Code:**

    o   Launch Visual Studio Code from your Start menu (Windows), Launchpad (macOS), or application launcher (Linux).

2. **Install the Python Extension:**

    o   Go to the Extensions view by clicking the Extensions icon on the sidebar (or press Ctrl+Shift+X).

    o   Search for "Python" and click the install button for the extension provided by Microsoft.

    o   Once installed, the Python extension enables syntax highlighting, code autocompletion, linting, debugging, and other Python-specific features.

Step 3: Configure Python Interpreter

1. **Select Python Interpreter:**

- o   Press Ctrl+Shift+P to open the Command Palette, then type "Python: Select Interpreter" and press Enter.

- o   VS Code will display a list of Python interpreters available on your system. Select the one you want to use for your project (e.g., the one installed in your virtual environment).

2. **Verify the Configuration:**

- o   Create a new Python file (e.g., main.py) and add a simple script:

```
print("VS Code is set up!")
```

- o   Run the script by pressing Ctrl+F5 (Run Without Debugging) or F5 (Run with Debugging). The output should appear in the integrated terminal.

Step 4: Set Up Additional Extensions (Optional)

1. **Python Linting:**

- o   Linting helps you catch syntax errors and enforce coding standards. VS Code's Python extension supports various linters, such as pylint, flake8, and mypy.

- o   To enable linting, press Ctrl+Shift+P, type "Python: Enable Linting," and select your preferred linter.

2. **Python Debugger:**

- o   VS Code provides a built-in debugger. To start debugging, set breakpoints by clicking on the left margin of the code editor, then press F5 to start the debugger.

o   The Debug view will open, allowing you to step through your code, inspect variables, and evaluate expressions.

3. **Version Control Integration:**

o   VS Code integrates seamlessly with Git. If you're using Git for version control, the Source Control view (accessible via the sidebar) provides tools for managing commits, branches, and repositories.

2. Setting Up PyCharm

PyCharm is a dedicated Python IDE developed by JetBrains. It comes in two versions: Community (free) and Professional (paid, with more advanced features). PyCharm is particularly powerful for Python developers due to its robust support for Django, Flask, and scientific libraries, as well as its advanced debugging and testing tools.

Step 1: Install PyCharm

1. **Download PyCharm:**

o   Visit the PyCharm website and download the installer. Choose the Community edition unless you require the additional features of the Professional edition.

2. **Run the Installer:**

o   For Windows, run the .exe file. On macOS, open the .dmg file and drag PyCharm to your Applications folder. For Linux, you might use a package manager or download and extract the tarball.

3. **Complete the Installation:**

   o Follow the prompts in the installer. You may be asked to configure options like creating a desktop shortcut, associating .py files with PyCharm, and adding PyCharm to your system PATH.

Step 2: Configure Python Interpreter in PyCharm

1. **Open PyCharm and Create a New Project:**

   o Launch PyCharm and choose "New Project" from the welcome screen.

2. **Configure the Project Interpreter:**

   o In the "New Project" dialog, you'll see an option to configure the project interpreter. Click on the drop-down menu and select the Python interpreter you wish to use, such as a virtual environment or the system interpreter.

   o You can also create a new virtual environment directly from this screen by selecting "New environment using Virtualenv" and specifying the location.

3. **Verify the Configuration:**

   o Once the project is created, add a new Python file (e.g., main.py) and write a simple script:

```python
print("PyCharm is set up!")
```

- o Run the script by right-clicking in the editor and selecting "Run main." The output should appear in the Run window at the bottom of the IDE.

Step 3: Explore PyCharm Features

1. **Code Navigation and Autocompletion:**

   - o PyCharm offers intelligent code autocompletion and navigation. As you type, PyCharm suggests completions based on the context, helping you write code faster and with fewer errors.

2. **Integrated Debugger:**

   - o Set breakpoints by clicking on the left margin next to the line numbers, and start debugging by selecting "Debug main" from the Run menu or by pressing Shift+F9.

   - o PyCharm's debugger provides advanced features like inline variable evaluation, step-through debugging, and a variable watch list.

3. **Version Control Integration:**

   - o PyCharm has built-in support for Git, SVN, Mercurial, and other version control systems. Access these tools via the VCS menu or the dedicated Version Control tool window.

   - o You can clone repositories, manage branches, and perform commits directly from within PyCharm.

4. **Test Runner:**

    o   PyCharm makes it easy to write and run unit
        tests using popular testing frameworks like
        unittest, pytest, or nose. You can run tests
        directly from the editor and view the results
        in the Test Runner tab.

5. **Database Tools (Professional Edition):**

    o   If you're using the Professional edition,
        PyCharm provides powerful database tools
        that allow you to manage SQL databases,
        execute queries, and view data directly
        within the IDE.

3. Choosing Between VS Code and PyCharm

Both VS Code and PyCharm are excellent choices for
Python development, but they cater to slightly different
needs and preferences:

- **VS Code:**

    o   Lightweight, highly customizable, and has a
        vast ecosystem of extensions.

    o   Ideal if you're looking for a versatile editor
        that supports multiple languages and
        development environments.

    o   Free and open-source.

- **PyCharm:**

    o   A more full-featured IDE with advanced
        tools specifically designed for Python
        development.

- o Preferred if you need robust support for complex Python projects, frameworks like Django or Flask, or scientific computing.

- o The Community edition is free, while the Professional edition offers additional features for a subscription fee.

Ultimately, the choice between VS Code and PyCharm depends on your specific needs, project complexity, and personal preference. Some developers even use both, depending on the task at hand.

Setting up your IDE is a crucial step in creating an efficient and effective development environment for Python-based mobile app development. Whether you choose VS Code or PyCharm, both offer powerful tools and features that will streamline your coding process, improve productivity, and help you avoid common errors. With your IDE configured, you're now ready to start coding, debugging, and deploying your mobile applications.

Installing Necessary Libraries and Frameworks:

Once you have Python and your IDE set up, the next step is to install the necessary libraries and frameworks that will enable you to build and run mobile applications using Python. Depending on the specific framework you plan to use (e.g., Kivy, BeeWare), you will need to install various libraries and dependencies.

1. Installing Kivy

Kivy is a popular Python framework for building cross-platform applications, including mobile apps. It's particularly known for its support of multi-touch and its ability to create highly interactive applications.

Step 1: Installing Kivy via pip

1. **Ensure pip is Installed:**

   o First, ensure that pip is installed and updated on your system. You can check by running:

pip –version

If pip is not installed, you can install it using the following command on Linux:

sudo apt install python3-pip

- On Windows or macOS, pip is usually installed automatically with Python.

2. **Install Kivy:**

- Open your terminal (or Command Prompt on Windows) and install Kivy using pip:

pip install kivy

   o This command installs Kivy and its dependencies. The installation may take a few minutes, as Kivy requires several additional packages, such as Cython and Pygame.

Step 2: Verifying the Installation

1. **Create a Test Script:**

   o After installing Kivy, it's a good idea to verify the installation by creating a simple test script. Open your IDE (VS Code or

PyCharm) and create a new Python file, kivy_test.py:

```python
from kivy.app import App

from kivy.uix.label import Label


class TestApp(App):

    def build(self):

        return Label(text="Kivy is installed correctly!")


if __name__ == '__main__':

    TestApp().run()
```

2. **Run the Script:**

- Run the script in your IDE or terminal:

```
python kivy_test.py
```

- If Kivy is installed correctly, a window will open displaying the text "Kivy is installed correctly!".

3. **Troubleshooting Installation Issues:**

- If you encounter errors during installation or when running the script, ensure that all dependencies are correctly installed. You can try reinstalling Kivy or checking for specific error messages related to dependencies like Cython or Pygame.

2. Installing BeeWare

BeeWare is a suite of tools for building native applications in Python. It includes Toga, a widget toolkit for creating native GUIs that run on multiple platforms, including iOS and Android.

Step 1: Installing Toga via pip

1. **Install Toga:**

    o   Toga is the core part of the BeeWare suite that you'll use to create the user interface of your applications. Install it via pip:

```
pip install toga
```

    o   This command will download and install Toga and its dependencies.

Step 2: Verifying the Installation

1. **Create a Test Script:**

    o   Similar to Kivy, you should verify the Toga installation by creating a simple test script. Create a new Python file, toga_test.py:

```python
import toga

from toga.style import Pack

from toga.style.pack import COLUMN, CENTER

def build(app):

    label = toga.Label('Toga is installed correctly!',
style=Pack(text_align=CENTER))
```

```python
    box = toga.Box(children=[label],
style=Pack(direction=COLUMN, alignment=CENTER))

    return toga.MainWindow(title='Test Toga App',
content=box)

def main():

    return toga.App('Test Toga', 'org.beeware.testtoga',
startup=build)

if __name__ == '__main__':

    main().main_loop()
```

2. **Run the Script:**

- Run the script in your IDE or terminal:

```
python toga_test.py
```

- A window should appear with the message "Toga is installed correctly!".

3. **Handling Platform-Specific Dependencies:**

- If you plan to deploy Toga applications on platforms like iOS or Android, you may need additional tools (such as Xcode for iOS or Android Studio for Android). Toga provides specific commands to package and deploy apps to these platforms.

3. Installing Additional Libraries

Depending on your project requirements, you may need to install additional Python libraries. Here are a few common ones that are often used in mobile app development:

a. Requests: For HTTP Requests

- The requests library is used for making HTTP requests, such as accessing web APIs from your mobile app.

1. Install Requests:

```
pip install requests
```

2. Example Usage:

```
import requests

response = requests.get('https://api.example.com/data')
print(response.json())
```

   o This script fetches data from a web API and prints it as JSON.

b. SQLAlchemy: For Database Management

- SQLAlchemy is a powerful SQL toolkit and Object-Relational Mapping (ORM) library for managing databases within your Python applications.

1. **Install SQLAlchemy:**

```
pip install sqlalchemy
```

2. Example Usage:

```
from sqlalchemy import create_engine, Column, Integer, String, Base
```

```python
engine = create_engine('sqlite:///app.db')
Base = declarative_base()

class User(Base):
    __tablename__ = 'users'
    id = Column(Integer, primary_key=True)
    name = Column(String)
```

Base.metadata.create_all(engine)

- o This script creates a simple SQLite database with a User table.

c. Pillow: For Image Processing

- Pillow is a popular library for opening, manipulating, and saving image files in various formats.

1. **Install Pillow:**

pip install pillow

2. Example Usage:

from PIL import Image

img = Image.open('example.jpg')

img.show()

This script opens and displays an image using the default image viewer.

4. Creating a Requirements File

As your project grows, you'll likely need to keep track of all the libraries and dependencies your application requires. Python's pip allows you to create a requirements.txt file that lists all the dependencies, which can be easily installed in one command.

Step 1: Generate a Requirements File

1. **Create the File:**

   o In your project directory, run the following command to generate a requirements.txt file:

pip freeze > requirements.txt

   - This file will list all the installed packages in your current environment.

2. **Example requirements.txt:**

kivy==2.0.0

requests==2.25.1

SQLAlchemy==1.4.15

Pillow==8.2.0

   o The file includes the library names and their versions.

Step 2: Installing from a Requirements File

1. **Install Dependencies:**

   o If you're setting up a new environment, you can install all the necessary packages from the requirements.txt file with a single command:

pip install -r requirements.txt

This command reads the file and installs all the listed packages.

5. Managing Dependencies with Virtual Environments

To avoid conflicts between different projects' dependencies, it's recommended to use virtual environments. This ensures that each project has its own isolated environment with the specific versions of libraries it requires.

Step 1: Creating a Virtual Environment

1. **Create the Environment:**

   o Navigate to your project directory and create a virtual environment:

python3 -m venv myenv

- Replace myenv with your preferred environment name.

2. **Activate the Environment:**

- On Windows:

myenv\Scripts\activate

On macOS/Linux:

source myenv/bin/activate

   o Your terminal prompt will change to show that the virtual environment is active.

Step 2: Installing Dependencies in the Virtual Environment

1. **Install Packages:**

   o   With the virtual environment activated, install the necessary libraries:

pip install kivy toga requests

2. **Deactivate the Environment:**

   • When you're done working in the virtual environment, deactivate it by running:

Deactivate

Setting up the necessary libraries and frameworks is a critical step in preparing your development environment for Python-based mobile app development. By following the steps outlined above, you ensure that you have all the tools you need to build, test, and deploy your applications efficiently. Whether you're using Kivy for cross-platform apps, BeeWare for native UIs, or other libraries for specific functionalities, your environment is now equipped to handle a wide range of development tasks.

<u>Configuring Emulators and Physical Devices for Testing:</u>

Testing is a crucial part of the mobile app development process. To ensure that your app works correctly on various devices, you can use both emulators and physical devices. Emulators allow you to simulate different devices and operating systems on your development machine, while testing on physical devices ensures that your app behaves as expected in a real-world environment.

1. Configuring Android Emulators

Android emulators are a part of Android Studio, which provides a comprehensive environment for developing and testing Android applications. You can simulate various devices with different screen sizes, resolutions, and Android versions.

Step 1: Install Android Studio

1. **Download Android Studio:**

   - Visit the Android Studio website and download the latest version.

2. **Install Android Studio:**

   - Run the installer and follow the setup wizard. During installation, ensure that the Android Virtual Device (AVD) Manager is selected. This tool is essential for creating and managing emulators.

Step 2: Setting Up an Android Emulator

1. **Launch Android Studio:**

   - Open Android Studio and select "AVD Manager" from the "Tools" menu or by clicking the AVD Manager icon in the toolbar.

2. **Create a New Virtual Device:**

   - In the AVD Manager, click on "Create Virtual Device."

3. **Select a Device Profile:**

- o Choose a device profile from the list. You can select popular devices like Pixel, Nexus, or even tablets. Click "Next."

4. **Choose a System Image:**

   - o Select the system image (Android version) you want to emulate. You can download additional system images if needed. Click "Next."

5. **Configure the Emulator:**

   - o Name your virtual device and adjust settings like orientation and advanced options if needed. Click "Finish" to create the emulator.

6. **Launch the Emulator:**

   - o Your new virtual device will appear in the AVD Manager. Click the "Play" button next to the device to launch the emulator.

   - o The emulator will start and display the Android home screen, simulating the device you selected.

Step 3: Running Your Python App on the Emulator

1. **Install Buildozer (For Kivy Apps):**

   - o If you are developing with Kivy, you can use Buildozer to package your Python code into an APK that can be installed on the emulator.

pip install buildozer

2. **Configure Buildozer:**

- Navigate to your Kivy project directory and initialize Buildozer:

buildozer init

- This command creates a buildozer.spec file that you can edit to configure your app.

3. **Build the APK:**

- Run Buildozer to create an APK:

buildozer -v android debug

- This process may take some time, as it compiles your app and packages it into an APK.

4. **Install and Run the APK on the Emulator:**

- Once the APK is built, Buildozer will automatically install it on the running emulator.

buildozer android deploy run

Your app will launch on the emulator, allowing you to test its functionality.

2. Configuring iOS Simulators

For iOS development, Apple provides iOS Simulators as part of Xcode, which you can use to test your applications on various iPhone and iPad models.

Step 1: Install Xcode

1. **Download Xcode:**

- o Xcode is available for free on the Mac App Store. Search for "Xcode" and click "Get" to download and install it.

2. **Install Xcode:**

   - o After the download is complete, open Xcode and follow the setup instructions. Xcode may prompt you to install additional components; allow it to do so.

Step 2: Setting Up an iOS Simulator

1. **Open the iOS Simulator:**

   - o You can launch the iOS Simulator directly from Xcode by selecting "Xcode > Open Developer Tool > Simulator" from the menu.

2. **Choose a Device:**

   - o The simulator will launch with a default device (e.g., iPhone 14). To change the device, go to "Hardware > Device" and select a different iPhone or iPad model.

3. **Launch the Simulator:**

   - o The simulator will start and display the iOS home screen.

Step 3: Running Your Python App on the Simulator

1. **Install Briefcase (For BeeWare Apps):**

   - o If you're using BeeWare's Toga to build your app, you can use Briefcase to package your Python code for iOS.

pip install briefcase

2. **Create a New BeeWare Project:**

- Start a new Toga project using Briefcase:

briefcase new

- Follow the prompts to set up your project.

3. **Build the iOS App:**

- Build your app for iOS:

briefcase build iOS

- This command will generate an Xcode project.

4. **Deploy the App to the Simulator:**

- Run the app on the iOS Simulator:

briefcase run iOS

Your app will be deployed to the simulator, allowing you to test its behavior on iOS devices.

3. Testing on Physical Devices

While emulators and simulators are useful for initial testing, it's essential to test your app on real devices to ensure it performs well in actual usage scenarios.

Testing on Android Devices

1. **Enable Developer Options:**

   - On your Android device, go to "Settings > About Phone" and tap "Build number" seven times to enable Developer Options.

2. **Enable USB Debugging:**

- o   Go to "Settings > Developer Options" and enable "USB Debugging."

3. **Connect the Device:**

   - o   Connect your Android device to your computer using a USB cable. You may be prompted to allow USB debugging on your device; click "OK."

4. **Deploy and Run Your App:**

   - o   Use Buildozer to deploy your APK directly to the connected device:

```
buildozer android deploy run
```

   - o   Your app will be installed and launched on the physical device, allowing you to test its real-world performance.

Testing on iOS Devices

1. **Register Your Device:**

   - To test on a physical iOS device, you need to register it with your Apple Developer account.

2. **Enable Developer Mode:**

   - Connect your iOS device to your Mac and open Xcode. The device will appear in the device list. Enable Developer Mode on your iOS device.

3. **Deploy the App to the Device:**

   - Use Xcode to build and run your app on the connected iPhone or iPad.

```
briefcase run iOS -d <device_name>
```

The app will be installed and launched on your iOS device, where you can test its performance and behavior.

4. Tips for Effective Testing

- **Test on Multiple Devices:** Ensure your app runs smoothly on different devices with various screen sizes, resolutions, and OS versions.

- **Check Performance:** Monitor your app's performance on both emulators and physical devices, focusing on CPU usage, memory consumption, and battery impact.

- **Use Real-World Scenarios:** Test your app in conditions that mimic real-world usage, including low connectivity, multitasking, and power-saving modes.

- **Automate Testing:** Consider setting up automated testing frameworks like Appium to perform routine tests on your app across multiple devices and platforms.

Conclusion

Setting up emulators and connecting physical devices are critical steps in the mobile app development process. By using emulators, you can quickly test your app across a wide range of devices and operating systems. However, real-world testing on physical devices is essential to ensure your app performs well under actual usage conditions. With both methods set up, you are well-equipped to thoroughly test your mobile applications, identify potential issues, and optimize the user experience.

Chapter 3: Understanding Mobile App Architecture

Introduction to Mobile App Architecture

Mobile app architecture refers to the structural design of a mobile application, including its layers, components, and the interaction between them. A well-designed architecture is crucial for building scalable, maintainable, and efficient mobile applications. Understanding the principles of mobile app architecture helps you organize your code, manage dependencies, and optimize performance.

1. The Basics of Mobile App Architecture

Mobile app architecture typically consists of multiple layers, each responsible for specific aspects of the application. These layers are designed to separate concerns, making the application easier to develop, test, and maintain. The most common layers include:

- **Presentation Layer (UI Layer)**

- **Business Logic Layer (Service Layer)**

- **Data Access Layer (Persistence Layer)**

Let's examine each of these layers in detail.

a. Presentation Layer (UI Layer)

The Presentation Layer is responsible for the user interface (UI) and user experience (UX). It includes all the components that the user interacts with, such as buttons, text fields, and other visual elements. This layer handles the input from the user and displays the output.

Example:

In a Kivy-based app, the Presentation Layer might include the UI components defined using widgets like Label, Button, and TextInput.

```python
from kivy.app import App

from kivy.uix.boxlayout import BoxLayout

from kivy.uix.button import Button

from kivy.uix.label import Label

from kivy.uix.textinput import TextInput

class MyApp(App):

    def build(self):

        layout = BoxLayout(orientation='vertical')

        self.label = Label(text="Enter your name:")

        self.text_input = TextInput()

        self.button = Button(text="Submit",
on_press=self.on_button_press)

        layout.add_widget(self.label)

        layout.add_widget(self.text_input)

        layout.add_widget(self.button)

        return layout

    def on_button_press(self, instance):

        self.label.text = f"Hello, {self.text_input.text}!"

if __name__ == '__main__':

    MyApp().run()
```

Explanation:

- The UI is defined using a vertical BoxLayout that contains a Label, TextInput, and Button.

- The on_button_press method updates the label based on user input, demonstrating the interaction within the Presentation Layer.

b. Business Logic Layer (Service Layer)

The Business Logic Layer handles the core functionality of the application. It processes user input, interacts with data sources, and applies the business rules that govern how the application behaves. This layer acts as the intermediary between the Presentation Layer and the Data Access Layer.

Example:

Let's enhance the previous example by adding a service layer that processes user data. We'll create a simple service that validates and formats the user's name.

```
class NameService:

    def format_name(self, name):

        return name.strip().title()

    def validate_name(self, name):

        return len(name.strip()) > 0
```

Incorporate this service into the Kivy app:

```
from kivy.app import App

from kivy.uix.boxlayout import BoxLayout

from kivy.uix.button import Button
```

```python
from kivy.uix.label import Label
from kivy.uix.textinput import TextInput
class NameService:
    def format_name(self, name):
        return name.strip().title()
    def validate_name(self, name):
        return len(name.strip()) > 0
class MyApp(App):
    def build(self):
        self.name_service = NameService()
        layout = BoxLayout(orientation='vertical')
        self.label = Label(text="Enter your name:")
        self.text_input = TextInput()
        self.button = Button(text="Submit",
on_press=self.on_button_press)
        layout.add_widget(self.label)
        layout.add_widget(self.text_input)
        layout.add_widget(self.button)
        return layout
    def on_button_press(self, instance):
        name = self.text_input.text
        if self.name_service.validate_name(name):
```

```
        formatted_name =
self.name_service.format_name(name)

        self.label.text = f"Hello, {formatted_name}!"

    else:

        self.label.text = "Please enter a valid name."

if __name__ == '__main__':

    MyApp().run()
```

Explanation:

- The NameService class encapsulates the business logic for validating and formatting names.

- The on_button_press method in MyApp uses NameService to process the user's input, separating the UI logic from the business logic.

c. Data Access Layer (Persistence Layer)

The Data Access Layer manages the storage and retrieval of data. It abstracts the underlying data sources (such as databases, file systems, or web services) and provides a consistent interface for the Business Logic Layer to interact with. This separation allows the application to easily adapt to different data storage mechanisms.

Example:

Let's add a simple data access layer that saves and retrieves user data. For this example, we'll use a JSON file to persist user information.

```
import json

import os
```

```python
class UserDataStore:

    def __init__(self, filepath='user_data.json'):

        self.filepath = filepath

    def save_user_data(self, name):

        data = {"name": name}

        with open(self.filepath, 'w') as file:

            json.dump(data, file)

    def load_user_data(self):

        if os.path.exists(self.filepath):

            with open(self.filepath, 'r') as file:

                data = json.load(file)

            return data.get("name", "")

        return ""
```

Integrate this data access layer into the Kivy app:

```python
from kivy.app import App

from kivy.uix.boxlayout import BoxLayout

from kivy.uix.button import Button

from kivy.uix.label import Label

from kivy.uix.textinput import TextInput

class NameService:

    def format_name(self, name):
```

```python
        return name.strip().title()
    def validate_name(self, name):
        return len(name.strip()) > 0
class UserDataStore:
    def __init__(self, filepath='user_data.json'):
        self.filepath = filepath
    def save_user_data(self, name):
        data = {"name": name}
        with open(self.filepath, 'w') as file:
            json.dump(data, file)
    def load_user_data(self):
        if os.path.exists(self.filepath):
            with open(self.filepath, 'r') as file:
                data = json.load(file)
            return data.get("name", "")
        return ""
class MyApp(App):
    def build(self):
        self.name_service = NameService()
        self.data_store = UserDataStore()
        layout = BoxLayout(orientation='vertical')
```

```python
        self.label = Label(text="Enter your name:")

        self.text_input =
TextInput(text=self.data_store.load_user_data())

        self.button = Button(text="Submit",
on_press=self.on_button_press)

        layout.add_widget(self.label)

        layout.add_widget(self.text_input)

        layout.add_widget(self.button)

        return layout

    def on_button_press(self, instance):

        name = self.text_input.text

        if self.name_service.validate_name(name):

            formatted_name =
self.name_service.format_name(name)

            self.data_store.save_user_data(formatted_name)

            self.label.text = f"Hello, {formatted_name}!"

        else:

            self.label.text = "Please enter a valid name."

if __name__ == '__main__':

    MyApp().run()
```

Explanation:

- The UserDataStore class provides methods to save and load user data from a JSON file.

- The MyApp class now uses UserDataStore to persist the user's name, demonstrating the separation of concerns between data access and other layers.

2. Common Architectural Patterns

Several architectural patterns are commonly used in mobile app development. These patterns help in organizing the code in a way that promotes scalability, maintainability, and testability.

a. Model-View-Controller (MVC)

MVC is a design pattern that separates an application into three main components:

- **Model:** Manages the data and business logic.

- **View:** Represents the UI and displays the data to the user.

- **Controller:** Acts as an intermediary between the Model and View, handling user input and updating the Model and View accordingly.

Example of MVC:

In a Kivy app, you might structure the code as follows:

- **Model:** UserDataStore (handles data)

- **View:** Kivy widgets like Label, Button, TextInput

- **Controller:** MyApp (manages the interaction between the view and model)

Example Code Snippet:

```
class MyApp(App):
```

```python
def build(self):
    # Model and View initialization
    self.user_data_store = UserDataStore()
    self.view = self.create_view()
    return self.view

def create_view(self):
    layout = BoxLayout(orientation='vertical')
    self.label = Label(text="Enter your name:")
    self.text_input = TextInput(text=self.user_data_store.load_user_data())
    self.button = Button(text="Submit", on_press=self.on_button_press)
    layout.add_widget(self.label)
    layout.add_widget(self.text_input)
    layout.add_widget(self.button)
    return layout

def on_button_press(self, instance):
    # Controller logic
    name = self.text_input.text
    self.user_data_store.save_user_data(name)
    self.label.text = f"Hello, {name}!"
```

b. Model-View-ViewModel (MVVM)

MVVM is another design pattern that separates the development of the graphical user interface from the business logic or back-end logic (the model). It introduces an additional layer called the ViewModel, which serves as a bridge between the View and the Model.

- **Model:** Manages the data and business logic.

- **View:** Represents the UI.

- **ViewModel:** Acts as a mediator between the View and the Model, handling the logic that governs how the UI interacts with the data.

Example Code Snippet:

```python
class UserViewModel:
    def __init__(self):
        self.user_data_store = UserDataStore()
    def get_user_name(self):
        return self.user_data_store.load_user_data()
    def set_user_name(self, name):
        self.user_data_store.save_user_data(name)
class MyApp(App):
    def build(self):
        self.view_model = UserViewModel()
        layout = BoxLayout(orientation='vertical')
        self.label = Label(text="Enter your name:")
```

```python
        self.text_input =
TextInput(text=self.view_model.get_user_name())

        self.button = Button(text="Submit",
on_press=self.on_button_press)

        layout.add_widget(self.label)

        layout.add_widget(self.text_input)

        layout.add_widget(self.button)

        return layout

    def on_button_press(self, instance):

        name = self.text_input.text

        self.view_model.set_user_name(name)

        self.label.text = f"Hello, {name}!"
```

Explanation:

- The UserViewModel handles interactions between
  the UI and the data, making the application easier to
  test and maintain.

c. Clean Architecture

Clean Architecture is a more advanced architectural
pattern that emphasizes a separation of concerns, where the
core business logic is independent of frameworks,
databases, and external libraries. This pattern is
characterized by concentric layers, where the innermost
layers (Entities, Use Cases) are independent of the outer
layers (Interface Adapters, Frameworks, and Drivers).

Example Code Snippet:

Implementing Clean Architecture in a mobile app requires a more complex structure, but the basic idea involves separating your code into layers such as:

- **Entities:** Core business objects.

- **Use Cases:** Application-specific business rules.

- **Interface Adapters:** Transforms data from the outer layers to a format that the inner layers can use.

- **Frameworks and Drivers:** The outermost layer, which includes UI, database, and other external systems.

```python
# Entities

class User:

    def __init__(self, name):

        self.name = name

# Use Cases

class UserService:

    def __init__(self, user_repo):

        self.user_repo = user_repo

    def save_user(self, user):

        self.user_repo.save(user)

    def get_user(self):

        return self.user_repo.load()

# Interface Adapters
```

```python
class UserRepository:
    def __init__(self, data_store):
        self.data_store = data_store
    def save(self, user):
        self.data_store.save_user_data(user.name)
    def load(self):
        name = self.data_store.load_user_data()
        return User(name)
# Frameworks and Drivers
class MyApp(App):
    def build(self):
        data_store = UserDataStore()
        user_repo = UserRepository(data_store)
        self.user_service = UserService(user_repo)
        layout = BoxLayout(orientation='vertical')
        self.label = Label(text="Enter your name:")
        user = self.user_service.get_user()
        self.text_input = TextInput(text=user.name if user else "")
        self.button = Button(text="Submit", on_press=self.on_button_press)
        layout.add_widget(self.label)
        layout.add_widget(self.text_input)
```

```
    layout.add_widget(self.button)

    return layout

def on_button_press(self, instance):

    name = self.text_input.text

    user = User(name)

    self.user_service.save_user(user)

    self.label.text = f"Hello, {name}!"
```

Explanation:

- The core business logic (User, UserService) is independent of the UI framework (Kivy) and data storage details (UserDataStore), adhering to the principles of Clean Architecture.

3. Visualizing Mobile App Architecture

Understanding mobile app architecture often requires visual aids to grasp the relationships between different components. Below are visual representations of the key layers and patterns discussed above.

Layered Architecture:

- **Presentation Layer:** Manages the UI and user interactions.

- **Business Logic Layer:** Handles the core application logic.

- **Data Access Layer:** Manages data storage and retrieval.

MVC Architecture:

- **Model:** Manages the application data and business rules.

- **View:** Handles the UI and user interactions.

- **Controller:** Facilitates communication between the Model and the View.

MVVM Architecture:

- **Model:** Represents the data.

- **View:** Represents the UI.

- **ViewModel:** Acts as an intermediary, managing the logic and data flow between the View and Model.

Clean Architecture:

- **Entities:** Core business rules.

- **Use Cases:** Application-specific business logic.

- **Interface Adapters:** Converts data for the use cases and entities.

- **Frameworks and Drivers:** Handles external operations like UI, database, and networking.

Client-Server Architecture:

Client-server architecture is a foundational concept in mobile app development, where the application (the client) interacts with a server to retrieve, process, and store data. This architecture is especially common in mobile applications that require real-time data, such as social media platforms, e-commerce apps, and online games. Understanding how client-server architecture works is essential for designing and building robust, scalable mobile applications.

1. What is Client-Server Architecture?

Client-server architecture is a distributed application structure that divides tasks between the client (front-end) and the server (back-end). The client is responsible for presenting the user interface and handling user interactions, while the server manages data storage, business logic, and the processing of requests from multiple clients.

Key Components:

- **Client:** The mobile application running on the user's device. It sends requests to the server and displays the data or results provided by the server.
- **Server:** A remote machine or a cloud service that processes client requests, performs operations (like querying a database), and returns the necessary data to the client.
- **API (Application Programming Interface):** The communication interface between the client and server, typically implemented using HTTP requests and responses in the form of JSON or XML.

Data Flow in Client-Server Architecture:

1. **Client Request:** The client sends a request to the server, usually via an HTTP request.
2. **Server Processing:** The server receives the request, processes it (e.g., querying a database, performing calculations), and generates a response.
3. **Server Response:** The server sends the response back to the client, typically in JSON format.

4. **Client Display:** The client processes the server's response and updates the user interface accordingly.

2. Implementing Client-Server Architecture

Let's build a simple example to demonstrate client-server architecture in a mobile app. We'll create a mobile client using Python (Kivy) that communicates with a Flask-based server. The server will handle requests to retrieve and update user data.

a. Setting Up the Server (Using Flask)

Step 1: Install Flask

First, we need to set up the server using Flask, a lightweight web framework for Python.

1. **Install Flask:**

```
pip install Flask
```

Step 2: Create a Simple Flask Server

Next, create a Flask application (server.py) that will handle HTTP requests from the client.

```python
from flask import Flask, jsonify, request

app = Flask(__name__)

# Mock database

users = {

    1: {"name": "Alice", "age": 25},
```

```python
    2: {"name": "Bob", "age": 30}
}

@app.route('/users', methods=['GET'])

def get_users():

    return jsonify(users)

@app.route('/users/<int:user_id>', methods=['GET'])

def get_user(user_id):

    user = users.get(user_id)

    if user:

        return jsonify(user)

    else:

        return jsonify({"error": "User not found"}), 404

@app.route('/users', methods=['POST'])

def add_user():

    new_user = request.json

    user_id = max(users.keys()) + 1

    users[user_id] = new_user

    return jsonify({"id": user_id, "user": new_user}), 201
```

```python
if __name__ == '__main__':

    app.run(debug=True)
```

Explanation:

- **/users:** A GET endpoint that returns all users.
- **/users/<int:user_id>:** A GET endpoint that returns a specific user by ID.
- **/users:** A POST endpoint that adds a new user to the database.

Step 3: Run the Server

Run the Flask server:

```
python server.py
```

The server will start and listen for requests on http://127.0.0.1:5000.

b. Building the Mobile Client (Using Kivy)

Now, we'll create a Kivy-based mobile client that communicates with the Flask server.

Step 1: Install Requests Library

We'll use the requests library to send HTTP requests from the client to the server.

1. **Install Requests:**

```
pip install requests
```

Step 2: Create the Mobile Client

Create a Kivy application (client.py) that interacts with the Flask server.

```python
import requests

from kivy.app import App

from kivy.uix.boxlayout import BoxLayout

from kivy.uix.button import Button

from kivy.uix.label import Label

from kivy.uix.textinput import TextInput

class MyApp(App):

    def build(self):

        self.layout = BoxLayout(orientation='vertical')

        self.label = Label(text="Enter User ID:")

        self.text_input = TextInput()

        self.get_button = Button(text="Get User",
on_press=self.get_user)

        self.result_label = Label(text="User data will be
displayed here.")

        self.layout.add_widget(self.label)

        self.layout.add_widget(self.text_input)

        self.layout.add_widget(self.get_button)

        self.layout.add_widget(self.result_label)

        return self.layout

    def get_user(self, instance):
```

```python
        user_id = self.text_input.text

        try:

            response =
requests.get(f'http://127.0.0.1:5000/users/{user_id}')

            if response.status_code == 200:

                user_data = response.json()

                self.result_label.text = f"Name:
{user_data['name']}, Age: {user_data['age']}"

            else:

                self.result_label.text = "User not found."

        except requests.exceptions.RequestException as e:

            self.result_label.text = f"Error: {e}"

if __name__ == '__main__':

    MyApp().run()
```

Explanation:

- **TextInput:** Allows the user to enter a user ID.

- **Button:** Triggers the get_user method to send a GET request to the Flask server.

- **Label:** Displays the retrieved user data or an error message.

Step 3: Run the Mobile Client

Run the Kivy application:

```
python client.py
```

When you enter a user ID (e.g., 1 or 2) and click the "Get User" button, the app will send a request to the Flask server, retrieve the user data, and display it.

3. Understanding Data Flow in Client-Server Architecture

To fully grasp client-server architecture, it's essential to understand how data flows between the client and server. Let's walk through the process using the example we just created:

1. **Client Sends a Request:**

   o The user enters a user ID and clicks the "Get User" button.

   o The Kivy app sends a GET request to http://127.0.0.1:5000/users/<user_id> using the requests library.

Request Example:

GET /users/1 HTTP/1.1

Host: 127.0.0.1:5000

2. **Server Processes the Request:**

   • The Flask server receives the request and processes it by looking up the user ID in the users dictionary.

   • If the user is found, the server generates a JSON response containing the user data.

Response Example:

{

"name": "Alice",

```
    "age": 25
}
```

3. **Client Receives the Response:**

- The Kivy app receives the response and processes the JSON data.

- The app updates the UI to display the user's name and age.

4. **Error Handling:**

- If the user ID does not exist, the server returns a 404 error, and the client displays an error message.

- If there's a network issue or server error, the client handles the exception and informs the user.

4. Benefits and Challenges of Client-Server Architecture

Benefits:

- **Scalability:** The server can handle requests from multiple clients, making it easier to scale the application.

- **Centralized Data Management:** All data is stored and managed on the server, ensuring consistency and reducing redundancy.

- **Security:** Sensitive operations and data processing occur on the server, reducing the risk of exposure on the client side.

Challenges:

- **Network Dependency:** The client must have a network connection to communicate with the server. Offline capabilities may require additional implementation.

- **Latency:** Communication between the client and server introduces latency, which can affect the app's performance.

- **Complexity:** Implementing client-server architecture adds complexity to the application, especially when handling authentication, error management, and data synchronization.

5. Extending the Example: Implementing POST Requests

To further understand client-server architecture, let's extend our example by adding functionality to create new users via a POST request.

Step 1: Update the Kivy Client

Add a new UI component and functionality to allow users to create a new user.

```python
class MyApp(App):

    def build(self):

        self.layout = BoxLayout(orientation='vertical')

        self.label = Label(text="Enter User ID:")

        self.text_input = TextInput()
```

```python
        self.get_button = Button(text="Get User",
on_press=self.get_user)

        self.result_label = Label(text="User data will be
displayed here.")

        self.name_input = TextInput(hint_text="Enter name")

        self.age_input = TextInput(hint_text="Enter age",
input_filter='int')

        self.add_button = Button(text="Add User",
on_press=self.add_user)

        self.layout.add_widget(self.label)

        self.layout.add_widget(self.text_input)

        self.layout.add_widget(self.get_button)

        self.layout.add_widget(self.result_label)

        self.layout.add_widget(self.name_input)

        self.layout.add_widget(self.age_input)

        self.layout.add_widget(self.add_button)

        return self.layout

    def get_user(self, instance):

        user_id = self.text_input.text

        try:
```

```python
        response =
requests.get(f'http://127.0.0.1:5000/users/{user_id}')

        if response.status_code == 200:

            user_data = response.json()

            self.result_label.text = f"Name:
{user_data['name']}, Age: {user_data['age']}"

        else:

            self.result_label.text = "User not found."

    except requests.exceptions.RequestException as e:

        self.result_label.text = f"Error: {e}"

def add_user(self, instance):

    name = self.name_input.text

    age = self.age_input.text

    if name and age:

        new_user = {"name": name, "age": int(age)}

        try:

            response =
requests.post('http://127.0.0.1:5000/users', json=new_user)

            if response.status_code == 201:
```

```
            self.result_label.text = "User added
successfully!"

        else:

            self.result_label.text = "Failed to add user."

        except requests.exceptions.RequestException as e:

            self.result_label.text = f"Error: {e}"

    else:

        self.result_label.text = "Please enter both name and
age."
```

Explanation:

- **Name and Age Inputs:** Additional TextInput widgets allow users to enter a new user's name and age.
- **Add User Button:** The add_user method sends a POST request to create a new user on the server.

Step 2: Test the New Functionality

Run the updated client and server applications. You can now create new users by entering a name and age and clicking the "Add User" button. The new user will be stored on the server and can be retrieved using the user ID.

Client-server architecture is a powerful and flexible design pattern that is essential for building modern mobile applications. By separating the client and server responsibilities, this architecture allows for scalable, maintainable, and secure applications. Understanding how to implement and manage client-server communication is crucial for any mobile app developer.

Architectural Patterns:

Architectural patterns like MVC (Model-View-Controller) and MVVM (Model-View-ViewModel) play a crucial role in organizing and structuring mobile applications. These patterns help developers manage the complexity of large applications by separating concerns, improving code maintainability, and facilitating easier testing. In this section, we will explore the MVC and MVVM patterns in depth, along with other common architectural patterns used in mobile app development.

1. Model-View-Controller (MVC)

MVC is one of the most widely used architectural patterns in software development, including mobile app development. It divides an application into three interconnected components:

- **Model:** Manages the data and business logic of the application.

- **View:** Represents the user interface and displays data to the user.

- **Controller:** Handles user input, updates the model, and refreshes the view.

How MVC Works:

- The **View** listens to user input (e.g., button clicks) and forwards it to the **Controller.**

- The **Controller** processes the input, updates the **Model**, and then instructs the **View** to update itself based on the new data in the **Model**.

- The **Model** notifies the **View** of any changes to the data, allowing the **View** to update accordingly.

Visual Representation:

MVC Example in a Kivy Application:

Let's create a simple Kivy app that uses the MVC pattern to manage user data.

Step 1: Define the Model

The **Model** in our MVC pattern will manage user data.

```python
class UserModel:

    def __init__(self):

        self.user_data = {"name": ""}

    def set_user_name(self, name):

        self.user_data["name"] = name

    def get_user_name(self):

        return self.user_data["name"]
```

Step 2: Define the View

The **View** will handle the user interface.

```python
from kivy.uix.boxlayout import BoxLayout

from kivy.uix.label import Label

from kivy.uix.textinput import TextInput
```

```python
from kivy.uix.button import Button

class UserView(BoxLayout):
    def __init__(self, controller, **kwargs):
        super(UserView, self).__init__(**kwargs)
        self.controller = controller
        self.orientation = 'vertical'
        self.label = Label(text="Enter your name:")
        self.text_input = TextInput()
        self.button = Button(text="Submit",
on_press=self.on_button_press)
        self.result_label = Label(text="Your name will be
displayed here.")
        self.add_widget(self.label)
        self.add_widget(self.text_input)
        self.add_widget(self.button)
        self.add_widget(self.result_label)
    def on_button_press(self, instance):
        name = self.text_input.text
        self.controller.update_user_name(name)
    def update_view(self, name):
        self.result_label.text = f"Hello, {name}!"
```

Step 3: Define the Controller

The **Controller** will manage the interaction between the **Model** and the **View**.

```python
class UserController:

    def __init__(self, model, view):

        self.model = model

        self.view = view

    def update_user_name(self, name):

        self.model.set_user_name(name)

        self.view.update_view(self.model.get_user_name())
```

Step 4: Integrate MVC in the Kivy App

Now, we integrate all the components into the Kivy app.

```python
from kivy.app import App

class MyApp(App):

    def build(self):

        model = UserModel()

        view = UserView(controller=None)

        controller = UserController(model, view)

        view.controller = controller

        return view

if __name__ == '__main__':

    MyApp().run()
```

Explanation:

- The **UserModel** manages the user's name.

- The **UserView** handles the UI and interacts with the user.

- The **UserController** processes user input, updates the model, and instructs the view to refresh.

2. Model-View-ViewModel (MVVM)

MVVM is another popular architectural pattern that is especially common in frameworks that support data binding. It separates the development of the graphical user interface from the business logic or back-end logic (the model).

- **Model:** Represents the data and business logic.

- **View:** Represents the UI, which is bound to properties of the ViewModel.

- **ViewModel:** Acts as an intermediary between the View and the Model, exposing data from the Model and handling user interactions.

How MVVM Works:

- The **ViewModel** exposes data and commands to the **View** through properties and methods.

- The **View** binds to these properties and commands, updating automatically when the data in the **ViewModel** changes.

- The **Model** provides the data, and the **ViewModel** manipulates this data for presentation in the **View**.

Visual Representation:

MVVM Example in a Kivy Application:

Let's implement the MVVM pattern in a Kivy application.

Step 1: Define the Model

```python
class UserModel:

    def __init__(self):

        self.user_data = {"name": ""}

    def set_user_name(self, name):

        self.user_data["name"] = name

    def get_user_name(self):

        return self.user_data["name"]
```

Step 2: Define the ViewModel

The **ViewModel** will act as a bridge between the **Model** and the **View**.

```python
from kivy.properties import StringProperty

from kivy.event import EventDispatcher

class UserViewModel(EventDispatcher):

    user_name = StringProperty()

    def __init__(self, model, **kwargs):

        super(UserViewModel, self).__init__(**kwargs)

        self.model = model

        self.user_name = self.model.get_user_name()
```

```python
def update_user_name(self, name):

    self.model.set_user_name(name)

    self.user_name = self.model.get_user_name()
```

Step 3: Define the View

The **View** in MVVM pattern uses data binding to automatically update the UI.

```python
from kivy.uix.boxlayout import BoxLayout

from kivy.uix.label import Label

from kivy.uix.textinput import TextInput

from kivy.uix.button import Button

class UserView(BoxLayout):

    def __init__(self, view_model, **kwargs):

        super(UserView, self).__init__(**kwargs)

        self.view_model = view_model

        self.orientation = 'vertical'

        self.label = Label(text="Enter your name:")

        self.text_input =
TextInput(text=self.view_model.user_name)

        self.button = Button(text="Submit",
on_press=self.on_button_press)

        self.result_label = Label(text="Your name will be
displayed here.")
```

```python
        self.add_widget(self.label)
        self.add_widget(self.text_input)
        self.add_widget(self.button)
        self.add_widget(self.result_label)
        self.view_model.bind(user_name=self.update_view)
    def on_button_press(self, instance):
        name = self.text_input.text
        self.view_model.update_user_name(name)
    def update_view(self, instance, value):
        self.result_label.text = f"Hello, {value}!"
```

Step 4: Integrate MVVM in the Kivy App

Integrate the components into the Kivy app.

```python
from kivy.app import App
class MyApp(App):
    def build(self):
        model = UserModel()
        view_model = UserViewModel(model)
        view = UserView(view_model=view_model)
        return view
if __name__ == '__main__':
    MyApp().run()
```

Explanation:

- The **UserViewModel** manages the interaction between the **Model** and the **View**.

- Data binding allows the **View** to automatically update when the **ViewModel** changes.

3. Other Architectural Patterns

Apart from MVC and MVVM, several other architectural patterns are commonly used in mobile app development. Each of these patterns offers different advantages depending on the specific requirements of your application.

a. Model-View-Presenter (MVP)

MVP is similar to MVC but with a clearer separation between the View and the Model. The Presenter acts as the middleman that manipulates the Model based on user input and updates the View.

- **Model:** Contains the data and business logic.

- **View:** Displays data to the user and forwards user actions to the Presenter.

- **Presenter:** Contains the logic to update the View based on interactions with the Model.

Visual Representation:

MVP Example Code Snippet:

```python
class UserModel:
    def __init__(self):
        self.user_data = {"name": ""}
```

```python
    def set_user_name(self, name):
        self.user_data["name"] = name
    def get_user_name(self):
        return self.user_data["name"]
class UserView:
    def display_user(self, name):
        print(f"Hello, {name}!")
class UserPresenter:
    def __init__(self, model, view):
        self.model = model
        self.view = view
    def set_user_name(self, name):
        self.model.set_user_name(name)
        self.view.display_user(self.model.get_user_name())
# Usage
model = UserModel()
view = UserView()
presenter = UserPresenter(model, view)
presenter.set_user_name("Alice")
```

Explanation:

- The **Presenter** takes user input from the **View** and updates the **Model** accordingly. It then updates the **View** with the new data.

b. Clean Architecture

Clean Architecture is a more advanced and flexible architectural pattern that emphasizes separation of concerns, where the core business logic is independent of frameworks, databases, and external libraries.

Core Concepts:

- **Entities:** Core business logic and data structures.

- **Use Cases:** Application-specific business logic.

- **Interface Adapters:** Transforms data from the outer layers (like frameworks and databases) to a format that the inner layers can use.

- **Frameworks and Drivers:** The outermost layer, which includes UI, databases, web frameworks, etc.

Visual Representation:

Clean Architecture Example Code Snippet:

```python
# Entities
class User:
    def __init__(self, name):
        self.name = name

# Use Cases
class UserService:
    def __init__(self, user_repo):
        self.user_repo = user_repo
```

```python
    def save_user(self, user):
        self.user_repo.save(user)
    def get_user(self):
        return self.user_repo.load()
# Interface Adapters
class UserRepository:
    def __init__(self, data_store):
        self.data_store = data_store
    def save(self, user):
        self.data_store.save_user_data(user.name)
    def load(self):
        name = self.data_store.load_user_data()
        return User(name)
# Frameworks and Drivers
class UserDataStore:
    def __init__(self, filepath='user_data.json'):
        self.filepath = filepath
    def save_user_data(self, name):
        data = {"name": name}
        with open(self.filepath, 'w') as file:
            json.dump(data, file)
    def load_user_data(self):
```

```python
    if os.path.exists(self.filepath):
        with open(self.filepath, 'r') as file:
            data = json.load(file)
        return data.get("name", "")
    return ""

# Putting it all together
data_store = UserDataStore()

user_repo = UserRepository(data_store)

user_service = UserService(user_repo)

# Example usage
user = User("Bob")

user_service.save_user(user)

retrieved_user = user_service.get_user()

print(retrieved_user.name)  # Output: Bob
```

Explanation:

- **Entities** and **Use Cases** form the core logic, independent of how data is stored or presented.

- **Interface Adapters** translate between the internal logic and the external frameworks.

- **Frameworks and Drivers** handle the actual implementation details (e.g., file storage, database access).

4. Choosing the Right Architecture

Choosing the right architectural pattern depends on various factors, such as the complexity of your application, team expertise, and specific project requirements:

- **MVC** is suitable for simple to moderately complex applications where the separation of concerns can be easily managed.

- **MVVM** is ideal when you have a framework that supports data binding and you want to separate the view logic from the business logic.

- **MVP** is useful in scenarios where you need a clear separation between the view and the model, with the presenter handling all the business logic.

- **Clean Architecture** is recommended for large, complex applications that require scalability, flexibility, and the ability to evolve over time.

Understanding and implementing architectural patterns like MVC, MVVM, MVP, and Clean Architecture are essential for developing scalable, maintainable, and testable mobile applications. Each pattern offers different benefits and is suitable for different scenarios. By choosing the right architecture, you can better manage your codebase, enhance collaboration within your development team, and create applications that are easier to maintain and extend over time.

Overview of App Components:

When building a mobile application, it's essential to understand the various components that make up the architecture. These components typically include the **User Interface (UI)**, the **Backend**, and the **Database**. Each component plays a critical role in ensuring the app functions smoothly, providing users with a seamless experience while managing data and business logic efficiently.

1. User Interface (UI)

The **User Interface (UI)** is the front-end part of a mobile application that users interact with directly. It includes all the visual elements, such as buttons, text fields, images, and navigation elements, that allow users to perform actions and receive feedback from the app.

Key Concepts:

- **Layout:** The arrangement of UI elements on the screen.

- **Widgets:** Interactive components like buttons, labels, and text inputs.

- **Navigation:** How users move between different screens or views within the app.

Example: Creating a Simple UI with Kivy

Let's create a basic UI for a mobile app using Kivy, a Python framework for building cross-platform applications.

```python
from kivy.app import App

from kivy.uix.boxlayout import BoxLayout

from kivy.uix.button import Button

from kivy.uix.label import Label
```

```python
from kivy.uix.textinput import TextInput
class MyUI(BoxLayout):
    def __init__(self, **kwargs):
        super(MyUI, self).__init__(**kwargs)
        self.orientation = 'vertical'
        self.label = Label(text="Enter your name:")
        self.text_input = TextInput()
        self.button = Button(text="Submit",
on_press=self.on_button_press)
        self.result_label = Label(text="Your name will be
displayed here.")
        self.add_widget(self.label)
        self.add_widget(self.text_input)
        self.add_widget(self.button)
        self.add_widget(self.result_label)
    def on_button_press(self, instance):
        name = self.text_input.text
        self.result_label.text = f"Hello, {name}!"
class MyApp(App):
    def build(self):
        return MyUI()
if __name__ == '__main__':
    MyApp().run()
```

Explanation:

- **BoxLayout:** Arranges UI elements vertically.

- **Label:** Displays text to the user.

- **TextInput:** Allows the user to enter text.

- **Button:** Triggers an action when pressed.

- **Result Label:** Updates with the user's input after the button is pressed.

UI in Action:

2. Backend

The **Backend** of a mobile app handles the business logic, processing, and interactions with external systems, such as databases or APIs. It's typically the server-side part of the application that performs operations requested by the client (UI), such as retrieving data, performing computations, or handling authentication.

Key Concepts:

- **Business Logic:** The rules that govern how data is processed and managed.

- **API (Application Programming Interface):** The interface through which the client communicates with the backend.

- **Middleware:** Software that acts as a bridge between the client and the backend, managing communication, security, and data processing.

Visual Representation:

Example: Creating a Simple Backend with Flask

Let's build a simple backend using Flask, a lightweight web framework for Python, to handle requests from the UI.

```python
from flask import Flask, jsonify, request

app = Flask(__name__)

# Mock database
users = {
    1: {"name": "Alice", "age": 25},
    2: {"name": "Bob", "age": 30}
}

@app.route('/users', methods=['GET'])
def get_users():
    return jsonify(users)

@app.route('/users/<int:user_id>', methods=['GET'])
def get_user(user_id):
    user = users.get(user_id)
    if user:
        return jsonify(user)
    else:
        return jsonify({"error": "User not found"}), 404

@app.route('/users', methods=['POST'])
def add_user():
    new_user = request.json
```

```
user_id = max(users.keys()) + 1

users[user_id] = new_user

return jsonify({"id": user_id, "user": new_user}), 201

if __name__ == '__main__':

app.run(debug=True)
```

Explanation:

- **/users (GET):** Returns a list of users.

- **/users/<int:user_id> (GET):** Returns data for a specific user.

- **/users (POST):** Adds a new user to the mock database.

Backend in Action:

You can run the Flask server and use tools like Postman or a simple Python script to test the endpoints.

```
python server.py
```

Testing the API with Python:

```
import requests

# Get all users

response = requests.get('http://127.0.0.1:5000/users')

print(response.json())

# Get a specific user

response = requests.get('http://127.0.0.1:5000/users/1')

print(response.json())
```

Add a new user

new_user = {"name": "Charlie", "age": 35}

response = requests.post('http://127.0.0.1:5000/users', json=new_user)

print(response.json())

3. Database

The **Database** is where the app's data is stored, managed, and retrieved. It is a crucial component of the backend and is responsible for persisting data, ensuring its integrity, and providing efficient access for read and write operations.

Key Concepts:

- **Database Management System (DBMS):** Software that manages the database (e.g., MySQL, PostgreSQL, SQLite).

- **Tables:** Structures within the database that store data in rows and columns.

- **Queries:** Requests to retrieve or manipulate data in the database, typically written in SQL (Structured Query Language).

Visual Representation:

Example: Setting Up a Simple SQLite Database

Let's create a simple SQLite database to store user information, and integrate it with our Flask backend.

Step 1: Create a Database

Create a file named database.db and a table users to store user data.

```python
import sqlite3

def init_db():

    conn = sqlite3.connect('database.db')

    cursor = conn.cursor()

    # Create table

    cursor.execute('''CREATE TABLE IF NOT EXISTS users

                (id INTEGER PRIMARY KEY, name TEXT,
age INTEGER)''')

    # Insert some users

    cursor.execute("INSERT INTO users (name, age)
VALUES ('Alice', 25)")

    cursor.execute("INSERT INTO users (name, age)
VALUES ('Bob', 30)")

    conn.commit()

    conn.close()

if __name__ == '__main__':

    init_db()
```

Step 2: Integrate the Database with Flask

Modify the Flask server to interact with the SQLite database instead of the mock dictionary.

```python
from flask import Flask, jsonify, request

import sqlite3
```

```python
app = Flask(__name__)
def query_db(query, args=(), one=False):
    conn = sqlite3.connect('database.db')
    cursor = conn.cursor()
    cursor.execute(query, args)
    rv = cursor.fetchall()
    conn.close()
    return (rv[0] if rv else None) if one else rv
@app.route('/users', methods=['GET'])
def get_users():
    users = query_db('SELECT * FROM users')
    return jsonify([{ "id": user[0], "name": user[1], "age":
user[2] } for user in users])
@app.route('/users/<int:user_id>', methods=['GET'])
def get_user(user_id):
    user = query_db('SELECT * FROM users WHERE id =
?', [user_id], one=True)
    if user:
        return jsonify({"id": user[0], "name": user[1], "age":
user[2]})
    else:
        return jsonify({"error": "User not found"}), 404
@app.route('/users', methods=['POST'])
```

```python
def add_user():
    new_user = request.json
    conn = sqlite3.connect('database.db')
    cursor = conn.cursor()
    cursor.execute("INSERT INTO users (name, age)
VALUES (?, ?)", (new_user['name'], new_user['age']))
    conn.commit()
    new_id = cursor.lastrowid
    conn.close()
    return jsonify({"id": new_id, "user": new_user}), 201

if __name__ == '__main__':
    app.run(debug=True)
```

Explanation:

- **query_db:** A helper function to interact with the SQLite database.

- **get_users:** Fetches all users from the database.

- **get_user:** Fetches a specific user by ID.

- **add_user:** Adds a new user to the database.

Database Interaction in Action:

You can run the updated Flask server and use the same API testing methods to interact with the SQLite database.

python server.py

4. Connecting the UI, Backend, and Database

Now that we have a clear understanding of the UI, Backend, and Database components, let's see how they interact in a complete mobile application.

Data Flow in a Mobile App:

1. **User Interaction:** The user interacts with the UI by entering data or pressing buttons.

2. **UI Requests Backend:** The UI sends a request to the backend (e.g., to fetch or update data).

3. **Backend Processes Request:** The backend processes the request, often querying the database.

4. **Database Operations:** The database retrieves or updates data as per the request.

5. **Backend Responds:** The backend sends the processed data back to the UI.

6. **UI Updates:** The UI updates to reflect the new data or state.

Visual Representation of Data Flow:

Example: Connecting All Components

Assume we have the following setup:

- **UI:** A Kivy app that interacts with the user.

- **Backend:** A Flask server that handles requests.

- **Database:** An SQLite database that stores user data.

Step 1: Create the UI (Kivy Client)

import requests

from kivy.app import App

```python
from kivy.uix.boxlayout import BoxLayout

from kivy.uix.button import Button

from kivy.uix.label import Label

from kivy.uix.textinput import TextInput

class MyUI(BoxLayout):

    def __init__(self, **kwargs):

        super(MyUI, self).__init__(**kwargs)

        self.orientation = 'vertical'

        self.label = Label(text="Enter User ID:")

        self.text_input = TextInput()

        self.get_button = Button(text="Get User",
on_press=self.get_user)

        self.result_label = Label(text="User data will be
displayed here.")

        self.add_widget(self.label)

        self.add_widget(self.text_input)

        self.add_widget(self.get_button)

        self.add_widget(self.result_label)

        self.name_input = TextInput(hint_text="Enter name")

        self.age_input = TextInput(hint_text="Enter age",
input_filter='int')

        self.add_button = Button(text="Add User",
on_press=self.add_user)
```

```python
        self.add_widget(self.name_input)
        self.add_widget(self.age_input)
        self.add_widget(self.add_button)
    def get_user(self, instance):
        user_id = self.text_input.text
        try:
            response =
requests.get(f'http://127.0.0.1:5000/users/{user_id}')
            if response.status_code == 200:
                user_data = response.json()
                self.result_label.text = f"Name:
{user_data['name']}, Age: {user_data['age']}"
            else:
                self.result_label.text = "User not found."
        except requests.exceptions.RequestException as e:
            self.result_label.text = f"Error: {e}"
    def add_user(self, instance):
        name = self.name_input.text
        age = self.age_input.text
        if name and age:
            new_user = {"name": name, "age": int(age)}
            try:
```

```
        response =
requests.post('http://127.0.0.1:5000/users', json=new_user)

        if response.status_code == 201:

            self.result_label.text = "User added
successfully!"

        else:

            self.result_label.text = "Failed to add user."

    except requests.exceptions.RequestException as e:

        self.result_label.text = f"Error: {e}"

else:

    self.result_label.text = "Please enter both name and
age."

class MyApp(App):

    def build(self):

        return MyUI()

if __name__ == '__main__':

    MyApp().run()
```

Explanation:

- The Kivy UI allows the user to get and add user data.

- The backend processes these requests and interacts with the SQLite database.

Running the Complete App:

1. Start the Flask server to handle requests:

python server.py

2.   Run the Kivy app to interact with the UI:

python client.py

When you enter a user ID and click "Get User," the app sends a request to the Flask backend, which retrieves the user data from the SQLite database and displays it in the UI. Similarly, you can add a new user by entering the name and age and clicking "Add User."

Understanding the interaction between the UI, Backend, and Database is fundamental to building robust mobile applications. The UI provides the interface for user interaction, the Backend handles the logic and communication with external systems, and the Database stores and retrieves data as needed. By effectively connecting these components, you can create applications that are scalable, maintainable, and provide a seamless user experience.

Conclusion

Understanding mobile app architecture is essential for building scalable, maintainable, and efficient applications. By adopting architectural patterns such as MVC, MVVM, or Clean Architecture, you can ensure that your application is well-organized and easier to develop, test, and extend. The separation of concerns between different layers—such as the Presentation Layer, Business Logic Layer, and Data Access Layer—allows you to focus on each part of your application independently, leading to better code quality and a more robust application.

Part II: Python Mobile Frameworks
Chapter 4: Introduction to Kivy

<u>What is Kivy?</u>

Kivy is an open-source Python library specifically designed for the rapid development of multitouch applications. It is a cross-platform framework, meaning that applications built with Kivy can run on various operating systems, including Windows, macOS, Linux, Android, and iOS, with minimal code changes. Kivy is particularly popular in the development of mobile applications, thanks to its rich set of user interface elements, robust event handling, and support for gestures and multitouch interactions.

Key Features of Kivy

1. **Cross-Platform Compatibility:**

   o   Kivy allows developers to write code once and deploy it across multiple platforms. This is particularly beneficial for mobile app development, where apps need to run on both Android and iOS devices.

2. **Multitouch Support:**

   o   Kivy natively supports multitouch gestures, making it ideal for creating interactive applications where users can use multiple fingers to interact with the app.

3. **OpenGL ES 2 Accelerated:**

   o Kivy leverages OpenGL ES 2, providing smooth and efficient rendering of complex user interfaces and animations.

4. **Customizable Widgets:**

   o Kivy includes a comprehensive set of widgets, such as buttons, labels, sliders, and more. These widgets are highly customizable, allowing developers to create unique and engaging user interfaces.

5. **Event-Driven Framework:**

   o Kivy operates on an event-driven architecture, where the app reacts to user input or other events, making it responsive and interactive.

How Kivy Works

Kivy applications are structured around an event loop and a tree of widgets. The core components of a Kivy app include the **App Class**, **Widgets**, **Layouts**, and optionally, the **KV Language**.

1. App Class:

- The App class is the entry point for every Kivy application. You create your application by subclassing the App class and overriding the build() method, where you define the root widget of your application.

2. Widgets:

- Widgets are the building blocks of Kivy's user interface. They are elements like buttons, labels, text inputs, and images. Widgets can respond to user input, such as touches, and are used to build up the interface of your app.

3. Layouts:

- Layouts are containers that organize widgets in a specific structure, such as vertically, horizontally, or in a grid. This allows you to control how widgets are displayed on the screen.

4. KV Language:

- Kivy includes an optional language called KV, which is used to describe the interface and interactions in a declarative way. KV language helps separate the design from the logic, making the code cleaner and more maintainable.

Visual Representation of Kivy's Structure

Here's a visual breakdown of how a Kivy application is structured:

Explanation:

- **App Class** is the root of your application, responsible for initializing and running the app.

- **Widgets** are the individual elements that make up the user interface.

- **Layouts** organize these widgets in a specific order or structure.

- **KV Language** can be used to define the user interface outside of the main Python code.

Example: Creating a Simple Kivy Application

Let's explore how Kivy works by creating a simple mobile application that displays a label and a button. When the user presses the button, the label's text changes.

Step 1: Define the App Class

First, define your Kivy app by subclassing the App class. This class will serve as the entry point of the application.

```python
from kivy.app import App

from kivy.uix.label import Label

from kivy.uix.button import Button

from kivy.uix.boxlayout import BoxLayout

class MyFirstApp(App):

    def build(self):

        # Create a vertical layout

        layout = BoxLayout(orientation='vertical')

        # Add a label

        self.label = Label(text="Hello, Kivy!")

        layout.add_widget(self.label)

        # Add a button

        button = Button(text="Click Me",
on_press=self.on_button_press)

        layout.add_widget(button)

        return layout
```

```python
def on_button_press(self, instance):

    # Change the label text when the button is pressed

    self.label.text = "Button Clicked!"

if __name__ == '__main__':

    MyFirstApp().run()
```

Explanation:

- **BoxLayout:** This is a layout that arranges widgets either vertically or horizontally. In this example, widgets are arranged vertically.

- **Label:** A widget that displays text. Here, it initially displays "Hello, Kivy!".

- **Button:** A widget that can be pressed. When pressed, it triggers the on_button_press method.

- **on_button_press:** A method that changes the text of the label when the button is clicked.

Step 2: Run the Application

To see the app in action, save the script as main.py and run it:

```
python main.py
```

UI in Action:

When you click the "Click Me" button, the label's text will change to "Button Clicked!".

KV Language: A Declarative Approach

Kivy also provides the **KV Language**, which is a simple language to define the layout of your application. It allows you to separate the presentation from the logic by placing the UI elements in a .kv file, making the codebase cleaner and more maintainable.

Example: Using KV Language

Here's how the same example could be written using KV Language.

Python Code (main.py):

```python
from kivy.app import App

from kivy.uix.boxlayout import BoxLayout

class MyFirstApp(App):

    pass

if __name__ == '__main__':

    MyFirstApp().run()
```

KV Language File (myfirst.kv):

```
BoxLayout:

    orientation: 'vertical'

        Label:

        id: my_label

        text: 'Hello, Kivy!'

        Button:

        text: 'Click Me'

        on_press: my_label.text = 'Button Clicked!'
```

Explanation:

- **BoxLayout:** The root widget, as before.

- **Label and Button:** Defined in the KV file with their properties.

- **on_press:** A shorthand in KV language to bind a function to the button press event.

Benefits of KV Language:

- **Separation of Concerns:** Keeps UI design separate from business logic, making the codebase cleaner.

- **Ease of Use:** Easier to define complex UIs declaratively.

KV Language in Action:

When you run the Python script with the KV file in the same directory, Kivy automatically loads the myfirst.kv file and builds the UI.

Kivy is a powerful framework for developing cross-platform applications in Python. Its support for multitouch, customizable widgets, and cross-platform compatibility make it an excellent choice for mobile app development. By understanding the core concepts such as the **App Class, Widgets, Layouts,** and **KV Language,** you can start building interactive and visually appealing applications that work seamlessly across various platforms.

Advantages of Using Kivy:

Kivy stands out as a powerful and versatile framework for building mobile applications in Python, offering a range of advantages that make it an attractive choice for developers.

Whether you're targeting Android, iOS, or desktop platforms, Kivy provides the tools needed to create interactive, visually appealing, and highly responsive applications.

1. Cross-Platform Compatibility

Kivy allows developers to write code once and deploy it across multiple platforms, including Android, iOS, Windows, macOS, and Linux. This cross-platform capability is one of Kivy's most significant advantages, reducing development time and effort.

Example: A Single Codebase for Multiple Platforms

Here's a simple Kivy app that can run on Android, iOS, and desktop platforms with no changes to the code.

```python
from kivy.app import App

from kivy.uix.button import Button

class MyApp(App):

    def build(self):

        return Button(text="Hello, Kivy!")

if __name__ == '__main__':

    MyApp().run()
```

Explanation:

- This app consists of a single button with the text "Hello, Kivy!".

- The same code runs on all supported platforms, demonstrating Kivy's cross-platform nature.

2. Rich User Interface with Customizable Widgets

Kivy provides a rich set of widgets that are highly customizable, allowing developers to create unique and interactive user interfaces. These widgets include buttons, labels, sliders, text inputs, and more, which can be easily styled and modified to suit the needs of the application.

Example: Customizing a Button Widget

```python
from kivy.app import App

from kivy.uix.button import Button

class MyApp(App):

    def build(self):

        return Button(

            text="Click Me!",

            font_size=24,

            background_color=(1, 0, 0, 1),

            color=(1, 1, 1, 1),

            size_hint=(0.5, 0.5),

            pos_hint={'center_x': 0.5, 'center_y': 0.5}

        )

if __name__ == '__main__':

    MyApp().run()
```

Explanation:

- **font_size:** Adjusts the size of the button text.

- **background_color:** Changes the button's background to red.

- **color:** Sets the text color to white.

- **size_hint and pos_hint:** Adjust the size and position of the button, making it centered and half the width/height of the screen.

3. Built-in Multitouch Support

Kivy has **native support for multitouch gestures**, which is essential for modern mobile applications. Whether it's pinch-to-zoom, swipe, or multiple finger taps, Kivy handles these interactions seamlessly.

Example: Implementing a Pinch-to-Zoom Gesture

```python
from kivy.app import App

from kivy.uix.image import Image

from kivy.uix.scatter import Scatter

class MyApp(App):

    def build(self):

        scatter = Scatter()

        image = Image(source='kivy_logo.png')

        scatter.add_widget(image)

        return scatter

if __name__ == '__main__':

    MyApp().run()
```

Explanation:

- **Scatter:** A widget that allows for multitouch gestures like scaling (pinch-to-zoom), rotating, and translating (moving) the child widget.

- **Image:** Displays an image that users can interact with.

4. OpenGL ES 2 Acceleration

Kivy is **OpenGL ES 2 accelerated**, which means it leverages the power of the GPU to render graphics, ensuring smooth performance even for complex UIs and animations. This is particularly beneficial for mobile applications where performance is crucial.

Example: Creating a Smooth Animation

from kivy.app import App

from kivy.uix.label import Label

from kivy.animation import Animation

class MyApp(App):

   def build(self):

      label = Label(text="Animated Text", font_size=50, pos_hint={'center_x': 0.5, 'center_y': 0.5})

      anim = Animation(pos_hint={'center_y': 0.9}, duration=2) + Animation(pos_hint={'center_y': 0.1}, duration=2)

      anim += Animation(pos_hint={'center_y': 0.5}, duration=1)

      anim.repeat = True

      anim.start(label)

```python
    return label
if __name__ == '__main__':
    MyApp().run()
```

Explanation:

- **Animation:** Kivy's Animation class allows for the creation of smooth animations by specifying properties to animate (like position, size, etc.) and the duration.

5. Rapid Development with KV Language

Kivy's **KV Language** allows for rapid development by separating the design of the UI from the application logic. This declarative language simplifies the creation of complex interfaces and promotes clean, maintainable code.

Example: Building a UI with KV Language

Python Code (main.py):

```python
from kivy.app import App
class MyFirstApp(App):
    pass
if __name__ == '__main__':
    MyFirstApp().run()
```

KV Language File (myfirst.kv):

```
BoxLayout:
    orientation: 'vertical'
```

```
Label:
id: my_label
text: 'Hello, Kivy!'
Button:
text: 'Click Me'
on_press: my_label.text = 'Button Clicked!'
```

Advantages of Using Kivy

Kivy stands out as a powerful and versatile framework for building mobile applications in Python, offering a range of advantages that make it an attractive choice for developers. Whether you're targeting Android, iOS, or desktop platforms, Kivy provides the tools needed to create interactive, visually appealing, and highly responsive applications. In this section, we will explore the key advantages of using Kivy, supported by examples, visual representations, and code snippets.

1. Cross-Platform Compatibility

Kivy allows developers to write code once and deploy it across multiple platforms, including Android, iOS, Windows, macOS, and Linux. This cross-platform capability is one of Kivy's most significant advantages, reducing development time and effort.

Example: A Single Codebase for Multiple Platforms

Here's a simple Kivy app that can run on Android, iOS, and desktop platforms with no changes to the code.

python

Copy code

```
from kivy.app import App

from kivy.uix.button import Button

class MyApp(App):

    def build(self):

        return Button(text="Hello, Kivy!")
```

```python
if __name__ == '__main__':
    MyApp().run()
```

Explanation:

- This app consists of a single button with the text "Hello, Kivy!".

- The same code runs on all supported platforms, demonstrating Kivy's cross-platform nature.

Visual Representation:

2. Rich User Interface with Customizable Widgets

Kivy provides a rich set of widgets that are highly customizable, allowing developers to create unique and interactive user interfaces. These widgets include buttons, labels, sliders, text inputs, and more, which can be easily styled and modified to suit the needs of the application.

Example: Customizing a Button Widget

python

Copy code

```python
from kivy.app import App
from kivy.uix.button import Button
class MyApp(App):
    def build(self):
        return Button(
            text="Click Me!",
            font_size=24,
```

```
        background_color=(1, 0, 0, 1),

        color=(1, 1, 1, 1),

        size_hint=(0.5, 0.5),

        pos_hint={'center_x': 0.5, 'center_y': 0.5}

    )

if __name__ == '__main__':

  MyApp().run()
```

Explanation:

- **font_size:** Adjusts the size of the button text.

- **background_color:** Changes the button's background to red.

- **color:** Sets the text color to white.

- **size_hint and pos_hint:** Adjust the size and position of the button, making it centered and half the width/height of the screen.

3. Built-in Multitouch Support

Kivy has **native support for multitouch gestures**, which is essential for modern mobile applications. Whether it's pinch-to-zoom, swipe, or multiple finger taps, Kivy handles these interactions seamlessly.

Example: Implementing a Pinch-to-Zoom Gesture

python

Copy code

```
from kivy.app import App
```

```python
from kivy.uix.image import Image
from kivy.uix.scatter import Scatter
class MyApp(App):
    def build(self):
        scatter = Scatter()
        image = Image(source='kivy_logo.png')
        scatter.add_widget(image)
        return scatter
if __name__ == '__main__':
    MyApp().run()
```

Explanation:

- **Scatter:** A widget that allows for multitouch gestures like scaling (pinch-to-zoom), rotating, and translating (moving) the child widget.

- **Image:** Displays an image that users can interact with.

4. OpenGL ES 2 Acceleration

Kivy is **OpenGL ES 2 accelerated**, which means it leverages the power of the GPU to render graphics, ensuring smooth performance even for complex UIs and animations. This is particularly beneficial for mobile applications where performance is crucial.

Example: Creating a Smooth Animation

python

Copy code

```python
from kivy.app import App

from kivy.uix.label import Label

from kivy.animation import Animation

class MyApp(App):

    def build(self):

        label = Label(text="Animated Text", font_size=50,
pos_hint={'center_x': 0.5, 'center_y': 0.5})

        anim = Animation(pos_hint={'center_y': 0.9},
duration=2) + Animation(pos_hint={'center_y': 0.1},
duration=2)

        anim += Animation(pos_hint={'center_y': 0.5},
duration=1)

        anim.repeat = True

        anim.start(label)

        return label

if __name__ == '__main__':

    MyApp().run()
```

Explanation:

- **Animation:** Kivy's Animation class allows for the creation of smooth animations by specifying properties to animate (like position, size, etc.) and the duration.

5. Rapid Development with KV Language

Kivy's **KV Language** allows for rapid development by separating the design of the UI from the application logic. This declarative language simplifies the creation of complex interfaces and promotes clean, maintainable code.

Example: Building a UI with KV Language

Python Code (main.py):

python

Copy code

```
from kivy.app import App

class MyFirstApp(App):
    pass

if __name__ == '__main__':
    MyFirstApp().run()
```

KV Language File (myfirst.kv):

yaml

Copy code

```
BoxLayout:
    orientation: 'vertical'
        Label:
        id: my_label
        text: 'Hello, Kivy!'
        Button:
```

text: 'Click Me'

on_press: my_label.text = 'Button Clicked!'

Explanation:

- **BoxLayout:** Defines the layout structure.

- **Label and Button:** The label's text changes when the button is pressed, demonstrating the use of KV language for creating interactive UIs.

6. Strong Community and Extensive Documentation

Kivy has a **strong, active community** and extensive documentation, making it easier for developers to find resources, tutorials, and help when needed. The community actively contributes to the framework's development, ensuring it stays up-to-date with the latest technology trends.

Access to Resources:

- **Official Documentation:** Kivy's official documentation is comprehensive and provides detailed information on every aspect of the framework.

- **Community Contributions:** Numerous tutorials, examples, and extensions are available, created by the Kivy community to help you get started and overcome challenges.

Example: Accessing the Kivy Documentation

You can explore the official Kivy documentation at:

https://kivy.org/doc/stable/

Kivy offers numerous advantages for mobile app development, making it a compelling choice for developers looking to build cross-platform applications. Its ability to run on multiple platforms with a single codebase, coupled with rich UI customization, multitouch support, OpenGL acceleration, and rapid development features, makes Kivy both powerful and flexible. Additionally, the strong community and extensive documentation further enhance its appeal, providing the support needed to create sophisticated mobile applications.

Installing and Setting Up Kivy

Before diving into mobile app development with Kivy, the first step is to install and set up the framework on your system. Kivy is compatible with various operating systems, including Windows, macOS, and Linux. In this section, we will walk through the process of installing Kivy, setting up your development environment, and verifying that everything is working correctly.

1. Prerequisites

Before you install Kivy, ensure that you have Python installed on your system. Kivy requires Python 3.6 or later. You can check your Python version by running the following command in your terminal or command prompt:

python –version

If Python is not installed, you can download it from the official website: python.org/downloads.

2. Installing Kivy

Kivy can be installed using pip, Python's package manager. The installation process varies slightly depending on your operating system. Follow the steps below according to your platform.

Installing Kivy on Windows

1. **Open Command Prompt**:

    o You can open the Command Prompt by searching for cmd in the Start menu.

2. **Create a Virtual Environment (Optional but Recommended)**:

    o It's good practice to create a virtual environment for your projects to manage dependencies separately. Navigate to your project directory and create a virtual environment:

```
python -m venv kivy_env
```

    o Activate the virtual environment:

```
kivy_env\Scripts\activate
```

3. **Install Kivy**:

    • Once the virtual environment is activated, install Kivy using pip:

```
pip install kivy
```

4. **Verify the Installation**:

- To ensure Kivy is installed correctly, create a simple Python script to test it:

```python
from kivy.app import App

from kivy.uix.label import Label


class TestApp(App):

    def build(self):

        return Label(text="Kivy is installed successfully!")

if __name__ == '__main__':

    TestApp().run()
```

  o Save this script as test_kivy.py and run it:

```
python test_kivy.py
```

  o If Kivy is installed correctly, a window should open displaying the text "Kivy is installed successfully!".

Installing Kivy on macOS

1. **Open Terminal**:

    o You can open the Terminal from the Launchpad or by searching for it in Spotlight.

2. **Create a Virtual Environment (Optional but Recommended)**:
   - Navigate to your project directory and create a virtual environment:

```
python3 -m venv kivy_env
```

Activate the virtual environment:

```
source kivy_env/bin/activate
```

3. **Install Kivy**:
   - With the virtual environment activated, install Kivy using pip:

```
pip install kivy
```

4. **Verify the Installation**:
   - Create a simple Python script to verify the installation:

```python
from kivy.app import App
from kivy.uix.label import Label
class TestApp(App):
    def build(self):
        return Label(text="Kivy is installed successfully!")
if __name__ == '__main__':
    TestApp().run()
```

Save this script as test_kivy.py and run it:

```
python3 test_kivy.py
```

- o ou should see a window displaying "Kivy is installed successfully!".

Installing Kivy on Linux

1. **Open Terminal**:

   - o Open your Terminal application.

2. **Install Dependencies**:

   - o Before installing Kivy, you need to install some dependencies:

sudo apt-get install python3-pip

sudo apt-get install python3-venv

sudo apt-get install python3-dev

sudo apt-get install build-essential libgl1-mesa-dev

3. **Create a Virtual Environment (Optional but Recommended)**:

- Navigate to your project directory and create a virtual environment:

python3 -m venv kivy_env

Activate the virtual environment:

source kivy_env/bin/activate

4. **Install Kivy**:

- With the virtual environment activated, install Kivy using pip:

pip install kivy

5. **Verify the Installation**:

- Test the installation by creating and running a simple Kivy script:

```
from kivy.app import App

from kivy.uix.label import Label

class TestApp(App):

  def build(self):

    return Label(text="Kivy is installed successfully!")

if __name__ == '__main__':

  TestApp().run()
```

Save the script as test_kivy.py and run it:

```
python3 test_kivy.py
```

  o A window should appear with the text "Kivy is installed successfully!".

3. Setting Up Your Development Environment

Once Kivy is installed, you might want to set up your development environment for more efficient coding. This involves choosing an Integrated Development Environment (IDE) or a text editor and configuring it to work with Kivy.

Using Visual Studio Code

Visual Studio Code (VS Code) is a popular choice for Python development due to its powerful features and extensive extensions.

1. **Install Visual Studio Code:**

     o Download and install VS Code from the official website: code.visualstudio.com.

190

2. **Install Python Extension**:

    - Open VS Code, go to the Extensions view by clicking the Extensions icon in the Activity Bar on the side of the window, and search for "Python". Install the extension provided by Microsoft.

3. **Configure VS Code for Kivy**:

    - Open your Kivy project in VS Code.

    - If you are using a virtual environment, make sure to select the correct Python interpreter. Press Ctrl + Shift + P, type "Python: Select Interpreter", and choose your virtual environment.

4. **Run Your Kivy App**:

    - You can run your Kivy app directly from VS Code by pressing F5 or by opening the terminal within VS Code (Ctrl +) and typing:

```
python test_kivy.py
```

The app should run and display the Kivy window as expected.

Using PyCharm

PyCharm is another excellent IDE for Python development, offering robust features such as intelligent code completion, debugging, and project management.

1. **Install PyCharm**:

- o Download and install PyCharm from the official website: jetbrains.com/pycharm.

2. **Create a New Project**:

   - o Open PyCharm and create a new Python project. If using a virtual environment, PyCharm will usually detect it automatically.

3. **Run Your Kivy App**:

   - o Write your Kivy code in a Python file within the PyCharm project.

   - o Right-click the file and select "Run" to execute the script.

4. Troubleshooting Common Issues

If you encounter any issues during installation or setup, here are some common problems and their solutions:

- **Issue:** Kivy window doesn't appear or shows an error.

  - o **Solution:** Ensure all dependencies are installed correctly, especially OpenGL-related libraries. Check the terminal or command prompt for specific error messages and install missing libraries.

- **Issue:** Python not recognized as an internal or external command.

  - o **Solution:** Ensure that Python is added to your system's PATH during installation. You can verify this by typing python --

version in your terminal or command prompt.

- **Issue:** Virtual environment activation fails.

    - **Solution:** Ensure that you are in the correct directory and that the virtual environment was created successfully. Check that you're using the right activation command based on your operating system.

5. Running Your First Kivy Application

Once Kivy is installed and your development environment is set up, you can start building Kivy applications. Let's go through running a simple "Hello, Kivy!" app to ensure everything is working.

Step 1: Create the Application

Here's a simple Kivy application:

```python
from kivy.app import App

from kivy.uix.label import Label

class HelloKivyApp(App):

    def build(self):

        return Label(text="Hello, Kivy!")

if __name__ == '__main__':

    HelloKivyApp().run()
```

Step 2: Run the Application

1. Save the script as hello_kivy.py.

2. Run it in your terminal or IDE:

python hello_kivy.py

Expected Output:

A window should open displaying the text "Hello, Kivy!" centered on the screen.

Installing and setting up Kivy is straightforward and can be done across various platforms with ease. Whether you're on Windows, macOS, or Linux, Kivy provides the tools you need to start building cross-platform mobile applications with Python. By setting up your development environment with IDEs like Visual Studio Code or PyCharm, you can further enhance your coding experience, making it easier to develop, debug, and manage your Kivy projects.

Basic Kivy Application Structure:

Understanding the basic structure of a Kivy application is essential for developing mobile apps using this powerful framework. A typical Kivy application consists of several key components, each playing a specific role in how the application is structured and functions. In this section, we will explore the foundational elements of a Kivy application, including the App class, widgets, layouts, and event handling. We will also provide code examples and explanations to help you understand how these components come together to create a functioning Kivy app.

1. The App Class

The App class is the starting point for any Kivy application. It is the main class that you subclass to define your application. The App class is responsible for managing the lifecycle of your application, including initialization, running the event loop, and cleanup.

Basic Structure of a Kivy App:

from kivy.app import App

class MyApp(App):

    def build(self):

        # This method should return the root widget of the application

        pass

if __name__ == '__main__':

    MyApp().run()

Explanation:

- **MyApp(App):** Here, MyApp is a subclass of the App class. This is where you define the main structure of your application.

- **build():** The build() method is overridden to return the root widget, which forms the main interface of the app. This method is called automatically when the app starts.

- **run():** The run() method starts the Kivy application, initializing everything and entering the main event loop.

2. Widgets in Kivy

Widgets are the basic building blocks of a Kivy application. They represent elements of the user interface, such as buttons, labels, sliders, and text inputs. Widgets are arranged in a hierarchy, forming a widget tree, where each widget can contain other widgets.

Example: Adding a Label Widget

from kivy.app import App

from kivy.uix.label import Label

class MyApp(App):

  def build(self):

    return Label(text="Hello, Kivy!")

if __name__ == '__main__':

  MyApp().run()

Explanation:

- **Label:** A widget that displays text on the screen. In this example, a Label widget is created with the text "Hello, Kivy!".

- **Return Statement in build():** The build() method returns the Label widget, which becomes the root widget of the application.

3. Layouts in Kivy

Layouts in Kivy are special widgets that manage the arrangement and positioning of other widgets. Kivy provides several layout options, such as BoxLayout, GridLayout, and AnchorLayout, each with its specific way of organizing widgets.

Example: Using BoxLayout

196

BoxLayout arranges widgets either vertically or horizontally.

```python
from kivy.app import App

from kivy.uix.label import Label

from kivy.uix.button import Button

from kivy.uix.boxlayout import BoxLayout

class MyApp(App):

    def build(self):

        layout = BoxLayout(orientation='vertical')

        label = Label(text="Hello, Kivy!")

        button = Button(text="Click Me")

        layout.add_widget(label)

        layout.add_widget(button)

        return layout

if __name__ == '__main__':

    MyApp().run()
```

Explanation:

- **BoxLayout:** A layout that arranges its children either vertically or horizontally. Here, the orientation is set to 'vertical', so the widgets are stacked on top of each other.

- **add_widget():** This method is used to add widgets (like Label and Button) to the layout.

4. Event Handling in Kivy

Event handling in Kivy allows your application to respond to user actions, such as button presses, text input, or gestures. You can bind methods to events like on_press or on_touch_down to define custom behavior.

Example: Handling Button Press Event

```python
from kivy.app import App
from kivy.uix.button import Button
from kivy.uix.boxlayout import BoxLayout
from kivy.uix.label import Label
class MyApp(App):
    def build(self):
        self.label = Label(text="Press the Button")
        button = Button(text="Click Me")
        button.bind(on_press=self.on_button_press)
        layout = BoxLayout(orientation='vertical')
        layout.add_widget(self.label)
        layout.add_widget(button)
        return layout
    def on_button_press(self, instance):
        self.label.text = "Button Pressed!"
if __name__ == '__main__':
    MyApp().run()
```

Explanation:

- **bind(on_press=self.on_button_press):** Binds the on_press event of the button to the on_button_press method.

- **on_button_press():** A method that changes the text of the label when the button is pressed.

5. Combining KV Language with Python

The KV Language is a declarative way to design Kivy interfaces, separating the UI design from the logic. You can define the structure of your UI in a .kv file and handle the logic in your Python code.

Example: Creating a UI with KV Language

Python Code (main.py):

```python
from kivy.app import App

from kivy.uix.boxlayout import BoxLayout

class MyRoot(BoxLayout):

    def on_button_press(self):

        self.ids.my_label.text = "Button Pressed!"

class MyApp(App):

    def build(self):

        return MyRoot()

if __name__ == '__main__':

    MyApp().run()
```

KV Language File (myroot.kv):

```
<MyRoot>:
```

```
orientation: 'vertical'
Label:
    id: my_label
    text: 'Press the Button'
Button:
    text: 'Click Me'
    on_press: root.on_button_press()
```

Explanation:

- **KV Language File:** Defines the UI components and their properties, such as orientation, text, and event bindings.

- **id:** The id allows you to reference widgets in your Python code.

- **on_button_press:** The method in the MyRoot class is called when the button is pressed.

6. The Widget Tree and Parent-Child Relationships

In Kivy, widgets are arranged in a hierarchical structure called the widget tree. Each widget can have children (other widgets) and a single parent (the widget it is contained within).

Example: Exploring the Widget Tree

```python
from kivy.app import App

from kivy.uix.boxlayout import BoxLayout

from kivy.uix.button import Button
```

```python
from kivy.uix.label import Label
class MyApp(App):
    def build(self):
        layout = BoxLayout(orientation='vertical')
        label = Label(text="Parent Widget")
        button = Button(text="Child Widget")
        layout.add_widget(label)
        layout.add_widget(button)
        return layout
if __name__ == '__main__':
    MyApp().run()
```

Explanation:

- **Parent-Child Relationships:** The BoxLayout is the parent widget, and it contains two child widgets: Label and Button.

Conclusion

The basic structure of a Kivy application is designed to be both intuitive and flexible, making it easy to start building interactive mobile apps with Python. By understanding the key components such as the App class, widgets, layouts, event handling, and the optional use of KV Language, you can structure your Kivy applications effectively.

Chapter 5: Deep Dive into Kivy

Kivy is a versatile framework that allows developers to build interactive, cross-platform applications with Python. After understanding the basics, it's crucial to dive deeper into the more advanced features and capabilities of Kivy to harness its full potential.

1. Advanced Widget Usage

While Kivy offers basic widgets like Label, Button, and TextInput, it also provides more complex widgets that can be customized and extended to create sophisticated user interfaces.

1.1. Custom Widgets

Custom widgets in Kivy allow you to create reusable components with specific behavior and appearance. By subclassing existing widgets or the Widget class, you can define your own custom widgets.

Example: Creating a Custom Toggle Button

```python
from kivy.app import App

from kivy.uix.boxlayout import BoxLayout

from kivy.uix.label import Label

from kivy.uix.togglebutton import ToggleButton

class MyToggleButton(ToggleButton):

    def __init__(self, **kwargs):

        super(MyToggleButton, self).__init__(**kwargs)

        self.bind(state=self.on_state_change)
```

```python
    def on_state_change(self, instance, value):
        if value == 'down':
            self.text = 'ON'
        else:
            self.text = 'OFF'
class MyApp(App):
    def build(self):
        layout = BoxLayout(orientation='vertical')
        toggle = MyToggleButton(text="OFF")
        label = Label(text="Custom Toggle Button")
        layout.add_widget(label)
        layout.add_widget(toggle)
        return layout
if __name__ == '__main__':
    MyApp().run()
```

Explanation:

- **MyToggleButton:** A custom toggle button that changes its text between "ON" and "OFF" when toggled.

- **on_state_change:** A method bound to the state property, which triggers whenever the button is pressed or released.

1.2. RecycleView

RecycleView is a powerful widget used for displaying large lists of data. Unlike ListView, RecycleView is optimized for performance by reusing widgets, making it ideal for handling large datasets.

Example: Implementing a RecycleView

```python
from kivy.app import App

from kivy.uix.recycleview import RecycleView

from kivy.uix.label import Label

from kivy.uix.boxlayout import BoxLayout

class RV(RecycleView):

    def __init__(self, **kwargs):

        super(RV, self).__init__(**kwargs)

        self.data = [{'text': str(x)} for x in range(100)]

class MyApp(App):

    def build(self):

        layout = BoxLayout(orientation='vertical')

        rv = RV()

        layout.add_widget(rv)

        return layout

if __name__ == '__main__':

    MyApp().run()
```

Explanation:

- **RecycleView:** Displays a list of 100 labels, each containing a number from 0 to 99.

- **self.data:** A list of dictionaries that defines the content of the RecycleView.

2. Animations

Kivy's Animation class provides a powerful way to create smooth and visually appealing animations. You can animate properties of widgets, such as size, position, color, and opacity.

2.1. Basic Animations

Example: Creating a Simple Animation

```python
from kivy.app import App

from kivy.uix.label import Label

from kivy.animation import Animation

class MyApp(App):
    def build(self):
        label = Label(text="Animating...", font_size=50,
pos_hint={'center_x': 0.5, 'center_y': 0.5})

        anim = Animation(font_size=100, duration=2) +
Animation(font_size=50, duration=2)

        anim.repeat = True

        anim.start(label)

        return label

if __name__ == '__main__':
```

MyApp().run()

Explanation:

- **Animation:** Animates the font_size of the label, growing and shrinking it repeatedly.

- **+ Operator:** Chains animations to run sequentially.

2.2. Complex Animations

Kivy allows for more complex animations by animating multiple properties at once or applying animations to nested widgets.

Example: Complex Animation on Multiple Widgets

from kivy.app import App

from kivy.uix.button import Button

from kivy.uix.boxlayout import BoxLayout

from kivy.animation import Animation

class MyApp(App):

    def build(self):

        layout = BoxLayout()

        btn1 = Button(text="Button 1")

        btn2 = Button(text="Button 2")

        layout.add_widget(btn1)

        layout.add_widget(btn2)

```python
    anim1 = Animation(pos_hint={'center_x': 0.3,
'center_y': 0.7}, duration=2)

    anim2 = Animation(pos_hint={'center_x': 0.7,
'center_y': 0.3}, duration=2)

    anim1.start(btn1)

    anim2.start(btn2)

    return layout

if __name__ == '__main__':

    MyApp().run()
```

Explanation:

- **Multiple Animations:** Animates the position of two buttons simultaneously, moving them to different positions on the screen.

- **pos_hint:** Adjusts the position of the widgets within their parent layout.

3. Gestures and Multitouch

Kivy has built-in support for handling gestures and multitouch interactions, which is critical for mobile applications. You can detect gestures like swiping, pinching, or rotating and respond accordingly.

3.1. Handling Touch Events

Example: Detecting Touch Events

```python
from kivy.app import App

from kivy.uix.widget import Widget

class TouchInput(Widget):
```

```python
def on_touch_down(self, touch):

    print("Touch down:", touch.pos)

    self.canvas.add(Color(1, 1, 0))

    self.canvas.add(Rectangle(pos=touch.pos, size=(10, 10)))

def on_touch_move(self, touch):

    print("Touch move:", touch.pos)

    self.canvas.add(Rectangle(pos=touch.pos, size=(10, 10)))


def on_touch_up(self, touch):

    print("Touch up:", touch.pos)

class MyApp(App):

    def build(self):

    return TouchInput()

if __name__ == '__main__':

    MyApp().run()
```

Explanation:

- **on_touch_down(), on_touch_move(), on_touch_up():** These methods detect when a touch starts, moves, or ends, and draw small rectangles at each touch point.

- **Canvas:** Kivy's Canvas is used to draw directly on the screen in response to touch events.

3.2. Pinch-to-Zoom Gesture

Example: Implementing Pinch-to-Zoom

```python
from kivy.app import App

from kivy.uix.scatter import Scatter

from kivy.uix.image import Image

class MyApp(App):

    def build(self):

        scatter = Scatter()

        image = Image(source='kivy_logo.png')

        scatter.add_widget(image)

        return scatter

if __name__ == '__main__':

    MyApp().run()
```

Explanation:

- **Scatter Widget:** Provides multitouch support, enabling pinch-to-zoom, rotation, and translation gestures on its child widget (in this case, an Image).

4. Canvas and Graphics

The Canvas is a key feature in Kivy that allows you to draw shapes, images, and text directly onto the screen. It provides low-level control over rendering, making it possible to create custom visual effects and graphics.

4.1. Drawing Shapes

Example: Drawing Basic Shapes on Canvas

```python
from kivy.app import App
from kivy.uix.widget import Widget
from kivy.graphics import Color, Rectangle, Ellipse, Line
class MyWidget(Widget):
    def __init__(self, **kwargs):
        super(MyWidget, self).__init__(**kwargs)
        with self.canvas:
            Color(1, 0, 0, 1)  # Red
            self.rect = Rectangle(pos=(100, 100), size=(200, 100))
            Color(0, 1, 0, 1)  # Green
            self.ellipse = Ellipse(pos=(200, 200), size=(100, 100))
            Color(0, 0, 1, 1)  # Blue
            self.line = Line(points=[300, 300, 500, 500, 700, 300], width=3)
class MyApp(App):
    def build(self):
        return MyWidget()
if __name__ == '__main__':
    MyApp().run()
```

Explanation:

- **Color:** Sets the drawing color for subsequent shapes.

- **Rectangle, Ellipse, Line:** Draws basic shapes like rectangles, ellipses, and lines.

4.2. Updating Canvas Dynamically

Example: Dynamically Updating Shapes

```python
from kivy.app import App

from kivy.uix.widget import Widget

from kivy.graphics import Color, Rectangle

class DynamicCanvas(Widget):

    def __init__(self, **kwargs):

        super(DynamicCanvas, self).__init__(**kwargs)

        with self.canvas:

            Color(1, 0, 0, 1)  # Red

            self.rect = Rectangle(pos=(100, 100), size=(200, 100))

        # Update the position and size of the rectangle

        self.bind(pos=self.update_rect, size=self.update_rect)

    def update_rect(self, *args):

        self.rect.pos = self.pos

        self.rect.size = self.size

class MyApp(App):

    def build(self):
```

```
    return DynamicCanvas()
if __name__ == '__main__':
    MyApp().run()
```

Explanation:

- **Dynamic Updates:** The rectangle's position and size update dynamically as the widget's position or size changes.

5. Integrating Kivy with Other Python Libraries

Kivy can be seamlessly integrated with other Python libraries, allowing you to extend its functionality. This is particularly useful for adding capabilities like data processing, networking, or machine learning.

5.1. Integrating Kivy with Matplotlib

Example: Displaying a Matplotlib Plot in Kivy

```python
from kivy.app import App
from kivy.uix.boxlayout import BoxLayout
from kivy.garden.matplotlib import FigureCanvasKivyAgg
import matplotlib.pyplot as plt
class MyApp(App):
    def build(self):
        layout = BoxLayout()
        fig, ax = plt.subplots()
        ax.plot([1, 2, 3, 4], [10, 20, 25, 30])
        ax.set_title('Simple Plot')
```

```python
    layout.add_widget(FigureCanvasKivyAgg(fig))

    return layout

if __name__ == '__main__':

    MyApp().run()
```

Explanation:

- **Matplotlib Integration:** This example shows how to embed a Matplotlib plot in a Kivy application using FigureCanvasKivyAgg.

Widgets and Layouts in Kivy:

Widgets and layouts are fundamental concepts in Kivy, allowing developers to create complex user interfaces. Widgets are the individual UI elements, such as buttons, labels, and sliders, while layouts are containers that organize and arrange these widgets on the screen. Understanding how to effectively use and customize widgets and layouts is key to building functional and visually appealing applications in Kivy.

In this section, we'll explore the different types of widgets and layouts available in Kivy, provide detailed explanations, and demonstrate their usage with practical examples.

1. Widgets in Kivy

Kivy provides a wide range of widgets that serve various purposes, from displaying text and images to handling user input. These widgets are the building blocks of your Kivy applications.

1.1. Basic Widgets

Here are some of the most commonly used basic widgets in Kivy:

- **Label:** Displays text on the screen.

- **Button:** A clickable button that can trigger actions.

- **TextInput:** A widget that allows the user to enter and edit text.

- **Slider:** A widget for selecting a value from a range by sliding a handle.

Example: Using Basic Widgets

from kivy.app import App

from kivy.uix.label import Label

from kivy.uix.button import Button

from kivy.uix.textinput import TextInput

from kivy.uix.slider import Slider

from kivy.uix.boxlayout import BoxLayout

class MyApp(App):

    def build(self):

        layout = BoxLayout(orientation='vertical', padding=10, spacing=10)

        # Label widget

        label = Label(text="Hello, Kivy!")

        # Button widget

        button = Button(text="Click Me", size_hint=(1, 0.2))

```python
# TextInput widget
text_input = TextInput(hint_text="Enter your name")
# Slider widget
slider = Slider(min=0, max=100, value=50)
# Add widgets to layout
layout.add_widget(label)
layout.add_widget(button)
layout.add_widget(text_input)
layout.add_widget(slider)
return layout

if __name__ == '__main__':
    MyApp().run()
```

Explanation:

- **Label:** Displays static text "Hello, Kivy!".

- **Button:** A button that can be clicked, with a size hint that makes it 20% of the height of the parent layout.

- **TextInput:** Allows users to input text, with a hint that appears when the text field is empty.

- **Slider:** A horizontal slider that ranges from 0 to 100, with the default value set to 50.

1.2. Advanced Widgets

Kivy also offers more advanced widgets that provide enhanced functionality or more complex behavior:

- **Image:** Displays images in various formats (e.g., PNG, JPEG).

- **Switch:** A widget similar to a toggle button, used for binary choices (on/off).

- **Spinner:** A dropdown list for selecting from multiple options.

- **ProgressBar:** A widget that visually represents progress as a horizontal bar.

Example: Using Advanced Widgets

```python
from kivy.app import App

from kivy.uix.image import Image

from kivy.uix.switch import Switch

from kivy.uix.spinner import Spinner

from kivy.uix.progressbar import ProgressBar

from kivy.uix.boxlayout import BoxLayout

class MyApp(App):

    def build(self):

        layout = BoxLayout(orientation='vertical',
padding=10, spacing=10)

        # Image widget

        image = Image(source='kivy_logo.png')

        # Switch widget

        switch = Switch(active=True)

        # Spinner widget
```

```python
spinner = Spinner(
    text='Option 1',
    values=('Option 1', 'Option 2', 'Option 3')
)
# ProgressBar widget
progress_bar = ProgressBar(value=50, max=100)
# Add widgets to layout
layout.add_widget(image)
layout.add_widget(switch)
layout.add_widget(spinner)
layout.add_widget(progress_bar)
return layout

if __name__ == '__main__':
    MyApp().run()
```

Explanation:

- **Image:** Displays the Kivy logo from a file named kivy_logo.png.

- **Switch:** Represents an on/off state, with the initial state set to "on".

- **Spinner:** A dropdown list with options "Option 1", "Option 2", and "Option 3".

- **ProgressBar:** Displays a progress bar halfway filled, with a maximum value of 100.

2. Layouts in Kivy

Layouts in Kivy are used to arrange widgets on the screen. Different layouts offer different ways of positioning and organizing widgets, allowing for flexible and responsive UI designs.

2.1. BoxLayout

BoxLayout is one of the most commonly used layouts in Kivy. It arranges its children widgets either vertically or horizontally.

Example: Using BoxLayout

```python
from kivy.app import App

from kivy.uix.label import Label

from kivy.uix.button import Button

from kivy.uix.boxlayout import BoxLayout

class MyApp(App):

    def build(self):

        layout = BoxLayout(orientation='horizontal')

        # Adding widgets to the BoxLayout

        layout.add_widget(Label(text="Label 1"))

        layout.add_widget(Button(text="Button 1"))

        layout.add_widget(Label(text="Label 2"))

        layout.add_widget(Button(text="Button 2"))

        return layout

if __name__ == '__main__':
```

MyApp().run()

Explanation:

- **BoxLayout:** Here, the BoxLayout is set to a horizontal orientation, so the widgets are placed side by side.

- **add_widget():** This method is used to add widgets to the layout.

2.2. GridLayout

GridLayout arranges widgets in a grid with a specified number of columns or rows.

Example: Using GridLayout

```
from kivy.app import App

from kivy.uix.gridlayout import GridLayout

from kivy.uix.button import Button

class MyApp(App):

    def build(self):

        layout = GridLayout(cols=2)

        # Adding buttons to the GridLayout

        layout.add_widget(Button(text="Button 1"))

        layout.add_widget(Button(text="Button 2"))

        layout.add_widget(Button(text="Button 3"))

        layout.add_widget(Button(text="Button 4"))

        return layout
```

```python
if __name__ == '__main__':
    MyApp().run()
```

Explanation:

- **GridLayout:** The layout is configured with two columns, so the buttons are arranged in a 2x2 grid.

- **cols:** Specifies the number of columns in the grid.

2.3. AnchorLayout

AnchorLayout positions its children relative to one of its corners or edges.

Example: Using AnchorLayout

```python
from kivy.app import App

from kivy.uix.anchorlayout import AnchorLayout

from kivy.uix.button import Button

class MyApp(App):

    def build(self):

        layout = AnchorLayout(anchor_x='right', anchor_y='bottom')

        # Adding a button to the AnchorLayout

        button = Button(text="Bottom Right", size_hint=(0.3, 0.2))

        layout.add_widget(button)

        return layout

if __name__ == '__main__':
```

MyApp().run()

Explanation:

- **AnchorLayout:** The button is anchored to the bottom-right corner of the layout.

- **anchor_x and anchor_y:** Determine the anchor point of the layout.

2.4. FloatLayout

FloatLayout allows you to position widgets using absolute coordinates or relative positions.

Example: Using FloatLayout

from kivy.app import App

from kivy.uix.floatlayout import FloatLayout

from kivy.uix.button import Button

class MyApp(App):

    def build(self):

        layout = FloatLayout()

        # Adding buttons to the FloatLayout

        button1 = Button(text="Top Left", size_hint=(0.3, 0.2), pos_hint={'x': 0, 'y': 0.8})

        button2 = Button(text="Center", size_hint=(0.3, 0.2), pos_hint={'center_x': 0.5, 'center_y': 0.5})

        button3 = Button(text="Bottom Right", size_hint=(0.3, 0.2), pos_hint={'right': 1, 'y': 0})

        layout.add_widget(button1)

```
        layout.add_widget(button2)

        layout.add_widget(button3)

        return layout

if __name__ == '__main__':

    MyApp().run()
```

Explanation:

- **FloatLayout:** Allows precise positioning of widgets within the layout.

- **pos_hint:** Used to specify the position of widgets within the layout using relative coordinates.

2.5. StackLayout

StackLayout arranges widgets in a horizontal or vertical stack, wrapping them to the next line when there is no more space.

Example: Using StackLayout

```
from kivy.app import App

from kivy.uix.stacklayout import StackLayout

from kivy.uix.button import Button

class MyApp(App):

    def build(self):

        layout = StackLayout()


        # Adding buttons to the StackLayout
```

```python
    for i in range(10):

        btn = Button(text=f"Button {i+1}", size_hint=(0.3, 0.2))

        layout.add_widget(btn)

    return layout

if __name__ == '__main__':

    MyApp().run()
```

Explanation:

- **StackLayout:** Stacks widgets horizontally or vertically, wrapping to the next line as needed.

- **size_hint:** Adjusts the size of each button, determining how much space it takes up in the layout.

3. Combining Widgets and Layouts

Often, you'll need to combine multiple layouts and widgets to create a more complex user interface. This involves nesting layouts within each other and carefully managing widget properties to achieve the desired design.

Example: Combining Layouts

```python
from kivy.app import App

from kivy.uix.label import Label

from kivy.uix.button import Button

from kivy.uix.textinput import TextInput

from kivy.uix.boxlayout import BoxLayout
```

```python
from kivy.uix.gridlayout import GridLayout

from kivy.uix.floatlayout import FloatLayout

class MyApp(App):

    def build(self):

        main_layout = BoxLayout(orientation='vertical',
padding=10, spacing=10)

        # Top layout with a label and a text input

        top_layout = BoxLayout(orientation='horizontal',
size_hint=(1, 0.2))

        label = Label(text="Enter your name:")

        text_input = TextInput()

        top_layout.add_widget(label)

        top_layout.add_widget(text_input)

        # Middle layout with buttons in a grid

        middle_layout = GridLayout(cols=2, spacing=10)

        middle_layout.add_widget(Button(text="Button 1"))

        middle_layout.add_widget(Button(text="Button 2"))

        middle_layout.add_widget(Button(text="Button 3"))

        middle_layout.add_widget(Button(text="Button 4"))


        # Bottom layout with a button anchored at the bottom-
right

        bottom_layout = FloatLayout(size_hint=(1, 0.3))
```

```python
    button = Button(text="Submit", size_hint=(0.3, 0.4),
pos_hint={'right': 1, 'y': 0})

    bottom_layout.add_widget(button)

    # Add all layouts to the main layout

    main_layout.add_widget(top_layout)

    main_layout.add_widget(middle_layout)

    main_layout.add_widget(bottom_layout)

    return main_layout

if __name__ == '__main__':

  MyApp().run()
```

Explanation:

- **Top Layout:** A BoxLayout that contains a label and a text input field.

- **Middle Layout:** A GridLayout that arranges buttons in a 2x2 grid.

- **Bottom Layout:** A FloatLayout with a button anchored at the bottom-right.

- **Main Layout:** A BoxLayout that combines the top, middle, and bottom layouts vertically.

Widgets and layouts are at the core of any Kivy application, and understanding how to use them effectively is crucial for building sophisticated and responsive user interfaces. By mastering basic and advanced widgets, as well as various layout types, you can create complex, dynamic UIs that meet the needs of your application.

Handling User Input and Events in Kivy:

Handling user input and events is a critical aspect of building interactive applications with Kivy. Kivy provides a robust system for managing various types of user interactions, including touch events, keyboard input, gestures, and more. Understanding how to effectively handle these inputs and events is key to creating responsive and engaging applications.

In this section, we will explore how to handle user input and events in Kivy, using practical examples and code to demonstrate how these features work in real applications.

1. Handling Touch and Mouse Events

Touch and mouse events are fundamental for mobile and desktop applications. Kivy supports touch and mouse interactions through built-in methods that you can override to customize behavior when the user interacts with widgets.

1.1. Basic Touch Events

Kivy widgets come with built-in methods to handle touch events:

- **on_touch_down:** Triggered when a touch or click begins.

- **on_touch_move:** Triggered when a touch or click moves.

- **on_touch_up:** Triggered when a touch or click ends.

Example: Handling Basic Touch Events

from kivy.app import App

226

```python
from kivy.uix.widget import Widget
from kivy.graphics import Color, Ellipse
class TouchInput(Widget):
    def on_touch_down(self, touch):
        with self.canvas:
            Color(1, 0, 0)
            d = 30.
            Ellipse(pos=(touch.x - d / 2, touch.y - d / 2),
size=(d, d))
            print(f"Touch down at {touch.pos}")
    def on_touch_move(self, touch):
        with self.canvas:
            Color(0, 1, 0)
            d = 20.
            Ellipse(pos=(touch.x - d / 2, touch.y - d / 2),
size=(d, d))
            print(f"Touch move at {touch.pos}")
    def on_touch_up(self, touch):
        print(f"Touch up at {touch.pos}")
class MyApp(App):
    def build(self):
        return TouchInput()
if __name__ == '__main__':
```

MyApp().run()

Explanation:

- **on_touch_down:** Creates a red circle at the touch point when the screen is touched or clicked.

- **on_touch_move:** Creates a green circle as the touch or click moves across the screen.

- **on_touch_up:** Prints the position where the touch or click ends.

1.2. Distinguishing Between Multiple Touches

Kivy supports multitouch gestures, which are crucial for modern mobile applications. You can track multiple touch points simultaneously.

Example: Handling Multiple Touch Points

```python
from kivy.app import App

from kivy.uix.widget import Widget

from kivy.graphics import Color, Ellipse

class MultiTouchInput(Widget):

    def on_touch_down(self, touch):

        if touch.is_double_tap:

            print(f"Double tap detected at {touch.pos}")

        elif touch.is_mouse_scrolling:

            print(f"Mouse scroll detected: {touch.button}")

        else:
```

```python
        with self.canvas:

            Color(0, 0, 1)

            d = 30.

            Ellipse(pos=(touch.x - d / 2, touch.y - d / 2),
size=(d, d))

        print(f"Touch down at {touch.pos} with ID
{touch.uid}")

    def on_touch_move(self, touch):

        with self.canvas:

            Color(0, 1, 1)

            d - 20.

            Ellipse(pos=(touch.x - d / 2, touch.y - d / 2),
size=(d, d))

        print(f"Touch move at {touch.pos} with ID
{touch.uid}")

    def on_touch_up(self, touch):

        print(f"Touch up at {touch.pos} with ID {touch.uid}")

class MyApp(App):

    def build(self):

        return MultiTouchInput()

if __name__ == '__main__':

    MyApp().run()
```

Explanation:

- **touch.is_double_tap:** Detects a double-tap gesture.

- **touch.is_mouse_scrolling:** Detects when the mouse wheel is scrolled.

- **touch.uid:** Unique identifier for each touch point, allowing you to distinguish between multiple touches.

2. Handling Keyboard Input

Kivy can also capture and respond to keyboard input, which is essential for applications that require text entry or keyboard shortcuts.

2.1. Basic Keyboard Handling

You can handle keyboard input by binding to the keyboard and defining methods to respond to key presses and releases.

Example: Capturing Keyboard Input

```python
from kivy.app import App

from kivy.uix.widget import Widget

from kivy.core.window import Window

class KeyboardInput(Widget):

    def __init__(self, **kwargs):

        super(KeyboardInput, self).__init__(**kwargs)

        self._keyboard =
Window.request_keyboard(self._keyboard_closed, self)

self._keyboard.bind(on_key_down=self._on_key_down)
```

```python
        self._keyboard.bind(on_key_up=self._on_key_up)

    def _keyboard_closed(self):

self._keyboard.unbind(on_key_down=self._on_key_down)

        self._keyboard = None

    def _on_key_down(self, keyboard, keycode, text,
modifiers):

        print(f"Key {keycode[1]} pressed")

        if keycode[1] == 'a':

            print("The 'A' key was pressed")

    def _on_key_up(self, keyboard, keycode):

        print(f"Key {keycode[1]} released")

class MyApp(App):

    def build(self):

        return KeyboardInput()

if __name__ == '__main__':

    MyApp().run()
```

Explanation:

- **Window.request_keyboard:** Requests control of
  the keyboard for input.

- **_on_key_down and _on_key_up:** Methods that
  handle key press and release events, respectively.

- **keycode:** Contains information about the key that
  was pressed or released.

2.2. TextInput Widget for Handling Text Entry

The TextInput widget in Kivy is designed for text entry and automatically handles keyboard input, including focus management and text editing.

Example: Using TextInput for User Input

```python
from kivy.app import App

from kivy.uix.boxlayout import BoxLayout

from kivy.uix.textinput import TextInput

from kivy.uix.label import Label

class MyApp(App):

    def build(self):

        layout = BoxLayout(orientation='vertical',
padding=10, spacing=10)

        label = Label(text="Enter text:")

        text_input = TextInput(multiline=False)

        text_input.bind(on_text_validate=self.on_enter)

        layout.add_widget(label)

        layout.add_widget(text_input)

        return layout

    def on_enter(self, instance):

        print(f"User entered: {instance.text}")

if __name__ == '__main__':

    MyApp().run()
```

Explanation:

- **TextInput(multiline=False):** A single-line text input field.

- **on_text_validate:** An event that triggers when the user presses the Enter key.

- **instance.text:** The text entered by the user.

3. Handling Gestures

Kivy's support for gestures such as swipes, pinches, and rotations makes it ideal for creating interactive mobile applications. You can detect these gestures and define custom behaviors in response to them.

3.1. Swipe Gestures

Swipe gestures are common in mobile applications for navigating through content or triggering specific actions.

Example: Detecting Swipe Gestures

```python
from kivy.app import App

from kivy.uix.label import Label

from kivy.uix.boxlayout import BoxLayout

from kivy.uix.widget import Widget

from kivy.uix.floatlayout import FloatLayout

class SwipeWidget(Widget):

    def on_touch_down(self, touch):

        self.start_x = touch.x

        self.start_y = touch.y
```

```python
        return super(SwipeWidget,
self).on_touch_down(touch)

    def on_touch_up(self, touch):

        dx = touch.x - self.start_x

        dy = touch.y - self.start_y

        if abs(dx) > abs(dy):

            if dx > 0:

                self.parent.label.text = "Swiped Right"

            else:

                self.parent.label.text = "Swiped Left"

        else:

            if dy > 0:

                self.parent.label.text = "Swiped Up"

            else:

                self.parent.label.text = "Swiped Down"

        return super(SwipeWidget, self).on_touch_up(touch)

class MyApp(App):

    def build(self):

        layout = FloatLayout()

        self.label = Label(text="Swipe in any direction",
size_hint=(None, None), size=(300, 50),
pos_hint={'center_x': 0.5, 'center_y': 0.9})

        swipe_widget = SwipeWidget()
```

```
    layout.add_widget(self.label)

    layout.add_widget(swipe_widget)

    layout.label = self.label

    return layout

if __name__ == '__main__':

    MyApp().run()
```

Explanation:

- **SwipeWidget:** Detects swipe gestures by comparing the start and end positions of a touch.

- **on_touch_down and on_touch_up:** Track the initial and final positions of the touch to determine the swipe direction.

- **dx and dy:** Calculate the distance moved horizontally and vertically to detect swipe direction.

3.2. Pinch-to-Zoom Gesture

The pinch-to-zoom gesture is commonly used for scaling images or other content.

Example: Implementing Pinch-to-Zoom

```
from kivy.app import App

from kivy.uix.scatter import Scatter

from kivy.uix.image import Image

from kivy.uix.floatlayout import FloatLayout

class MyApp(App):

    def build(self):
```

```
    layout = FloatLayout()

    scatter = Scatter()

    image = Image(source='kivy_logo.png')

    scatter.add_widget(image)

    layout.add_widget(scatter)

    return layout

if __name__ == '__main__':

    MyApp().run()
```

Explanation:

- **Scatter:** Provides multitouch support, enabling gestures like pinch-to-zoom.

- **Image:** The image is added to the Scatter widget, allowing it to be scaled, rotated, and moved.

4. Customizing Event Handling

Kivy allows you to customize event handling to suit the specific needs of your application. You can define custom events or modify existing ones to create more dynamic and responsive interfaces.

4.1. Creating Custom Events

Custom events can be created and dispatched in Kivy to trigger specific actions in your application.

Example: Defining and Dispatching a Custom Event

```
from kivy.app import App

from kivy.uix.button import Button
```

```python
from kivy.uix.boxlayout import BoxLayout

from kivy.uix.label import Label

class CustomEventButton(Button):

    def on_press(self):

        self.dispatch('on_custom_event')

    def on_custom_event(self, *args):

        print("Custom event triggered")

class MyApp(App):

    def build(self):

        layout = BoxLayout(orientation='vertical',
padding=10, spacing=10)

        button = CustomEventButton(text="Press Me")

button.bind(on_custom_event=self.on_custom_event_trigg
ered)

        label = Label(text="Custom event demo")

            layout.add_widget(button)

        layout.add_widget(label)

        return layout

    def on_custom_event_triggered(self, *args):

        print("Custom event handled in the app")

if __name__ == '__main__':

    MyApp().run()
```

Explanation:

- **CustomEventButton:** A button that triggers a custom event (on_custom_event) when pressed.

- **dispatch:** Dispatches the custom event when the button is pressed.

- **on_custom_event:** A method that handles the custom event.

Handling user input and events in Kivy is a powerful feature that enables developers to create highly interactive and responsive applications. Whether you're dealing with touch events, keyboard input, gestures, or custom events, Kivy provides the tools needed to manage these interactions effectively.

Styling and Theming Your App in Kivy:

Styling and theming are essential aspects of mobile app development that determine the look and feel of an application. Kivy provides a flexible framework for customizing the appearance of your app, allowing you to apply styles, themes, and custom graphics to create a unique user interface.

1. Basic Styling with Kivy Properties

Kivy widgets come with various properties that can be used to style elements such as text, background color, font size, and more. These properties can be set directly in Python code or defined in KV language.

1.1. Styling Widgets with Properties

You can customize the appearance of Kivy widgets by setting properties like color, font_size, background_color, and others.

238

Example: Basic Styling with Kivy Properties

```python
from kivy.app import App

from kivy.uix.button import Button

from kivy.uix.label import Label

from kivy.uix.boxlayout import BoxLayout

class MyApp(App):

    def build(self):

        layout = BoxLayout(orientation='vertical',
padding=10, spacing=10)

        # Styled Label

        label = Label(

            text="Welcome to My App",

            font_size=24,

            color=(1, 0, 0, 1)  # Red text

        )

        # Styled Button

        button = Button(

            text="Click Me",

            font_size=20,

            background_color=(0, 1, 0, 1),  # Green background

            color=(1, 1, 1, 1),  # White text

            size_hint=(1, 0.5)
```

```
    )

    layout.add_widget(label)

    layout.add_widget(button)

    return layout

if __name__ == '__main__':

  MyApp().run()
```

Explanation:

- **font_size:** Adjusts the size of the text.

- **color:** Changes the color of the text (RGBA format).

- **background_color:** Sets the background color of the button.

- **size_hint:** Controls the button's size relative to its parent layout.

2. Advanced Styling with KV Language

The KV language in Kivy provides a more structured way to define the appearance of widgets, separating the UI design from the logic. This allows for more maintainable and readable code, especially when dealing with complex UIs.

2.1. Using KV Language for Styling

KV language allows you to define the properties of widgets directly in a KV file, making it easy to manage and modify the appearance of your application.

Example: Styling with KV Language

Python Code (main.py):

```python
from kivy.app import App

from kivy.uix.boxlayout import BoxLayout

class MyRoot(BoxLayout):

    pass

class MyApp(App):

    def build(self):

        return MyRoot()

if __name__ == '__main__':

    MyApp().run()
```

KV Language File (myroot.kv):

```
<MyRoot>:

    orientation: 'vertical'

    padding: 10

    spacing: 10

    Label:

        text: "Welcome to My Themed App"

        font_size: 32

        color: 1, 0.5, 0, 1  # Orange text

    Button:

        text: "Press Me"

        font_size: 24
```

    background_color: 0.3, 0.6, 1, 1 # Light blue
background

    color: 1, 1, 1, 1 # White text

    size_hint: 1, 0.4

Explanation:

- **Label and Button:** Widgets are styled directly in the KV file, with properties like font_size, color, and background_color defined in a clean, declarative manner.

- **<MyRoot>:** Defines the layout and general styling for the root widget.

3. Custom Fonts and Images

Custom fonts and images can greatly enhance the visual appeal of your app. Kivy allows you to use custom fonts for text and easily integrate images into your UI.

3.1. Using Custom Fonts

You can specify custom fonts for text elements in your Kivy application, either in the Python code or KV language.

Example: Applying Custom Fonts

Python Code (main.py):

```python
from kivy.app import App

from kivy.uix.label import Label

from kivy.uix.boxlayout import BoxLayout

class MyApp(App):
```

```python
def build(self):

    layout = BoxLayout(orientation='vertical', padding=10, spacing=10)

    # Custom Font Label

    label = Label(

        text="Hello with Custom Font",

        font_size=24,

        font_name='Roboto-Bold.ttf'  # Custom font file

    )

    layout.add_widget(label)

    return layout

if __name__ == '__main__':

    MyApp().run()
```

Explanation:

- **font_name:** Specifies the path to the custom font file (e.g., Roboto-Bold.ttf).

- **font_size:** Sets the size of the custom font.

3.2. Integrating Images

Images can be used as backgrounds, icons, or decorative elements in your Kivy app. Kivy's Image widget makes it easy to load and display images.

Example: Using Images in the UI

KV Language File (myroot.kv):

```
<MyRoot>:
    orientation: 'vertical'
    padding: 10
    spacing: 10
    Image:
        source: 'background.png'
        allow_stretch: True
        keep_ratio: False
    Label:
        text: "Hello with a Background Image"
        font_size: 32
        color: 1, 1, 1, 1  # White text
```

Explanation:

- **source:** Specifies the path to the image file (e.g., background.png).

- **allow_stretch:** Allows the image to be stretched to fill the widget's size.

- **keep_ratio:** Maintains the aspect ratio of the image.

4. Theming Your Application

Theming allows you to apply a consistent visual style across your entire application. By defining a theme, you can standardize colors, fonts, and other visual elements, making your app more cohesive and professional.

4.1. Creating a Theme with KV Language

You can define a theme in KV language by setting up global variables or defining reusable styles that can be applied across different widgets.

Example: Defining a Global Theme

KV Language File (theme.kv):

```
#:set primary_color 0.3, 0.6, 1, 1  # Light blue

#:set secondary_color 0.1, 0.3, 0.8, 1  # Darker blue

#:set text_color 1, 1, 1, 1  # White

<MyRoot>:
    orientation: 'vertical'
    padding: 10
    spacing: 10
    canvas.before:
        Color:
            rgba: primary_color
        Rectangle:
            pos: self.pos
            size: self.size
    Label:
        text: "Themed Application"
        font_size: 32
        color: text_color
```

Button:

    text: "Themed Button"

    font_size: 24

    background_color: secondary_color

    color: text_color

    size_hint: 1, 0.4

Explanation:

- **#:set:** Defines global variables (e.g., primary_color, secondary_color, text_color) that can be reused throughout the KV file.

- **canvas.before:** Draws a background color behind the widget using the primary_color defined in the theme.

- **Label and Button:** Use the text_color and secondary_color to ensure a consistent look.

4.2. Applying Themes Dynamically

You can also switch themes dynamically based on user preferences or app settings.

Example: Switching Themes Dynamically

from kivy.app import App

from kivy.uix.boxlayout import BoxLayout

from kivy.uix.button import Button

from kivy.uix.label import Label

class MyApp(App):

```python
def build(self):
    self.theme = {
        "primary_color": (0.3, 0.6, 1, 1),
        "secondary_color": (0.1, 0.3, 0.8, 1),
        "text_color": (1, 1, 1, 1)
    }
    layout = BoxLayout(orientation='vertical',
padding=10, spacing=10)
    self.label = Label(
        text="Current Theme",
        font_size=32,
        color=self.theme['text_color']
    )
    button = Button(
        text="Switch Theme",
        font_size=24,
        background_color=self.theme['secondary_color'],
        color=self.theme['text_color'],
        size_hint=(1, 0.4)
    )
    button.bind(on_press=self.switch_theme)
    layout.add_widget(self.label)
```

```python
        layout.add_widget(button)

        return layout

    def switch_theme(self, instance):
        # Toggle between two themes
        if self.theme['primary_color'] == (0.3, 0.6, 1, 1):
            self.theme['primary_color'] = (1, 0.5, 0.3, 1)  # Orange
            self.theme['secondary_color'] = (0.8, 0.3, 0.1, 1)  # Darker orange
        else:
            self.theme['primary_color'] = (0.3, 0.6, 1, 1)  # Light blue
            self.theme['secondary_color'] = (0.1, 0.3, 0.8, 1)  # Darker blue

        # Apply the new theme to the widgets
        self.label.color = self.theme['text_color']
        instance.background_color = self.theme['secondary_color']


if __name__ == '__main__':
    MyApp().run()
```

Explanation:

- **self.theme:** A dictionary storing theme colors.

- **switch_theme:** Toggles between two different themes (blue and orange) when the button is pressed, and applies the changes dynamically.

5. Using Custom Graphics and Canvas

For more advanced styling, you can draw custom graphics using Kivy's Canvas class. This allows for the creation of complex visual elements like gradients, shadows, and custom shapes.

5.1. Drawing Custom Graphics

The Canvas class allows you to draw directly onto widgets, creating custom backgrounds, borders, and other graphic elements.

Example: Custom Background with Canvas

```python
from kivy.app import App

from kivy.uix.label import Label

from kivy.uix.boxlayout import BoxLayout

from kivy.graphics import Color, Rectangle


class MyCustomLabel(Label):

    def __init__(self, **kwargs):

        super(MyCustomLabel, self).__init__(**kwargs)

        with self.canvas.before:

            Color(0, 0, 1, 1)  # Blue background

            self.rect = Rectangle(pos=self.pos, size=self.size)
```

```python
        self.bind(pos=self.update_rect,
size=self.update_rect)


    def update_rect(self, *args):

        self.rect.pos = self.pos

        self.rect.size = self.size


class MyApp(App):

    def build(self):

        layout = BoxLayout(orientation='vertical',
padding=10, spacing=10)


        # Custom styled label with a blue background
        custom_label = MyCustomLabel(

            text="Custom Styled Label",

            font_size=24,

            color=(1, 1, 1, 1)  # White text

        )


        layout.add_widget(custom_label)

        return layout


if __name__ == '__main__':
```

MyApp().run()

Explanation:

- **Canvas.before:** Draws a blue rectangle behind the label, creating a custom background.

- **update_rect:** Ensures that the background rectangle resizes and repositions with the label.

6. Implementing Responsive Design

Responsive design is crucial for mobile apps that need to adapt to different screen sizes and orientations. Kivy provides tools like size_hint, pos_hint, and layouts to create responsive UIs.

6.1. Responsive Layouts

By using size_hint and pos_hint, you can create layouts that automatically adjust based on the screen size.

Example: Responsive Layout

```python
from kivy.app import App

from kivy.uix.button import Button

from kivy.uix.boxlayout import BoxLayout


class MyApp(App):

    def build(self):

        layout = BoxLayout(padding=10, spacing=10)


        # Buttons that resize according to the screen size
```

```python
    button1 = Button(text="Button 1", size_hint=(0.5, 0.5))

    button2 = Button(text="Button 2", size_hint=(0.5, 0.5))


    layout.add_widget(button1)

    layout.add_widget(button2)

    return layout


if __name__ == '__main__':

  MyApp().run()
```

Explanation:

- **size_hint:** Controls how much space a widget should take relative to its parent. Here, both buttons take up 50% of the width and height of their parent layout.

Styling and theming are powerful tools in Kivy that allow you to create visually appealing and user-friendly applications. By using Kivy properties, KV language, custom fonts, images, themes, and custom graphics, you can tailor the appearance of your app to meet the needs of your users and the aesthetic goals of your project.

Building Responsive UIs in Kivy:

Building responsive user interfaces (UIs) is essential for creating applications that work well across different screen sizes, resolutions, and orientations. Kivy provides various tools and techniques to design responsive UIs that adapt dynamically to changes in the environment, ensuring a consistent and user-friendly experience on both mobile devices and desktops.

In this section, we will explore how to build responsive UIs in Kivy using layouts, size hints, position hints, and other Kivy features. We will provide practical examples and code snippets to demonstrate how to create flexible and adaptive interfaces.

1. Understanding Responsive Design in Kivy

Responsive design in Kivy involves creating UIs that adjust their layout, size, and position based on the available screen space. This is crucial for applications that need to run on multiple devices with varying screen dimensions.

Key Concepts:

- **size_hint:** Defines how much space a widget should take relative to its parent layout.

- **pos_hint:** Controls the positioning of a widget within its parent layout.

- **Layouts:** Kivy's layouts (like BoxLayout, GridLayout, AnchorLayout, etc.) help organize widgets in a way that adapts to different screen sizes.

2. Using Size Hints and Position Hints

Size hints and position hints are central to making widgets responsive in Kivy. They allow you to define the size and position of widgets as a proportion of the parent layout, rather than using fixed pixel values.

2.1. Size Hints

size_hint is a tuple ((width, height)) where each value is a proportion of the parent widget's size. For example, a size_hint of (0.5, 0.5) means the widget will take up 50% of the parent widget's width and height.

Example: Using Size Hints

from kivy.app import App

from kivy.uix.button import Button

from kivy.uix.boxlayout import BoxLayout

class MyApp(App):

  def build(self):

    layout = BoxLayout(padding=10, spacing=10)

    # Buttons with size hints

    button1 = Button(text="Button 1", size_hint=(0.7, 0.5)) # 70% width, 50% height

    button2 = Button(text="Button 2", size_hint=(0.3, 0.5)) # 30% width, 50% height

    layout.add_widget(button1)

```
layout.add_widget(button2)

return layout


if __name__ == '__main__':

    MyApp().run()
```

Explanation:

- **size_hint=(0.7, 0.5):** Button 1 takes up 70% of the width and 50% of the height of its parent layout.

- **size_hint=(0.3, 0.5):** Button 2 takes up the remaining 30% of the width and 50% of the height.

2.2. Position Hints

pos_hint allows you to position a widget relative to its parent layout using relative coordinates (ranging from 0 to 1).

Example: Using Position Hints

```
from kivy.app import App

from kivy.uix.button import Button

from kivy.uix.floatlayout import FloatLayout


class MyApp(App):

    def build(self):

        layout = FloatLayout()
```

```python
    # Buttons with position hints

    button1 = Button(text="Top Left", size_hint=(0.3, 0.3), pos_hint={'x': 0, 'top': 1})

    button2 = Button(text="Center", size_hint=(0.3, 0.3), pos_hint={'center_x': 0.5, 'center_y': 0.5})

    button3 = Button(text="Bottom Right", size_hint=(0.3, 0.3), pos_hint={'right': 1, 'y': 0})


    layout.add_widget(button1)

    layout.add_widget(button2)

    layout.add_widget(button3)


    return layout


if __name__ == '__main__':

    MyApp().run()
```

Explanation:

- **pos_hint={'x': 0, 'top': 1}:** Positions Button 1 in the top-left corner of the parent layout.

- **pos_hint={'center_x': 0.5, 'center_y': 0.5}:** Centers Button 2 within the parent layout.

- **pos_hint={'right': 1, 'y': 0}:** Positions Button 3 in the bottom-right corner of the parent layout.

3. Using Responsive Layouts

Kivy offers several layouts that inherently support responsive design by managing the placement and sizing of widgets within them. These layouts can adapt to different screen sizes and orientations.

3.1. BoxLayout for Responsive Design

BoxLayout arranges widgets in a horizontal or vertical stack. By combining size_hint with BoxLayout, you can create responsive UIs that adjust to screen changes.

Example: Responsive BoxLayout

```python
from kivy.app import App

from kivy.uix.button import Button

from kivy.uix.boxlayout import BoxLayout

class MyApp(App):

    def build(self):

        layout = BoxLayout(orientation='horizontal',
padding=10, spacing=10)

            # Buttons with size hints in a BoxLayout

        button1 = Button(text="Button 1", size_hint=(0.5, 1))

        button2 = Button(text="Button 2", size_hint=(0.5, 1))

        layout.add_widget(button1)

        layout.add_widget(button2)

        return layout
```

```
if __name__ == '__main__':

    MyApp().run()
```

Explanation:

- **orientation='horizontal':** The BoxLayout arranges widgets horizontally.

- **size_hint=(0.5, 1):** Each button takes up 50% of the width and 100% of the height, adjusting dynamically as the window resizes.

3.2. GridLayout for Adaptive Grids

GridLayout is useful for creating grids where each cell can adapt to the available space. It automatically arranges widgets into a grid based on the number of rows or columns specified.

Example: Adaptive GridLayout

```
from kivy.app import App

from kivy.uix.button import Button

from kivy.uix.gridlayout import GridLayout


class MyApp(App):

    def build(self):

        layout = GridLayout(cols=2, padding=10, spacing=10)


        # Adding buttons to the GridLayout

        for i in range(1, 5):
```

```
        layout.add_widget(Button(text=f"Button {i}"))


    return layout


if __name__ == '__main__':

    MyApp().run()
```

Explanation:

- **cols=2:** The layout arranges widgets in two columns.

- **GridLayout:** Automatically adjusts the size and position of the buttons to fit within the grid cells.

4. Adapting to Screen Orientation Changes

Responsive UIs must handle screen orientation changes, especially on mobile devices where users frequently switch between portrait and landscape modes. Kivy layouts, combined with size and position hints, can help you create interfaces that adapt smoothly to these changes.

Example: Adapting to Orientation Changes

```
from kivy.app import App

from kivy.uix.button import Button

from kivy.uix.boxlayout import BoxLayout

from kivy.core.window import Window


class MyApp(App):
```

```python
def build(self):

    layout = BoxLayout(orientation='horizontal',
padding=10, spacing=10)


    # Buttons that adapt to orientation

    button1 = Button(text="Button 1", size_hint=(0.5, 1))

    button2 = Button(text="Button 2", size_hint=(0.5, 1))


    layout.add_widget(button1)

    layout.add_widget(button2)


    Window.bind(on_resize=self.on_window_resize)


    return layout


def on_window_resize(self, window, width, height):
    # Change layout orientation based on aspect ratio
    if width > height:
        self.root.orientation = 'horizontal'
    else:
        self.root.orientation = 'vertical'
```

```python
if __name__ == '__main__':
    MyApp().run()
```

Explanation:

- **Window.bind(on_resize=self.on_window_resize):** Binds the window resize event to a custom handler.

- **on_window_resize:** Changes the orientation of the BoxLayout based on the window's aspect ratio (horizontal for landscape, vertical for portrait).

5. Using FloatLayout for Precise Control

FloatLayout provides absolute positioning control over widgets, allowing you to place widgets anywhere on the screen using pos_hint and size_hint. This is useful when you need precise control over widget placement.

Example: Creating a Responsive UI with FloatLayout

```python
from kivy.app import App

from kivy.uix.floatlayout import FloatLayout

from kivy.uix.button import Button


class MyApp(App):
    def build(self):
        layout = FloatLayout()


        # Button positioned at top-right corner
```

```python
    button1 = Button(text="Top Right", size_hint=(0.3,
0.3), pos_hint={'right': 1, 'top': 1})

    # Button positioned at center
    button2 = Button(text="Center", size_hint=(0.4, 0.4),
pos_hint={'center_x': 0.5, 'center_y': 0.5})

    # Button positioned at bottom-left corner
    button3 = Button(text="Bottom Left", size_hint=(0.3,
0.3), pos_hint={'x': 0, 'y': 0})

    layout.add_widget(button1)
    layout.add_widget(button2)
    layout.add_widget(button3)

    return layout

if __name__ == '__main__':
    MyApp().run()
```

- **FloatLayout:** Provides a flexible layout where widgets can be positioned anywhere on the screen.

- **pos_hint and size_hint:** Used to control the placement and size of buttons within the FloatLayout.

6. Implementing Scrollable Views

In responsive designs, especially for mobile apps, it's common to have content that doesn't fit on the screen and requires scrolling. Kivy's ScrollView allows you to create scrollable areas in your UI.

Example: Creating a Scrollable View

```python
from kivy.app import App

from kivy.uix.scrollview import ScrollView

from kivy.uix.gridlayout import GridLayout

from kivy.uix.button import Button


class MyApp(App):

    def build(self):

        # Create a ScrollView

        scroll_view = ScrollView(size_hint=(1, None), size=(Window.width, Window.height))


        # Create a GridLayout for the scrollable content

        grid = GridLayout(cols=1, spacing=10, size_hint_y=None)

        grid.bind(minimum_height=grid.setter('height'))


        # Add many buttons to the GridLayout

        for i in range(20):
```

```python
        btn = Button(text=f"Button {i + 1}",
size_hint_y=None, height=40)

        grid.add_widget(btn)


    scroll_view.add_widget(grid)


    return scroll_view


if __name__ == '__main__':

    MyApp().run()
```

Explanation:

- **ScrollView:** A container that allows scrolling of its content.

- **GridLayout:** Holds the scrollable content, with size_hint_y=None and height set to accommodate the content height.

- **bind(minimum_height=grid.setter('height')):** Ensures that the GridLayout expands to fit its content, enabling scrolling.

Building responsive UIs in Kivy is essential for creating applications that provide a consistent and user-friendly experience across a wide range of devices and screen sizes. By leveraging Kivy's layouts, size hints, position hints, and scrollable views, you can design interfaces that dynamically adapt to different environments, ensuring your app looks and works great on any device.

Conclusion

Diving deeper into Kivy reveals the framework's full potential, enabling developers to create more sophisticated and interactive applications. By exploring advanced widget usage, animations, gesture handling, canvas operations, and integration with other Python libraries, you can take your Kivy applications to the next level.

Chapter 6: Exploring BeeWare

<u>What is BeeWare?</u>

BeeWare is an open-source suite of tools and libraries that enables Python developers to write, package, and deploy native applications across multiple platforms, including mobile (iOS and Android), desktop (Windows, macOS, Linux), and web environments. The core philosophy behind BeeWare is to empower developers to build truly native applications using Python while adhering to the look and feel of the platform they're targeting. This means that applications built with BeeWare use native widgets and controls, providing a seamless user experience that integrates naturally with the operating system.

Key Components of BeeWare

1. **Toga:** The core UI toolkit of BeeWare, allowing developers to create native user interfaces in Python. Toga provides a consistent API across platforms, while rendering the native widgets of each operating system.

2. **Briefcase:** A tool for packaging Python projects into standalone applications that can be distributed to end-users. Briefcase handles the intricacies of packaging for various platforms, including building and signing iOS and Android apps.

3. **Rubicon Java:** A library that facilitates communication between Python and Java, enabling the creation of Android apps with native UI components.

4. **Batavia:** A JavaScript implementation of the Python virtual machine, allowing Python code to run in the browser. This is particularly useful for web-based applications.

5. **Voc:** A transpiler that converts Python bytecode into Java bytecode, enabling Python code to be executed as a native Android app.

Why Use BeeWare?

BeeWare offers several advantages for developers who want to write native applications in Python:

- **Cross-Platform Compatibility:** Write your application once in Python and deploy it across multiple platforms with minimal changes.

- **Native Look and Feel:** BeeWare applications use native widgets, ensuring that your app looks and behaves like other applications on the target platform.

- **Open Source:** BeeWare is free to use and actively maintained by a community of developers.

- **Python Ecosystem:** Leverage the rich ecosystem of Python libraries and tools while building your application.

Getting Started with BeeWare

To get started with BeeWare, you'll need to set up your development environment, install the necessary tools, and create a simple application using Toga and Briefcase.

1. Installing BeeWare

267

You can install BeeWare's components using pip. The primary tools you'll need to start with are Toga and Briefcase.

Step 1: Set Up a Virtual Environment (Optional but Recommended)

python -m venv beeware_env

source beeware_env/bin/activate # On Windows, use: beeware_env\Scripts\activate

Step 2: Install Toga and Briefcase

pip install toga briefcase

This will install the Toga UI toolkit and the Briefcase packaging tool.

2. Creating Your First BeeWare Application

Let's create a simple cross-platform application using Toga. This application will display a window with a button that, when clicked, shows a message.

Step 1: Create a New BeeWare Project

briefcase new

This command will prompt you to enter details about your project, such as the app name, package name, and version. Once completed, it will create a new directory with the necessary project structure.

Step 2: Modify the app.py File

Navigate to the src/<package_name> directory (where <package_name> is the package name you provided during project creation) and open the app.py file. Replace its contents with the following code:

```python
import toga

from toga.style import Pack

from toga.style.pack import COLUMN, CENTER


class HelloWorldApp(toga.App):
    def startup(self):
        # Create the main window with a title
        main_box = toga.Box(style=Pack(direction=COLUMN, alignment=CENTER, padding=10))


        # Create a label
        self.label = toga.Label("Hello, World!", style=Pack(padding=(0, 5)))


        # Create a button and bind it to a callback function
        button = toga.Button("Click Me", on_press=self.say_hello, style=Pack(padding=5))


        # Add the label and button to the main box
        main_box.add(self.label)

        main_box.add(button)
```

```python
        # Set the main window content

    self.main_window =
toga.MainWindow(title=self.formal_name)

        self.main_window.content = main_box

        self.main_window.show()


    def say_hello(self, widget):

        # Update the label when the button is clicked

        self.label.text = "Button Clicked!"


def main():

    return HelloWorldApp()


if __name__ == '__main__':

    main().main_loop()
```

Explanation:

- **toga.App:** The base class for a Toga application. You subclass this to define your app's behavior.

- **toga.MainWindow:** Represents the main window of your application.

- **toga.Box:** A layout container that arranges widgets in a column or row.

- **toga.Label:** Displays text in the application.

- **toga.Button:** A clickable button that triggers the say_hello method when pressed.

Step 3: Build and Run the Application

To run the application, you can use the following command:

briefcase dev

This command will start the application in development mode, allowing you to see it running on your desktop.

3. Packaging and Deploying the Application

Once your application is ready, you can package it for distribution using Briefcase. Briefcase supports packaging for various platforms, including iOS, Android, Windows, macOS, and Linux.

Example: Packaging for macOS

briefcase build macOS

briefcase run macOS

Example: Packaging for iOS

briefcase build iOS

briefcase run iOS

Explanation:

- **briefcase build:** Compiles your application for the specified platform.

- **briefcase run:** Runs the packaged application on the specified platform (e.g., macOS or iOS).

Key Components of BeeWare:

BeeWare is a collection of tools and libraries designed to help Python developers create native applications that can run on multiple platforms, including mobile, desktop, and web. Each component of BeeWare serves a specific purpose in the development process, from building the user interface to packaging the application for distribution.

1. Toga: The Cross-Platform UI Toolkit

Toga is the core UI toolkit within the BeeWare suite. It allows developers to create native user interfaces using Python. Toga provides a consistent API across all platforms, while still rendering the native widgets and controls of each operating system. This ensures that applications built with Toga look and feel native on every platform.

1.1. Toga Basics

Toga is designed to be simple and intuitive, allowing developers to create UIs by defining windows, widgets, and layouts. Here's an example of how to create a basic Toga application with a label and a button.

Example: Basic Toga Application

```python
import toga

from toga.style import Pack

from toga.style.pack import COLUMN, CENTER


class SimpleApp(toga.App):
```

```python
def startup(self):
    # Create the main window with a title
    main_box =
toga.Box(style=Pack(direction=COLUMN,
alignment=CENTER, padding=10))


    # Create a label
    self.label = toga.Label("Hello, BeeWare!",
style=Pack(padding=(0, 5)))


    # Create a button and bind it to a callback function
    button = toga.Button("Click Me",
on_press=self.on_button_click, style=Pack(padding=5))


    # Add the label and button to the main box
    main_box.add(self.label)
    main_box.add(button)


    # Set the main window content
    self.main_window =
toga.MainWindow(title=self.formal_name)
    self.main_window.content = main_box
    self.main_window.show()
```

```python
def on_button_click(self, widget):

    # Update the label text when the button is clicked

    self.label.text = "Button Clicked!"


def main():

    return SimpleApp()


if __name__ == '__main__':

    main().main_loop()
```

Explanation:

- **toga.Box:** A layout container that organizes widgets vertically or horizontally.

- **toga.Label:** A widget that displays text.

- **toga.Button:** A clickable button that triggers an event handler (on_button_click) when pressed.

- **toga.MainWindow:** Represents the main window of the application.

- **style=Pack:** Toga's styling system that allows you to define layout properties such as padding, alignment, and direction.

Running the Example:

When you run this code, you will see a window with a label that says "Hello, BeeWare!" and a button labeled "Click Me." Clicking the button will change the label text to "Button Clicked!"

274

1.2. Toga Widgets and Layouts

Toga offers a wide range of widgets, such as Button, Label, TextInput, Table, and Tree, along with various layout containers like Box, SplitContainer, and ScrollContainer. These components can be combined to create complex user interfaces.

Example: Creating a More Complex Layout

```python
import toga

from toga.style import Pack

from toga.style.pack import COLUMN, ROW, CENTER, LEFT


class ComplexApp(toga.App):
    def startup(self):
        # Create the main window
        main_box = toga.Box(style=Pack(direction=COLUMN, alignment=CENTER, padding=10))


        # Create a title label
        title_label = toga.Label("User Information", style=Pack(font_size=20, padding=(0, 5)))


        # Create input fields
```

```python
        name_label = toga.Label("Name:",
style=Pack(padding=(0, 5), alignment=LEFT))

        name_input = toga.TextInput(style=Pack(flex=1))


        email_label = toga.Label("Email:",
style=Pack(padding=(0, 5), alignment=LEFT))

        email_input = toga.TextInput(style=Pack(flex=1))


        # Create a horizontal box for the input fields

        form_box = toga.Box(style=Pack(direction=ROW,
padding=5))

        form_box.add(name_label)

        form_box.add(name_input)

        form_box.add(email_label)

        form_box.add(email_input)


        # Create a submit button

        submit_button = toga.Button("Submit",
on_press=self.on_submit, style=Pack(padding=5))


        # Add widgets to the main box

        main_box.add(title_label)

        main_box.add(form_box)
```

```python
    main_box.add(submit_button)

    # Set the main window content
    self.main_window = toga.MainWindow(title=self.formal_name)
    self.main_window.content = main_box
    self.main_window.show()


def on_submit(self, widget):
    # Placeholder for form submission logic
    self.main_window.info_dialog("Form Submitted", "Your information has been submitted.")


def main():
    return ComplexApp()


if __name__ == '__main__':
    main().main_loop()
```

Explanation:

- **toga.TextInput:** A widget that allows the user to enter text.

- **toga.Box(direction=ROW):** A Box layout that arranges its children horizontally.

- **toga.MainWindow.info_dialog:** Displays a simple dialog box with a message.

Running the Example:

This example creates a more complex UI with input fields for the user's name and email, and a submit button that displays a confirmation dialog when clicked.

2. Briefcase: Packaging Python Applications

Briefcase is a tool within the BeeWare suite that helps developers package their Python code into standalone applications that can be distributed to end-users. Briefcase takes care of the intricacies involved in building and signing applications for various platforms, including iOS, Android, macOS, Windows, and Linux.

2.1. Setting Up a Briefcase Project

Creating a new BeeWare project with Briefcase is straightforward. The briefcase new command initializes a project with the necessary structure and configuration files.

Example: Creating a New BeeWare Project

briefcase new

Explanation:

- **briefcase new:** This command creates a new BeeWare project. It prompts the user for details such as the application name, package name, and project description. After answering the prompts, Briefcase generates the project files and directory structure.

2.2. Building and Running the Application

Once your project is set up, you can build and run the application using Briefcase.

Example: Running the Application in Development Mode

briefcase dev

Explanation:

- **briefcase dev:** Runs the application in development mode, allowing you to test it on your local machine before packaging it for distribution.

Example: Packaging the Application for Distribution

briefcase build macOS

briefcase run macOS

Explanation:

- **briefcase build macOS:** Packages the application for macOS. Similar commands are available for other platforms (e.g., briefcase build iOS).

- **briefcase run macOS:** Runs the packaged macOS application.

3. Rubicon Java: Bridging Python and Java for Android Development

Rubicon Java is a library that allows Python code to interface with Java, making it possible to develop Android applications using Python. Rubicon Java is particularly useful for calling Android-specific APIs from Python code, enabling seamless integration with the Android operating system.

3.1. Using Rubicon Java

Rubicon Java provides a straightforward way to interact with Java classes and methods from Python. Here's a basic example of using Rubicon Java to interact with an Android API.

Example: Accessing Android System Properties with Rubicon Java

```python
from rubicon.java import JavaClass


# Access the Android Build class
Build = JavaClass('android/os/Build')


# Print the Android device model
print(f"Device Model: {Build.MODEL}")
```

Explanation:

- **JavaClass:** A Rubicon Java function that allows you to load and interact with a Java class. In this case, it loads the android.os.Build class, which contains information about the Android device.

- **Build.MODEL:** Accesses the MODEL field of the Build class, which provides the model name of the Android device.

Running the Example:

This code, when run on an Android device, will print the model name of the device.

4. Batavia: Running Python in the Browser

Batavia is a JavaScript implementation of the Python virtual machine that enables Python code to run in the browser. This is particularly useful for web applications that need to execute Python code on the client side.

4.1. Using Batavia

Batavia allows you to embed Python code directly into HTML pages, enabling rich, interactive web applications that leverage Python's capabilities.

Example: Running Python in the Browser with Batavia

```html
<!DOCTYPE html>

<html>

<head>

    <title>Python in the Browser with Batavia</title>

    <script
src="https://batavia.beeware.org/static/batavia.min.js"></script>

</head>

<body>

    <h1>Python in the Browser</h1>

    <div id="output"></div>

    <script type="text/x-python">

        def main():

            document.getElementById('output').innerHTML =
'Hello from Python!'
```

```
    </script>

    <script>

      batavia.run();

    </script>

</body>

</html>
```

Explanation:

- **Batavia:** The Batavia library is included in the HTML page, allowing Python code to be executed in the browser.

- **<script type="text/x-python">:** Embeds Python code directly into the HTML page.

- **batavia.run():** Executes the embedded Python code.

Running the Example:

When you load this HTML page in a browser, the embedded Python code will run, and the message "Hello from Python!" will be displayed on the page.

5. Voc: Transpiling Python to Java Bytecode

Voc is a tool that converts Python bytecode into Java bytecode, enabling Python code to be executed as a native Android app. This allows you to write Android apps entirely in Python, which are then transpiled into Java bytecode for execution on Android devices.

5.1. Using Voc

Voc is typically used in conjunction with Rubicon Java and Briefcase to create Android apps. It handles the conversion of Python code into a format that can be run by the Android runtime.

Example: Basic Python to Java Bytecode Transpilation

voc -o build/path/to/output -p your_python_module.py

Explanation:

- **voc -o build/path/to/output -p your_python_module.py:** Transpiles the specified Python module (your_python_module.py) into Java bytecode and outputs it to the specified directory.

Running the Example:

After transpiling your Python code with Voc, you can integrate the generated bytecode into an Android project and run it on an Android device.

BeeWare's key components—**Toga, Briefcase, Rubicon Java, Batavia**, and **Voc**—provide a comprehensive toolkit for developing native applications across multiple platforms using Python. Whether you're building desktop apps, mobile apps, or even web apps, BeeWare allows you to write your application once and deploy it everywhere, all while maintaining a native look and feel.

Installing and Setting Up BeeWare:

To begin developing cross-platform native applications with BeeWare, you need to install and set up the necessary tools and libraries on your system. BeeWare provides a straightforward setup process that enables you to start building applications for platforms like iOS, Android, macOS, Windows, Linux, and even the web.

1. Prerequisites

Before you begin, ensure that you have the following prerequisites installed on your system:

- **Python 3.6+**: BeeWare requires Python 3.6 or later. You can download the latest version of Python from python.org.

- **pip**: Python's package manager, which is usually included with Python installations.

- **Git**: Version control software, which is required for managing BeeWare projects.

You can verify that Python and pip are installed by running the following commands in your terminal or command prompt:

python --version

pip –version

If you don't have Git installed, you can download it from git-scm.com.

2. Setting Up a Virtual Environment (Optional but Recommended)

It's a good practice to create a virtual environment for your BeeWare project. A virtual environment helps you manage project-specific dependencies and avoid conflicts with other Python packages installed globally on your system.

Step 1: Create a Virtual Environment

python -m venv beeware_env

Step 2: Activate the Virtual Environment

- **On macOS/Linux:**

source beeware_env/bin/activate

On Windows:

beeware_env\Scripts\activate

Once the virtual environment is activated, your terminal prompt should change to indicate that you are now working within the virtual environment.

3. Installing Toga and Briefcase

With your virtual environment activated (if you chose to use one), you can now install Toga and Briefcase, the core components of BeeWare.

Step 1: Install Toga

Toga is the UI toolkit used to create native user interfaces in BeeWare. Install Toga using pip:

pip install toga

Step 2: Install Briefcase

Briefcase is the tool used to package and deploy your BeeWare applications. Install Briefcase using pip:

pip install briefcase

This will install the latest versions of Toga and Briefcase, along with their dependencies.

4. Verifying the Installation

After installing Toga and Briefcase, it's important to verify that they were installed correctly. You can do this by checking the versions of Toga and Briefcase installed on your system.

Step 1: Verify Toga Installation

Run the following command to check the installed version of Toga:

```
python -c "import toga; print(toga.__version__)"
```

Step 2: Verify Briefcase Installation

Run the following command to check the installed version of Briefcase:

```
briefcase --version
```

If both commands return version numbers without any errors, you have successfully installed Toga and Briefcase.

5. Creating Your First BeeWare Project

Now that you've installed Toga and Briefcase, you're ready to create your first BeeWare project. Briefcase provides a convenient command to scaffold a new project with the necessary files and directories.

Step 1: Create a New Project

Navigate to the directory where you want to create your project, and run the following command:

```
briefcase new
```

Briefcase will prompt you for some basic information about your project, such as the application name, package name, and version. Once you've provided this information, Briefcase will generate the project structure.

Example: Briefcase New Project Prompts

Briefcase project generator

This wizard will ask you some questions to generate a new application.

Formal name: My First BeeWare App

App name: my_first_beeware_app

Bundle: com.example

Author: Your Name

Briefcase app template: org.beeware.app

After completing the prompts, you'll have a new directory containing your BeeWare project files.

6. Running Your BeeWare Application

With your project scaffolded, you can now run the application in development mode using Briefcase.

Step 1: Navigate to the Project Directory

cd my_first_beeware_app

Step 2: Run the Application

briefcase dev

This command launches the application on your development machine, allowing you to see it in action.

Briefcase sets up everything needed to run the application in development mode, including dependencies and configurations.

Example: Running a Simple BeeWare App

The default project created by Briefcase includes a basic Toga application that opens a window with a simple label. When you run briefcase dev, you should see a window similar to this:

7. Building and Packaging Your Application

Once you've developed your application, Briefcase can package it for distribution. This involves compiling your application into a standalone executable for the target platform(s).

Example: Building and Running on macOS

briefcase build macOS

briefcase run macOS

Example: Building and Running on Windows

briefcase build Windows

briefcase run Windows

Explanation:

- **briefcase build <platform>:** Compiles the application for the specified platform.

- **briefcase run <platform>:** Runs the compiled application on the specified platform.

8. Troubleshooting Installation Issues

If you encounter issues during installation, here are a few common problems and solutions:

- **Issue:** pip command not found.

  - o **Solution:** Ensure that Python and pip are installed correctly and added to your system's PATH.

- **Issue:** briefcase command not found.

  - o **Solution:** Ensure that Briefcase was installed in the correct environment. If using a virtual environment, make sure it's activated.

- **Issue:** Errors when running briefcase dev.

  - o **Solution:** Check that all dependencies are installed correctly. Running pip install -r requirements.txt inside your project directory can help resolve missing dependencies.

Installing and setting up BeeWare is a straightforward process that enables you to start building cross-platform native applications using Python. By following the steps outlined in this section, you've installed the core components of BeeWare—Toga and Briefcase—verified your installation, and created your first BeeWare project. You've also learned how to run your application in development mode and package it for distribution.

Creating Your First BeeWare App:

BeeWare enables Python developers to create cross-platform native applications using a unified codebase. In this section, we will walk you through the process of creating your first BeeWare app using Toga and Briefcase. We will cover the basics of setting up a new project, writing the application code, running it in development mode, and packaging it for distribution.

1. Setting Up Your First BeeWare Project

The first step in creating a BeeWare app is to set up a new project using Briefcase, which generates the necessary files and directory structure.

1.1. Initializing a New Project

Open your terminal or command prompt and navigate to the directory where you want to create your project. Then, run the following command to initialize a new BeeWare project:

briefcase new

This command will launch a project creation wizard that prompts you for information about your project. The following are typical prompts and their descriptions:

- **Formal name:** The full name of your application as it will appear to users.

- **App name:** A short, lowercase name for your app, typically used in the package name.

- **Bundle:** A reverse domain name identifier, often your domain name in reverse (e.g., com.example).

- **Author:** Your name or the name of your organization.

- **Briefcase app template:** The app template to use, typically org.beeware.app.

Example: Sample Input

Formal name: Hello World BeeWare

App name: hello_world_beeware

Bundle: com.example

Author: Your Name

Briefcase app template: org.beeware.app

Once you've provided the necessary information, Briefcase will generate a new directory with the following structure:

```
hello_world_beeware/
├── .gitignore
├── LICENSE
├── README.md
├── pyproject.toml
└── src/
    └── hello_world_beeware/
        ├── __init__.py
        ├── app.py
        ├── resources/
        └── templates/
```

2. Writing Your First BeeWare App

With the project initialized, the next step is to write the code for your application. The main application logic is typically placed in the app.py file within the src/<app_name>/ directory.

2.1. Understanding the App Structure

Open the src/hello_world_beeware/app.py file. By default, this file contains boilerplate code to get you started. The code is based on Toga, BeeWare's native UI toolkit.

Default app.py Structure:

```python
import toga

from toga.style import Pack

from toga.style.pack import COLUMN, CENTER


class HelloWorldApp(toga.App):

    def startup(self):

        # Create the main window with a title

        main_box =
toga.Box(style=Pack(direction=COLUMN,
alignment=CENTER, padding=10))


        # Create a label

        self.label = toga.Label("Hello, World!",
style=Pack(padding=(0, 5)))


        # Create a button and bind it to a callback function
```

```python
        button = toga.Button("Click Me",
on_press=self.on_button_click, style=Pack(padding=5))


        # Add the label and button to the main box

        main_box.add(self.label)

        main_box.add(button)


        # Set the main window content

        self.main_window =
toga.MainWindow(title=self.formal_name)

        self.main_window.content = main_box

        self.main_window.show()


    def on_button_click(self, widget):

        # Update the label text when the button is clicked

        self.label.text = "Button Clicked!"


def main():

    return HelloWorldApp()


if __name__ == '__main__':

    main().main_loop()
```

Explanation:

- **toga.App:** The base class for a Toga application. Your application logic is built within a subclass of toga.App.

- **startup():** The entry point of your application, where you define the UI and set up the main window.

- **toga.Box:** A layout container that arranges widgets either vertically or horizontally. Here, it's set to arrange widgets in a vertical column.

- **toga.Label:** Displays text on the screen. In this case, the label initially displays "Hello, World!".

- **toga.Button:** A clickable button that triggers the on_button_click method when pressed.

- **on_button_click():** This method changes the label's text to "Button Clicked!" when the button is pressed.

- **main_window.show():** Displays the main window with the defined content.

3. Running Your BeeWare App

After writing your application code, you can run it using Briefcase's development mode. This allows you to test your application on your local machine before packaging it for distribution.

3.1. Running the App in Development Mode

Navigate to your project's root directory and run the following command:

briefcase dev

This command compiles and runs your application in development mode. You should see a window open with the following elements:

- A label displaying "Hello, World!"

- A button labeled "Click Me"

When you click the button, the label's text changes to "Button Clicked!".

4. Modifying and Expanding Your BeeWare App

You can expand your BeeWare application by adding more widgets, handling different events, and organizing your UI more effectively. Below is an example of how to modify the initial application to include an additional text input field and display the user's input when the button is clicked.

4.1. Expanding the UI

Modify the app.py file to include a TextInput widget and update the on_button_click() method to display the user's input.

Updated app.py:

import toga

from toga.style import Pack

from toga.style.pack import COLUMN, CENTER

class HelloWorldApp(toga.App):

    def startup(self):

```python
        # Create the main window with a title

        main_box =
toga.Box(style=Pack(direction=COLUMN,
alignment=CENTER, padding=10))


        # Create a label

        self.label = toga.Label("Enter your name:",
style=Pack(padding=(0, 5)))


        # Create a text input field

        self.name_input =
toga.TextInput(style=Pack(padding=5, flex=1))


        # Create a button and bind it to a callback function

        button = toga.Button("Greet Me",
on_press=self.on_button_click, style=Pack(padding=5))


        # Add the label, text input, and button to the main box

        main_box.add(self.label)

        main_box.add(self.name_input)

        main_box.add(button)


        # Set the main window content
```

```python
        self.main_window =
toga.MainWindow(title=self.formal_name)

        self.main_window.content = main_box

        self.main_window.show()


    def on_button_click(self, widget):

        # Update the label text to greet the user with their
input

        self.label.text = f"Hello, {self.name_input.value}!"


def main():

    return HelloWorldApp()


if __name__ == '__main__':

    main().main_loop()
```

Explanation:

- **toga.TextInput:** A widget that allows users to enter text. The user's input is stored in self.name_input.value.

- **on_button_click():** The method now retrieves the text from self.name_input and updates the label to greet the user by name.

Running the Updated App:

When you run the updated application, you will see a label prompting you to enter your name, a text input field, and a button. After entering your name and clicking the button, the label will update to greet you by name.

5. Packaging Your BeeWare App

After testing your app in development mode, you can package it for distribution. BeeWare's Briefcase tool handles the packaging process, allowing you to create standalone executables for various platforms.

5.1. Building the Application

To package your application, use the following commands:

For macOS:

briefcase build macOS

For Windows:

briefcase build Windows

For Linux:

briefcase build Linux

These commands will compile your application and create a package that can be distributed and installed on the respective platform.

5.2. Running the Packaged Application

Once the build process is complete, you can run the packaged application using:

briefcase run macOS

Replace macOS with Windows or Linux if you are building for those platforms.

Explanation:

- **briefcase build <platform>:** Compiles the application for the specified platform.

- **briefcase run <platform>:** Runs the compiled application on the specified platform.

Creating your first BeeWare app is a straightforward process that introduces you to the core concepts of the BeeWare suite, including Toga for building the user interface and Briefcase for packaging the application. By following the steps outlined in this section, you have learned how to set up a new BeeWare project, write application logic, run the app in development mode, and package it for distribution.

Conclusion

BeeWare is a powerful framework for developing native applications in Python that can run across multiple platforms, including mobile devices. By leveraging Toga for the user interface and Briefcase for packaging, you can create applications that look and feel native on each platform. This section provided an introduction to what BeeWare is, how to set up your development environment, and how to create and package a simple application.

Chapter 7: Other Python Mobile Frameworks

Other Python Mobile Frameworks

While BeeWare offers a robust solution for creating cross-platform native applications with Python, other Python mobile frameworks are available that cater to different development needs and use cases. This section will explore some of the most popular Python mobile frameworks: **Kivy**, **Pyqtdeploy**, **Pygame**, and **PyJNIus**. Each framework has its own strengths and unique features, making it suitable for specific types of mobile applications. We'll provide an overview of each framework, followed by code examples to help you get started.

1. Kivy: A Versatile Cross-Platform Framework

Kivy is a powerful open-source Python framework designed for developing multitouch applications. It allows developers to create applications that run on multiple platforms, including iOS, Android, Windows, macOS, and Linux, using a single codebase. Kivy is particularly well-suited for applications that require a rich graphical interface or advanced touch input, such as games, multimedia apps, and custom UI-heavy applications.

1.1. Installing Kivy

To get started with Kivy, you need to install it using pip. It's recommended to create a virtual environment before installing Kivy to manage dependencies.

Installation Command:

pip install kivy

1.2. Creating a Simple Kivy Application

Let's create a simple Kivy application that displays a button. When the button is clicked, the text on the button changes.

Example: Basic Kivy App

```python
from kivy.app import App

from kivy.uix.button import Button

from kivy.uix.boxlayout import BoxLayout


class MyApp(App):
    def build(self):
        layout = BoxLayout(padding=10)
        self.button = Button(text="Click Me!", font_size=24)
        self.button.bind(on_press=self.change_text)
        layout.add_widget(self.button)
        return layout


    def change_text(self, instance):
        self.button.text = "Button Clicked!"


if __name__ == '__main__':
    MyApp().run()
```

Explanation:

- **BoxLayout:** A layout container that arranges its children in a linear fashion, either vertically or horizontally.

- **Button:** A widget that the user can click. The bind method attaches an event handler (change_text) that updates the button's text when clicked.

Running the Example:

When you run this code, a window appears with a button labeled "Click Me!". Clicking the button changes the label to "Button Clicked!".

2. Pyqtdeploy: Deploying PyQt Applications to Mobile

Pyqtdeploy is a deployment tool that helps package PyQt applications into standalone executables for various platforms, including iOS and Android. PyQt is a set of Python bindings for the Qt application framework, which is widely used for creating desktop and mobile applications with a native look and feel.

2.1. Installing Pyqtdeploy

You need to install Pyqtdeploy and the required PyQt libraries using pip. Note that Pyqtdeploy is usually used in combination with other tools for building and deploying applications.

Installation Command:

pip install pyqtdeploy PyQt5

2.2. Creating a Simple PyQt Application

Here is a simple example of a PyQt application that displays a window with a button. When the button is clicked, the button's label changes.

Example: Basic PyQt App

```python
import sys

from PyQt5.QtWidgets import QApplication, QWidget, QPushButton, QVBoxLayout


class MyApp(QWidget):
    def __init__(self):
        super().__init__()
        self.init_ui()

    def init_ui(self):
        self.setWindowTitle('PyQt App')
        layout = QVBoxLayout()

        self.button = QPushButton('Click Me!', self)
        self.button.clicked.connect(self.change_text)

        layout.addWidget(self.button)
        self.setLayout(layout)
```

```python
def change_text(self):

    self.button.setText('Button Clicked!')


def main():

    app = QApplication(sys.argv)

    window = MyApp()

    window.show()

    sys.exit(app.exec_())


if __name__ == '__main__':

    main()
```

Explanation:

- **QWidget:** The base class for all UI objects in PyQt. It represents the main window of the application.

- **QPushButton:** A widget that represents a clickable button.

- **QVBoxLayout:** A layout manager that arranges widgets vertically.

Running the Example:

Running this code opens a window with a button labeled "Click Me!". When you click the button, the label changes to "Button Clicked!".

3. Pygame: Game Development with Python

Pygame is a popular framework for developing 2D games using Python. While Pygame is primarily focused on game development, it can also be used to create simple graphical applications. Pygame applications can run on multiple platforms, including Android, using tools like Pygame Subset for Android (pgs4a).

3.1. Installing Pygame

To install Pygame, use pip:

Installation Command:

pip install pygame

3.2. Creating a Simple Pygame Application

Here is an example of a basic Pygame application that displays a window with a button. When the button is clicked, the button's label changes.

Example: Basic Pygame App

import pygame

import sys

pygame.init()

Set up the display

screen = pygame.display.set_mode((400, 300))

pygame.display.set_caption("Pygame App")

```python
# Set up the font
font = pygame.font.Font(None, 36)

# Set up the button
button_rect = pygame.Rect(100, 100, 200, 50)
button_color = (0, 128, 255)
button_text = "Click Me!"

# Main loop
running = True
while running:
    screen.fill((255, 255, 255))
    pygame.draw.rect(screen, button_color, button_rect)
    text_surface = font.render(button_text, True, (255, 255, 255))
    screen.blit(text_surface, (button_rect.x + 50, button_rect.y + 10))

    for event in pygame.event.get():
        if event.type == pygame.QUIT:
            running = False
        elif event.type == pygame.MOUSEBUTTONDOWN:
            if button_rect.collidepoint(event.pos):
```

```
button_text = "Button Clicked!"


pygame.display.flip()


pygame.quit()

sys.exit()
```

Explanation:

- **pygame.Rect:** Defines the position and size of the button.

- **pygame.draw.rect:** Draws the button rectangle on the screen.

- **pygame.font.Font:** Creates a font object for rendering text.

Running the Example:

Running this code opens a Pygame window with a button. When you click the button, the text changes to "Button Clicked!".

4. PyJNIus: Accessing Java APIs in Python for Android

PyJNIus is a Python library that allows you to access Java classes and methods from within Python code. It is particularly useful for Android development, where you may need to interact with Android's Java-based APIs directly.

4.1. Installing PyJNIus

To use PyJNIus, you need to have a working Python environment that includes a Java Development Kit (JDK). You can install PyJNIus using pip:

Installation Command:

pip install pyjnius

4.2. Using PyJNIus to Access Android APIs

Here's an example of using PyJNIus to access the Android Build class and retrieve the device's model name.

Example: Accessing Android APIs with PyJNIus

from jnius import autoclass

Access the Android Build class

Build = autoclass('android.os.Build')

Print the device model

print(f"Device Model: {Build.MODEL}")

Explanation:

- **autoclass:** A PyJNIus function that loads and returns a reference to a Java class.

- **Build.MODEL:** Retrieves the model name of the Android device from the Build class.

Running the Example:

This code, when run on an Android device, will print the model name of the device to the console.

Overview of Frameworks Like PyMob and SL4A:

In addition to the more well-known Python mobile frameworks like Kivy, PyQt, and BeeWare, there are other frameworks and tools that cater to specific use cases in mobile development. Two such tools are **PyMob** and **SL4A (Scripting Layer for Android)**. These frameworks offer different approaches to mobile development, each with its own set of features and limitations. In this section, we will explore these frameworks, providing an overview, installation steps, and examples of how to use them to develop mobile applications with Python.

1. PyMob: Simplified Mobile Development with Python

PyMob is a lesser-known Python framework that aims to simplify the development of mobile applications. It is particularly focused on making it easy to create simple, cross-platform apps using Python with minimal setup and boilerplate code. PyMob abstracts much of the complexity involved in mobile app development, allowing developers to focus on the core functionality of their apps.

1.1. Installing PyMob

PyMob is not as widely used or maintained as some other frameworks, so installation might require additional steps or manual setup. However, the basic installation can be done using pip.

Installation Command:

pip install pymob

1.2. Creating a Simple PyMob Application

Let's create a simple PyMob application that displays a message on the screen. Given the simplicity of PyMob, this example will be straightforward and easy to follow.

Example: Basic PyMob App

```python
import pymob


# Define the main function that sets up the application
def main():
    app = pymob.Application("My PyMob App")


    # Create a label widget to display text
    label = pymob.Label("Hello, PyMob!")


    # Add the label to the application's main window
    app.add_widget(label)


    # Run the application
    app.run()


if __name__ == '__main__':
    main()
```

Explanation:

- **pymob.Application:** Represents the main application object. It handles the creation of the main window and the event loop.

- **pymob.Label:** A simple widget that displays text on the screen.

- **app.add_widget(label):** Adds the label to the application's main window.

- **app.run():** Starts the application and displays the main window.

Running the Example:

Running this code opens a window with a label that says "Hello, PyMob!". The simplicity of PyMob makes it ideal for quick prototypes or simple applications.

2. SL4A: Scripting Layer for Android

SL4A (Scripting Layer for Android) is a framework that provides a simple API for Android, allowing developers to write Android applications using various scripting languages, including Python. SL4A is particularly useful for automating tasks, creating quick scripts, or developing simple Android apps without diving deep into Java or the Android SDK. While SL4A is not actively maintained anymore, it still serves as a valuable tool for specific use cases in Android development.

2.1. Setting Up SL4A for Python Development

To use SL4A for Python development on Android, you need to install the SL4A APK on your Android device, along with the Python for Android (Py4A) interpreter.

Step 1: Install SL4A on Your Android Device

1. Download the SL4A APK from a trusted source (such as GitHub or older repositories).

2. Install the APK on your Android device.

Step 2: Install Python for Android (Py4A)

1. Download the Python for Android APK from the same source where you obtained SL4A.

2. Install the APK on your Android device.

2.2. Writing and Running Python Scripts with SL4A

Once SL4A and Python for Android are set up on your device, you can write and execute Python scripts directly on your Android device.

Example: Basic SL4A Script to Display a Toast Message

import android

Initialize the Android interface

droid = android.Android()

Display a toast message

droid.makeToast("Hello, SL4A!")

Explanation:

- **android.Android():** Initializes the SL4A interface, allowing you to interact with Android APIs.

- **droid.makeToast:** Displays a toast message (a small popup message) on the Android device.

Running the Example:

To run this script, save it as a .py file on your Android device. Open the SL4A app, navigate to the script, and execute it. You should see a toast message on your screen that says "Hello, SL4A!".

2.3. SL4A Capabilities

SL4A allows Python scripts to interact with various Android features, such as:

- **Accessing Sensors:** Retrieve data from accelerometers, gyroscopes, and other sensors.

- **Sending SMS Messages:** Automate the process of sending SMS messages.

- **Making Phone Calls:** Initiate phone calls directly from a script.

- **Accessing GPS:** Retrieve location data from the device's GPS module.

- **Interacting with the File System:** Read and write files stored on the device.

Example: Accessing Device Location with SL4A

```python
import android


# Initialize the Android interface

droid = android.Android()


# Get the current location
```

```python
location = droid.getLastKnownLocation().result


# Display the location in a toast message
if location:
    lat = location['gps']['latitude']
    lon = location['gps']['longitude']
    droid.makeToast(f"Latitude: {lat}, Longitude: {lon}")
else:
    droid.makeToast("Unable to retrieve location")
```

Explanation:

- **droid.getLastKnownLocation():** Retrieves the last known GPS location of the device.

- **droid.makeToast:** Displays the latitude and longitude in a toast message.

PyMob and SL4A offer unique approaches to Python mobile development, catering to different needs and use cases. **PyMob** is ideal for developers who want a simplified, cross-platform framework for creating basic applications quickly. **SL4A** is particularly useful for automating tasks and writing scripts on Android devices using Python, providing easy access to Android's APIs without requiring extensive knowledge of Java or the Android SDK.

Comparing Frameworks:

When choosing a Python mobile framework, it's essential to consider the strengths and weaknesses of each option to determine which best suits your project's requirements. This section will compare some of the most popular Python mobile frameworks—**Kivy**, **BeeWare**, **Pyqtdeploy**, **Pygame**, **PyMob**, and **SL4A**—highlighting their key features, advantages, and limitations. We will also include code examples to illustrate how each framework is used in practice.

1. Kivy: A Versatile Cross-Platform Framework

Kivy is one of the most popular Python frameworks for developing cross-platform mobile applications. It is particularly well-suited for applications that require a rich graphical interface and advanced touch input, such as games, multimedia apps, and custom UI-heavy applications.

Strengths:

- **Cross-Platform Support:** Kivy apps run on iOS, Android, Windows, macOS, and Linux.

- **Rich Graphical Interface:** Ideal for creating visually appealing applications with support for multitouch gestures and complex layouts.

- **Active Community:** Kivy has an active community and extensive documentation, making it easier to find help and resources.

- **OpenGL Integration:** Leverages OpenGL for rendering, providing hardware-accelerated graphics.

Weaknesses:

- **Steeper Learning Curve:** Kivy's API can be complex for beginners, especially when dealing

315

with advanced features like custom widgets and animations.

- **Performance:** While Kivy is powerful, it may not offer the same level of performance as native development or frameworks that directly leverage native controls.

- **Larger App Size:** Kivy applications can be relatively large because they include the Kivy runtime and dependencies.

Example: Creating a Button with Kivy

```python
from kivy.app import App

from kivy.uix.button import Button

from kivy.uix.boxlayout import BoxLayout


class MyApp(App):
    def build(self):
        layout = BoxLayout(padding=10)
        self.button = Button(text="Click Me!", font_size=24)
        self.button.bind(on_press=self.change_text)
        layout.add_widget(self.button)
        return layout


    def change_text(self, instance):
        self.button.text = "Button Clicked!"
```

```
if __name__ == '__main__':

    MyApp().run()
```

Explanation: This example creates a simple Kivy app with a button that changes its text when clicked. The BoxLayout arranges the button in a linear fashion, and the bind method connects the button to an event handler that changes its label.

2. BeeWare: Native Look and Feel Across Platforms

BeeWare is a collection of tools and libraries for building native applications in Python that work across multiple platforms, including iOS, Android, Windows, macOS, and Linux. The core of BeeWare is the **Toga** UI toolkit, which provides a consistent API while rendering native widgets for each platform.

Strengths:

- **Native Look and Feel:** BeeWare applications use native controls, ensuring that your app looks and feels like a true native app on each platform.

- **Cross-Platform Consistency:** Write your application once and deploy it across multiple platforms with minimal changes.

- **Active Development:** BeeWare is actively maintained and continues to evolve with new features and improvements.

- **Comprehensive Tooling:** BeeWare includes tools like Briefcase for packaging and deploying apps, making the entire development process seamless.

Weaknesses:

- **Early Stage:** BeeWare is relatively young compared to other frameworks, which means it may lack some features and maturity found in more established tools.

- **Limited Community Resources:** While growing, the BeeWare community is still smaller than that of Kivy or PyQt, which can make finding help and resources more challenging.

- **Platform-Specific Issues:** Because BeeWare relies on platform-specific native widgets, there can be inconsistencies or bugs that vary between platforms.

Example: Creating a Button with BeeWare

```python
import toga

from toga.style import Pack

from toga.style.pack import COLUMN, CENTER


class HelloWorldApp(toga.App):

    def startup(self):

        main_box =
toga.Box(style=Pack(direction=COLUMN,
alignment=CENTER, padding=10))

        self.label = toga.Label("Hello, World!",
style=Pack(padding=(0, 5)))

        button = toga.Button("Click Me",
on_press=self.change_text, style=Pack(padding=5))
```

```python
        main_box.add(self.label)

        main_box.add(button)


        self.main_window =
toga.MainWindow(title=self.formal_name)

        self.main_window.content = main_box

        self.main_window.show()


    def change_text(self, widget):

        self.label.text = "Button Clicked!"


def main():

    return HelloWorldApp()


if __name__ == '__main__':

    main().main_loop()
```

Explanation: This BeeWare example creates a simple application with a button that changes its text when clicked. The Box layout arranges widgets in a column, and the Label widget displays the text that is updated when the button is pressed.

3. Pyqtdeploy: Deploying PyQt Applications to Mobile

Pyqtdeploy is a deployment tool that packages PyQt applications into standalone executables that can be distributed on various platforms, including iOS and Android. PyQt provides Python bindings for the Qt framework, which is known for its extensive widget library and support for creating complex desktop applications.

Strengths:

- **Rich Widget Library:** PyQt offers a wide range of widgets, making it suitable for building complex user interfaces.

- **Cross-Platform:** PyQt applications can be deployed across multiple platforms, including mobile, with Pyqtdeploy.

- **Native Performance:** Applications built with PyQt have performance similar to native applications, especially on desktop platforms.

Weaknesses:

- **Complex Setup:** Setting up PyQt and deploying applications with Pyqtdeploy can be more complex than using other frameworks.

- **Larger App Size:** PyQt applications can be large because they include the Qt runtime and other dependencies.

- **Limited Mobile Focus:** While PyQt is excellent for desktop applications, it is not specifically optimized for mobile development, and some mobile-specific features may be harder to implement.

Example: Creating a Button with PyQt

import sys

```python
from PyQt5.QtWidgets import QApplication, QWidget,
QPushButton, QVBoxLayout


class MyApp(QWidget):
    def __init__(self):
        super().__init__()
        self.init_ui()

    def init_ui(self):
        self.setWindowTitle('PyQt App')
        layout = QVBoxLayout()
        self.button = QPushButton('Click Me!', self)
        self.button.clicked.connect(self.change_text)
        layout.addWidget(self.button)
        self.setLayout(layout)

    def change_text(self):
        self.button.setText('Button Clicked!')


def main():
    app = QApplication(sys.argv)
    window = MyApp()
```

```python
window.show()

sys.exit(app.exec_())


if __name__ == '__main__':
    main()
```

Explanation: This PyQt example creates a simple application with a button that changes its text when clicked. The QVBoxLayout arranges widgets vertically, and the QPushButton widget represents the clickable button.

4. Pygame: Simple Game Development with Python

Pygame is a popular framework for developing 2D games using Python. While it is primarily focused on game development, it can also be used to create simple graphical applications. Pygame applications can run on multiple platforms, including Android, using tools like Pygame Subset for Android (pgs4a).

Strengths:

- **Easy to Learn:** Pygame is beginner-friendly and has a straightforward API, making it accessible for new developers.

- **Focused on Games:** Pygame is optimized for game development, with support for sprites, collision detection, and sound playback.

- **Cross-Platform:** Pygame applications can run on Windows, macOS, Linux, and Android.

Weaknesses:

- **Limited to 2D:** Pygame is not suitable for 3D game development or applications requiring advanced graphical capabilities.

- **Outdated:** Pygame has not seen significant updates in recent years, and some aspects of the framework may feel outdated compared to more modern game engines.

- **Not Optimized for Mobile:** While Pygame can run on mobile platforms, it is not specifically optimized for mobile performance or user interfaces.

Example: Creating a Button with Pygame

```python
import pygame

import sys


pygame.init()


screen = pygame.display.set_mode((400, 300))

pygame.display.set_caption("Pygame App")


font = pygame.font.Font(None, 36)

button_rect = pygame.Rect(100, 100, 200, 50)

button_color = (0, 128, 255)

button_text = "Click Me!"
```

```python
running = True

while running:

    screen.fill((255, 255, 255))

    pygame.draw.rect(screen, button_color, button_rect)

    text_surface = font.render(button_text, True, (255, 255, 255))

    screen.blit(text_surface, (button_rect.x + 50, button_rect.y + 10))


    for event in pygame.event.get():

        if event.type == pygame.QUIT:

            running = False

        elif event.type == pygame.MOUSEBUTTONDOWN:

            if button_rect.collidepoint(event.pos):

                button_text = "Button Clicked!"


    pygame.display.flip()


pygame.quit()

sys.exit()
```

Explanation: This Pygame example creates a simple window with a button. When the button is clicked, the text changes to "Button Clicked!". The pygame.draw.rect function draws the button, and pygame.font.Font is used to render the text.

5. PyMob: Simplified Mobile Development with Python

PyMob is a lightweight Python framework that simplifies the development of mobile applications. It is designed to allow developers to quickly prototype and build simple mobile apps with minimal setup and boilerplate code.

Strengths:

- **Ease of Use:** PyMob is straightforward and easy to learn, making it ideal for rapid prototyping and simple applications.

- **Cross-Platform:** PyMob allows for cross-platform development, though it is more limited compared to other frameworks like Kivy or BeeWare.

- **Minimal Boilerplate:** PyMob abstracts much of the complexity involved in mobile app development, allowing developers to focus on functionality.

Weaknesses:

- **Limited Features:** PyMob is not as feature-rich as other frameworks, making it unsuitable for complex or performance-intensive applications.

- **Small Community:** PyMob has a smaller user base and fewer resources available, which can make it challenging to find help or examples.

- **Lack of Updates:** PyMob may not be actively maintained, leading to potential issues with compatibility and bugs.

Example: Creating a Button with PyMob

```python
import pymob


def main():
    app = pymob.Application("My PyMob App")
    label = pymob.Label("Hello, PyMob!")
    app.add_widget(label)
    app.run()


if __name__ == '__main__':
    main()
```

Explanation: This simple PyMob example creates an application with a label that says "Hello, PyMob!". PyMob's minimalistic approach is evident in the concise and easy-to-understand code.

6. SL4A: Scripting Layer for Android

SL4A (Scripting Layer for Android) is a framework that allows you to write Android applications using scripting languages like Python. SL4A is useful for automating tasks, writing quick scripts, or developing simple Android apps without needing deep knowledge of Java or the Android SDK.

Strengths:

- **Access to Android APIs:** SL4A provides access to various Android APIs, enabling interaction with the device's hardware and system features.

- **Ease of Use:** SL4A simplifies Android development by allowing scripts to be written in Python, reducing the need to learn Java.

- **Automation:** Ideal for automating tasks on Android devices, such as sending SMS messages, accessing GPS, or managing files.

Weaknesses:

- **Not Actively Maintained:** SL4A is no longer actively maintained, which means it may not be compatible with newer versions of Android.

- **Limited to Android:** SL4A is specifically designed for Android, so it does not support other platforms.

- **Simple Applications Only:** SL4A is best suited for simple applications and scripts. It is not designed for developing complex or performance-intensive apps.

Example: Displaying a Toast Message with SL4A

```python
import android


droid = android.Android()

droid.makeToast("Hello, SL4A!")
```

Explanation: This SL4A example creates a simple script that displays a toast message on an Android device. The makeToast method is used to show the message "Hello, SL4A!" on the screen.

Each Python mobile framework has its own strengths and weaknesses, making them suitable for different types of projects:

- **Kivy:** Ideal for cross-platform applications with rich graphical interfaces and advanced touch input.

- **BeeWare:** Great for creating native applications that look and feel like they belong on each platform.

- **Pyqtdeploy:** Best suited for deploying PyQt applications across multiple platforms, particularly desktop.

- **Pygame:** A solid choice for simple 2D game development with Python.

- **PyMob:** Perfect for rapid prototyping and simple mobile apps with minimal setup.

- **SL4A:** Useful for automating tasks on Android devices using Python scripts.

Choosing the Right Framework for Your Project:

Choosing the right Python mobile framework for your project depends on various factors, including your specific project requirements, the platforms you want to target, your experience level, and the type of application you are building. In this section, we will guide you through the decision-making process by comparing the key Python mobile frameworks—**Kivy, BeeWare, Pyqtdeploy, Pygame, PyMob,** and **SL4A**—and providing scenarios where each framework might be the best choice. We'll also provide code snippets to illustrate the typical use cases of each framework.

1. Kivy: Best for Graphically Rich and Multitouch Applications

Kivy is ideal for projects that require advanced graphical interfaces, custom UI elements, and multitouch capabilities. It's particularly well-suited for developing games, multimedia applications, and other interactive apps that need to run on multiple platforms, including iOS, Android, Windows, macOS, and Linux.

When to Choose Kivy:

- **Cross-Platform Needs:** You need your application to run on multiple platforms with minimal changes.

- **Rich Graphical Interfaces:** Your app requires advanced graphics, animations, or multitouch gestures.

- **Community and Support:** You want to leverage a large community and extensive documentation.

Example: Creating a Drawing App with Kivy

```python
from kivy.app import App

from kivy.uix.widget import Widget

from kivy.graphics import Line


class DrawingWidget(Widget):
    def on_touch_down(self, touch):
        with self.canvas:
            touch.ud['line'] = Line(points=(touch.x, touch.y))
```

```python
    def on_touch_move(self, touch):

        touch.ud['line'].points += [touch.x, touch.y]


class DrawingApp(App):

    def build(self):

        return DrawingWidget()


if __name__ == '__main__':

    DrawingApp().run()
```

Explanation: This example creates a simple drawing app where users can draw lines on the screen by touching and dragging. Kivy's multitouch support and canvas-based drawing make it an excellent choice for such interactive applications.

2. BeeWare: Best for Native Look and Feel Across Platforms

BeeWare is the right choice when you need to create native applications that look and feel like they belong on each platform. With BeeWare, you can write your application once and deploy it to multiple platforms, including mobile and desktop, while ensuring that the UI uses native widgets and controls.

When to Choose BeeWare:

- **Native Look and Feel:** You want your app to have a native appearance and behavior on each platform.

- **Cross-Platform Development:** You need to target multiple platforms with a single codebase.

- **Integration with Native APIs:** Your app requires integration with native platform features.

Example: Creating a Simple Form with BeeWare

```python
import toga

from toga.style import Pack

from toga.style.pack import COLUMN, ROW


class SimpleFormApp(toga.App):
    def startup(self):
        name_label = toga.Label('Name:',
style=Pack(padding=(0, 5)))

        self.name_input = toga.TextInput(style=Pack(flex=1))

        button = toga.Button('Submit', on_press=self.submit,
style=Pack(padding=5))


        box = toga.Box(style=Pack(direction=COLUMN,
padding=10))

        row = toga.Box(style=Pack(direction=ROW,
padding=5))

        row.add(name_label)

        row.add(self.name_input)
```

```python
        box.add(row)

        box.add(button)


        self.main_window =
toga.MainWindow(title=self.formal_name)

        self.main_window.content = box

        self.main_window.show()


    def submit(self, widget):

        print(f"Submitted name: {self.name_input.value}")


def main():

    return SimpleFormApp()


if __name__ == '__main__':

    main().main_loop()
```

Explanation: This example demonstrates a simple form where users can input their name. The form is built using native widgets, ensuring it looks consistent with other applications on the platform.

3. Pyqtdeploy: Best for Complex Desktop Applications

Pyqtdeploy is particularly suitable for deploying complex desktop applications built with PyQt to mobile and desktop platforms. If your project involves creating a feature-rich application with a complex user interface, and you need the flexibility and power of the Qt framework, Pyqtdeploy is the right choice.

When to Choose Pyqtdeploy:

- **Complex UIs:** Your application requires a sophisticated user interface with advanced widgets.

- **Desktop and Mobile Deployment:** You want to deploy your application across both desktop and mobile platforms.

- **Qt Framework:** You are familiar with or prefer using the Qt framework for building UIs.

Example: Creating a Simple Calculator with PyQt

```python
import sys

from PyQt5.QtWidgets import QApplication, QWidget, QVBoxLayout, QLineEdit, QPushButton


class CalculatorApp(QWidget):
    def __init__(self):
        super().__init__()
        self.init_ui()


    def init_ui(self):
        self.setWindowTitle('Calculator')
        layout = QVBoxLayout()
```

```python
        self.display = QLineEdit()
        layout.addWidget(self.display)

        button = QPushButton('Calculate', self)
        button.clicked.connect(self.calculate)
        layout.addWidget(button)

        self.setLayout(layout)

    def calculate(self):
        expression = self.display.text()
        try:
            result = eval(expression)
            self.display.setText(str(result))
        except Exception as e:
            self.display.setText('Error')

def main():
    app = QApplication(sys.argv)
    window = CalculatorApp()
    window.show()
```

```
sys.exit(app.exec_())
```

```
if __name__ == '__main__':
    main()
```

Explanation: This PyQt example implements a simple calculator. The app allows users to enter mathematical expressions and displays the result when the "Calculate" button is pressed.

4. Pygame: Best for 2D Game Development

Pygame is the best choice if you are developing 2D games or simple graphical applications. Pygame provides a straightforward API for creating games and handling input, graphics, and sound, making it a popular choice for game developers who want to work with Python.

When to Choose Pygame:

- **2D Game Development:** You are developing a 2D game or a simple graphical application.

- **Cross-Platform Games:** You want your game to run on multiple platforms, including Windows, macOS, and Linux.

- **Simple and Fast Prototyping:** You need to prototype a game quickly with minimal setup.

Example: Creating a Simple Pygame with Moving Object

```
import pygame

import sys
```

```python
pygame.init()

screen = pygame.display.set_mode((600, 400))
pygame.display.set_caption("Simple Pygame Example")

x, y = 50, 50
speed = 5

running = True
while running:
    screen.fill((0, 0, 0))

    for event in pygame.event.get():
        if event.type == pygame.QUIT:
            running = False

    keys = pygame.key.get_pressed()
    if keys[pygame.K_LEFT]:
        x -= speed
    if keys[pygame.K_RIGHT]:
        x += speed
    if keys[pygame.K_UP]:
```

```
    y -= speed

  if keys[pygame.K_DOWN]:

    y += speed


  pygame.draw.rect(screen, (0, 128, 255), pygame.Rect(x, y, 60, 60))


  pygame.display.flip()


pygame.quit()

sys.exit()
```

Explanation: This Pygame example creates a simple window with a rectangle that can be moved using the arrow keys. Pygame's event handling and rendering capabilities make it ideal for such interactive applications.

5. PyMob: Best for Simple Cross-Platform Apps

PyMob is a lightweight framework that is ideal for developers who need to quickly prototype or build simple mobile apps with minimal setup. PyMob abstracts much of the complexity involved in mobile app development, making it a good choice for straightforward applications.

When to Choose PyMob:

- **Rapid Prototyping:** You need to quickly create a simple mobile app without dealing with complex configurations.

- **Cross-Platform Simplicity:** You want a framework that allows for basic cross-platform development with minimal code.

- **Minimalist Approach:** Your application requirements are simple, and you prefer an easy-to-learn framework.

Example: Creating a Simple PyMob App

```python
import pymob


def main():
    app = pymob.Application("Simple PyMob App")
    label = pymob.Label("Hello, PyMob!")
    app.add_widget(label)
    app.run()


if __name__ == '__main__':
    main()
```

Explanation: This PyMob example demonstrates the creation of a basic application with a label. The code is simple and straightforward, reflecting PyMob's focus on ease of use.

6. SL4A: Best for Automating Android Tasks with Python

SL4A (Scripting Layer for Android) is ideal for developers who need to automate tasks on Android devices using Python scripts. It provides access to various Android APIs, enabling developers to perform tasks such as sending SMS messages, accessing GPS data, and interacting with the file system.

When to Choose SL4A:

- **Android Automation:** You need to automate tasks on an Android device using Python.

- **Simple Android Apps:** You want to develop simple Android apps or scripts without diving deep into Java.

- **Access to Android APIs:** Your project requires direct interaction with Android's system features.

Example: Sending an SMS with SL4A

import android

droid = android.Android()

droid.smsSend('1234567890', 'Hello from SL4A!')

Explanation: This SL4A script sends an SMS message to a specified phone number. SL4A makes it easy to access Android's APIs using Python.

Choosing the right Python mobile framework depends on your project's specific needs:

- **Kivy** is the best choice for graphically rich, cross-platform applications, especially those requiring multitouch support.

- **BeeWare** is ideal for developers who want their applications to have a native look and feel across multiple platforms.

- **Pyqtdeploy** is suitable for complex desktop and mobile applications that leverage the power of the Qt framework.

- **Pygame** is perfect for 2D game development and simple graphical applications.

- **PyMob** is great for rapid prototyping and building simple mobile apps with minimal setup.

- **SL4A** is the go-to tool for automating tasks on Android devices using Python.

Conclusion

While BeeWare provides a comprehensive solution for developing cross-platform native applications with Python, several other Python mobile frameworks cater to different use cases and preferences. **Kivy** is ideal for building multitouch applications and games, **Pyqtdeploy** excels in deploying PyQt applications to mobile platforms, **Pygame** is the go-to framework for 2D game development, and **PyJNIus** allows for deep integration with Android's Java APIs.

Part III: Core Concepts and Tools
Chapter 8: Designing User Interfaces

Designing user interfaces (UIs) is a critical aspect of mobile application development. A well-designed UI ensures that your app is not only functional but also intuitive and aesthetically pleasing, enhancing the user experience. In this part, we will explore the core concepts and tools involved in designing user interfaces for mobile applications using Python frameworks like Kivy, BeeWare, and PyQt. We'll cover the fundamental principles of UI design, layout management, widget usage, and provide examples with code to illustrate these concepts.

Principles of Good UI Design:

Designing a user interface (UI) is about creating an experience that is both functional and enjoyable for users. Good UI design ensures that users can interact with your application efficiently and effectively, reducing frustration and increasing satisfaction.

1. Consistency

Consistency in UI design means maintaining uniformity in the visual and functional aspects of your application. This includes using consistent colors, fonts, button styles, and interactions throughout the app. Consistency helps users learn the interface more quickly and reduces confusion.

Key Aspects of Consistency:

- **Visual Consistency:** Ensure that colors, fonts, and spacing are uniform across all screens and components.

- **Functional Consistency:** Similar actions should produce similar results. For example, all buttons that perform an action should behave similarly.

- **Behavioral Consistency:** Predictable interactions help users build familiarity with the app.

Example: Consistent Button Design in Kivy

```python
from kivy.app import App

from kivy.uix.button import Button

from kivy.uix.boxlayout import BoxLayout


class ConsistencyApp(App):
    def build(self):
        layout = BoxLayout(orientation='vertical', padding=10, spacing=10)


        button1 = Button(text="Save", background_color=(0, 0.5, 0.5, 1), font_size=20)
        button2 = Button(text="Cancel", background_color=(0.5, 0, 0, 1), font_size=20)


        layout.add_widget(button1)
```

```
layout.add_widget(button2)

return layout
```

```
if __name__ == '__main__':

    ConsistencyApp().run()
```

Explanation:

- **Consistent Styles:** Both buttons use similar font sizes and padding, but with different background colors to indicate different actions. The consistent styling ensures that users recognize these as buttons that perform actions.

2. Simplicity

Simplicity in UI design involves presenting the user with only the information and controls they need at any given time. A simple, uncluttered interface allows users to focus on their tasks without being overwhelmed by unnecessary options or distractions.

Key Aspects of Simplicity:

- **Minimalist Design:** Use only essential elements in the UI. Avoid adding extra features that don't contribute to the user's primary goal.

- **Clear Hierarchy:** Organize content in a way that guides users naturally through tasks, with the most important actions given prominence.

- **Intuitive Navigation:** Design navigation that is straightforward and easy to understand.

Example: Simple and Focused UI in BeeWare

```python
import toga

from toga.style import Pack

from toga.style.pack import COLUMN, CENTER


class SimpleApp(toga.App):

    def startup(self):

        main_box = toga.Box(style=Pack(direction=COLUMN, alignment=CENTER, padding=10))


        label = toga.Label('Enter your name:', style=Pack(padding=(0, 5)))

        name_input = toga.TextInput(style=Pack(flex=1))

        button = toga.Button('Submit', on_press=self.submit, style=Pack(padding=5))


        main_box.add(label)

        main_box.add(name_input)

        main_box.add(button)


        self.main_window = toga.MainWindow(title=self.formal_name)

        self.main_window.content = main_box
```

```python
        self.main_window.show()

    def submit(self, widget):
        print("Name submitted.")


def main():
    return SimpleApp()


if __name__ == '__main__':
    main().main_loop()
```

Explanation:

- **Minimalism:** This simple form consists of a label, a text input, and a button, without any additional or unnecessary elements. This makes it easy for users to focus on the task of entering and submitting their name.

3. Feedback

Feedback in UI design is about giving users immediate and clear responses to their actions. When users interact with the UI—by clicking a button, submitting a form, or entering text—they should receive feedback that their action was registered and what the result of that action was.

Key Aspects of Feedback:

- **Visual Feedback:** Changes in the UI, such as button states or loading indicators, signal that an action is being processed.

- **Auditory Feedback:** Sounds or tones can confirm actions, especially useful in mobile applications.

- **Message Alerts:** Pop-ups, toast messages, or dialog boxes that inform users of the result of their actions, such as errors or successes.

Example: Providing Feedback in Kivy

from kivy.app import App

from kivy.uix.button import Button

from kivy.uix.label import Label

from kivy.uix.boxlayout import BoxLayout

class FeedbackApp(App):

  def build(self):

    self.layout = BoxLayout(orientation='vertical', padding=10, spacing=10)

    self.label = Label(text="Press the button", font_size=20)

    button = Button(text="Click Me!", font_size=20)

    button.bind(on_press=self.on_button_press)

```
self.layout.add_widget(self.label)

self.layout.add_widget(button)

return self.layout


def on_button_press(self, instance):

self.label.text = "Button clicked!"


if __name__ == '__main__':

FeedbackApp().run()
```

Explanation:

- **Immediate Feedback:** When the button is clicked, the label text changes to "Button clicked!", providing immediate visual feedback to the user.

4. Accessibility

Accessibility ensures that your UI is usable by people with a wide range of abilities and disabilities. This involves designing your application to be navigable via keyboard, using readable fonts, and ensuring sufficient color contrast, among other considerations.

Key Aspects of Accessibility:

- **Keyboard Navigation:** Ensure all interactive elements can be accessed via keyboard shortcuts or tab navigation.

- **Readable Fonts:** Use fonts that are legible at various sizes and avoid overly complex or decorative fonts.

- **Color Contrast:** Ensure sufficient contrast between text and background colors to make content readable for users with visual impairments.

Example: Accessible UI in Kivy

```python
from kivy.app import App

from kivy.uix.button import Button

from kivy.uix.boxlayout import BoxLayout


class AccessibleApp(App):

    def build(self):

        layout = BoxLayout(orientation='vertical', padding=10, spacing=10)


        button = Button(text="Submit", font_size=24, background_color=(0, 0.6, 0, 1))

        layout.add_widget(button)


        return layout


if __name__ == '__main__':

    AccessibleApp().run()
```

Explanation:

- **Color Contrast:** The button has a high contrast background color (green) with white text, making it easily readable. The button's size and clear label also contribute to accessibility.

5. Responsive Design

Responsive Design involves creating a UI that adapts to different screen sizes and orientations. This is particularly important for mobile applications that may be used on a variety of devices, from small smartphones to large tablets.

Key Aspects of Responsive Design:

- **Fluid Layouts:** Use flexible layouts that adjust based on the screen size.

- **Adaptive Elements:** UI elements should resize, reposition, or hide based on the available screen real estate.

- **Consistent Experience:** Ensure that the user experience remains consistent across different devices.

Example: Responsive UI in Kivy

```python
from kivy.app import App

from kivy.uix.button import Button

from kivy.uix.boxlayout import BoxLayout


class ResponsiveApp(App):

    def build(self):
```

```python
        layout = BoxLayout(orientation='horizontal',
padding=10, spacing=10)

        button1 = Button(text="Button 1", size_hint=(0.5, 1))

        button2 = Button(text="Button 2", size_hint=(0.5, 1))

        layout.add_widget(button1)

        layout.add_widget(button2)

        return layout

if __name__ == '__main__':

    ResponsiveApp().run()
```

Explanation:

- **Fluid Layout:** The BoxLayout with size_hint ensures that the buttons resize proportionally to the screen size. This provides a consistent experience on devices of different sizes.

The principles of good UI design—**Consistency, Simplicity, Feedback, Accessibility**, and **Responsive Design**—are essential for creating user-friendly applications that provide a positive user experience. By applying these principles in your Python mobile applications using frameworks like Kivy and BeeWare, you can create interfaces that are intuitive, efficient, and accessible to a broad audience. Each example provided here illustrates how these principles can be implemented in practice, helping you build applications that not only function well but also delight users.

Using Kivy's Kv Language for UI Design:

Kivy's Kv language is a powerful tool for designing user interfaces in Kivy applications. It allows you to define the layout and behavior of your UI elements in a separate, declarative syntax, which helps to keep your code organized and your UI design more readable. By using Kv language, you can separate the UI design from the logic, making your application easier to maintain and extend.

1. Introduction to Kv Language

Kv language is a domain-specific language (DSL) designed to describe the structure and behavior of Kivy widgets. It is similar to other markup languages like HTML or XML but is specifically tailored for Kivy.

1.1. Basic Kv Language Structure

Kv files typically have the same name as the corresponding Python class but with a .kv extension. The Kv file defines the UI layout and binds it to the Python logic.

Example: Simple Kv File Structure

Python:

```python
# main.py

from kivy.app import App

from kivy.uix.boxlayout import BoxLayout

class MyWidget(BoxLayout):

    pass
```

```python
class MyApp(App):
    def build(self):
        return MyWidget()
if __name__ == '__main__':
    MyApp().run()
```

Yaml:

```yaml
# mywidget.kv
<MyWidget>:
    orientation: 'vertical'
    padding: 10
    spacing: 10
    Label:
        text: "Hello, Kv!"
        font_size: 24
    Button:
        text: "Click Me"
        font_size: 24
```

Explanation:

- **<MyWidget>:** The Kv language defines a root widget class (MyWidget) that extends BoxLayout. This widget is linked to the MyWidget class in the Python file.

- **Label and Button:** The Kv file defines a label and a button inside the BoxLayout. The Kv syntax specifies properties such as text and font_size.

When you run the MyApp, it will display a vertical layout with a label and a button.

2. Defining and Using Properties in Kv Language

Kv language allows you to bind properties of widgets to variables or functions in your Python code. This enables dynamic updates to the UI when the underlying data changes.

2.1. Binding Properties

You can bind widget properties to Python class variables or methods using the Kv language. This is particularly useful for creating responsive UIs that automatically update when data changes.

Example: Binding Properties

Python:

```python
# main.py

from kivy.app import App

from kivy.uix.boxlayout import BoxLayout

from kivy.properties import StringProperty

class MyWidget(BoxLayout):

    label_text = StringProperty("Hello, Kv!")

    def change_text(self):

        self.label_text = "Button Clicked!"
```

```python
class MyApp(App):
    def build(self):
        return MyWidget()

if __name__ == '__main__':
    MyApp().run()
```

Yaml:

```yaml
# mywidget.kv
<MyWidget>:
    orientation: 'vertical'
    padding: 10
    spacing: 10
    Label:
        text: root.label_text
        font_size: 24

    Button:
        text: "Click Me"
        font_size: 24
        on_press: root.change_text()
```

Explanation:

- **StringProperty:** The label_text property is a StringProperty in the MyWidget class. It is bound to the text property of the Label widget in the Kv file.

- **Dynamic Updates:** When the button is pressed, the change_text method is called, updating the label_text, which in turn updates the label in the UI.

3. Creating and Using Custom Widgets in Kv Language

Kv language allows you to create custom widgets and reuse them across your application. This promotes modularity and code reuse.

3.1. Defining Custom Widgets

You can define custom widgets directly in the Kv file and use them as you would any other widget.

Example: Custom Widget in Kv Language

Python:

```python
# main.py

from kivy.app import App

from kivy.uix.boxlayout import BoxLayout

class MyWidget(BoxLayout):

    pass

class MyApp(App):

    def build(self):

        return MyWidget()

if __name__ == '__main__':

    MyApp().run()
```

Yaml:

```yaml
# mywidget.kv
```

```
<MyWidget>:
    orientation: 'vertical'
    padding: 10
    spacing: 10
    CustomButton:
        text: "Custom Button 1"
    CustomButton:
        text: "Custom Button 2"
<CustomButton@Button>:
    font_size: 24
    background_color: 0, 0.6, 0, 1
```

Explanation:

- **Conditional Styling:** The Label text and Button background color change based on the is_active property. This allows the UI to dynamically reflect the current state.

5. Best Practices for Using Kv Language

To make the most of Kv language, it's important to follow best practices that ensure your UI design is maintainable, efficient, and scalable.

5.1. Separate Logic from Design

Keep the UI design in the Kv file and the application logic in the Python file. This separation of concerns makes your code easier to maintain.

5.2. Use Reusable Components

Create reusable components (widgets) in Kv language to avoid duplication and make your UI design more modular.

5.3. Optimize Performance

Avoid overly complex Kv structures that could slow down your application. Use Kv language for layout and styling, but keep complex logic in your Python code.

Kivy's Kv language is a powerful tool for designing user interfaces that are both flexible and easy to manage. By separating the UI layout from the application logic, Kv language allows developers to create clean, maintainable codebases. Whether you're binding properties, creating custom widgets, or managing dynamic layouts, Kv language provides a robust framework for building sophisticated user interfaces in Kivy. The examples provided illustrate how you can leverage Kv language to create responsive and interactive UIs that enhance the user experience of your mobile applications.

Creating Dynamic and Interactive Interfaces:

Dynamic and interactive interfaces are essential for modern mobile applications, as they allow users to engage with the app in a more meaningful way. These interfaces respond to user input, display real-time data, and adapt to different contexts within the application.

1. Event Handling

Event handling is the foundation of interactivity in a user interface. It involves responding to user actions such as clicks, swipes, key presses, and other gestures. In Python

UI frameworks, event handling is typically managed by binding events to callback functions.

1.1. Handling Button Clicks in Kivy

Buttons are a common UI element that users interact with frequently. You can bind a button's on_press event to a function that executes when the button is clicked.

Example: Handling Button Clicks

```python
from kivy.app import App

from kivy.uix.button import Button

from kivy.uix.label import Label

from kivy.uix.boxlayout import BoxLayout

class MyWidget(BoxLayout):

    def __init__(self, **kwargs):

        super().__init__(**kwargs)

        self.orientation = 'vertical'

        self.label = Label(text="Press the button", font_size=24)

        self.button = Button(text="Click Me", font_size=24)

        self.button.bind(on_press=self.on_button_press)

            self.add_widget(self.label)

        self.add_widget(self.button)

    def on_button_press(self, instance):

        self.label.text = "Button Clicked!"
```

```python
class MyApp(App):

    def build(self):

        return MyWidget()

if __name__ == '__main__':

    MyApp().run()
```

Explanation:

- **Button Event Binding:** The bind method connects the on_press event of the Button to the on_button_press method. When the button is clicked, the label's text is updated.

- **Immediate Feedback:** The interface provides immediate feedback to the user, making it interactive and responsive.

2. Dynamic Updates

Dynamic interfaces update the UI in response to changes in data or user input without requiring a full reload of the screen. This is crucial for applications that display real-time information or that need to reflect changes immediately.

2.1. Updating UI Elements in Real-Time

You can dynamically update UI elements in response to changes in application state or data. This is often done by binding properties in your Python code to UI components.

Example: Real-Time Data Display

```python
from kivy.app import App

from kivy.uix.boxlayout import BoxLayout
```

```python
from kivy.uix.label import Label
from kivy.uix.slider import Slider
from kivy.properties import StringProperty
class MyWidget(BoxLayout):
    slider_value = StringProperty("50")
    def __init__(self, **kwargs):
        super().__init__(**kwargs)
        self.orientation = 'vertical'
        self.label = Label(text=self.slider_value,
font_size=24)
        self.slider = Slider(min=0, max=100, value=50)
        self.slider.bind(value=self.on_value_change)
        self.add_widget(self.label)
        self.add_widget(self.slider)
    def on_value_change(self, instance, value):
        self.slider_value = str(int(value))
class MyApp(App):
    def build(self):
        return MyWidget()
if __name__ == '__main__':
    MyApp().run()
```

Explanation:

- **Slider Binding:** The Slider widget is bound to the on_value_change method, which updates the slider_value property whenever the slider is moved.

- **Dynamic Label Update:** The label's text is bound to the slider_value property, so it updates in real-time as the slider is adjusted.

3. Creating Animations

Animations make the UI more engaging by providing visual feedback and transitions. In Kivy, animations can be used to move, resize, rotate, or fade UI elements in response to user interactions or changes in the application state.

3.1. Basic Animations in Kivy

Kivy's Animation class allows you to animate the properties of widgets over time, creating smooth transitions.

Example: Moving a Widget with Animation

```
from kivy.app import App

from kivy.uix.button import Button

from kivy.uix.boxlayout import BoxLayout

from kivy.animation import Animation

class MyWidget(BoxLayout):

    def __init__(self, **kwargs):

        super().__init__(**kwargs)
```

```python
        self.orientation = 'vertical'

        self.button = Button(text="Move Me",
size_hint=(None, None), size=(200, 50))

        self.button.bind(on_press=self.animate_button)

        self.add_widget(self.button)

    def animate_button(self, instance):

        anim = Animation(x=300, duration=1) +
Animation(x=0, duration=1)

        anim.start(instance)

class MyApp(App):

    def build(self):

        return MyWidget()

if __name__ == '__main__':

    MyApp().run()
```

Explanation:

- **Animation Chaining:** The Animation class is used to move the button from its starting position to x=300 and then back to its original position. The animation plays over 2 seconds, with the button moving out and returning smoothly.

- **Interactive Animation:** The animation is triggered by a button press, making the UI interactive and visually engaging.

4. Gesture Recognition

Gesture recognition allows you to create more advanced interactions by detecting user gestures like swipes, pinches, or long presses. Kivy provides built-in support for handling gestures, which is particularly useful in mobile applications.

4.1. Detecting Swipes in Kivy

Swipes are common gestures in mobile applications, often used for navigation or revealing additional content.

Example: Swipe Gesture Detection

```python
from kivy.app import App

from kivy.uix.label import Label

from kivy.uix.boxlayout import BoxLayout

class MyWidget(BoxLayout):

    def __init__(self, **kwargs):

        super().__init__(**kwargs)

        self.orientation = 'vertical'

        self.label = Label(text="Swipe Me", font_size=24)

        self.add_widget(self.label)

        self.bind(on_touch_move=self.on_swipe)

    def on_swipe(self, instance, touch):

        if touch.dx > 40:

            self.label.text = "Swiped Right!"

        elif touch.dx < -40:
```

```python
        self.label.text = "Swiped Left!"
class MyApp(App):
    def build(self):
        return MyWidget()
if __name__ == '__main__':
    MyApp().run()
```

Explanation:

- **Swipe Detection:** The on_touch_move method detects the direction of the swipe based on the dx property of the touch event. If the swipe is significant enough (greater than 40 pixels), the label text updates to indicate the swipe direction.

- **User Interaction:** This gesture recognition adds another layer of interactivity, allowing users to navigate or trigger actions with simple swipes.

5. Creating Custom Interactions

Sometimes, standard widgets and interactions are not enough to meet the specific needs of your application. In these cases, you can create custom interactions by defining your own event handlers and UI logic.

5.1. Building a Custom Drag-and-Drop Interface

Drag-and-drop interactions can be used to allow users to rearrange items, move objects, or transfer data between different parts of the application.

Example: Implementing Drag-and-Drop

```python
from kivy.app import App
```

```python
from kivy.uix.button import Button

from kivy.uix.boxlayout import BoxLayout

from kivy.uix.label import Label

class DraggableButton(Button):

    def on_touch_move(self, touch):

        if self.collide_point(*touch.pos):

            self.center_x = touch.x

            self.center_y = touch.y

        return super().on_touch_move(touch)

class MyWidget(BoxLayout):

    def __init__(self, **kwargs):

        super().__init__(**kwargs)

        self.orientation = 'vertical'

        self.label = Label(text="Drag the button",
font_size=24)

        self.button = DraggableButton(text="Drag Me",
size_hint=(None, None), size=(200, 50))


        self.add_widget(self.label)

        self.add_widget(self.button)

class MyApp(App):

    def build(self):

        return MyWidget()
```

```
if __name__ == '__main__':

  MyApp().run()
```

Explanation:

- **Custom Drag-and-Drop:** The DraggableButton class extends Button and overrides the on_touch_move method to make the button draggable. The button's position updates based on the touch coordinates, allowing the user to drag it around the screen.

- **Interactive Customization:** This example shows how you can create custom interactions that go beyond the standard widgets provided by Kivy.

Creating dynamic and interactive user interfaces is key to developing engaging and responsive mobile applications. By mastering event handling, dynamic updates, animations, gesture recognition, and custom interactions, you can build UIs that not only look great but also provide a rich user experience. The examples provided illustrate how to implement these concepts using Python and Kivy, empowering you to create sophisticated, user-friendly interfaces in your mobile applications.

Accessibility Considerations:

Designing accessible user interfaces (UIs) is crucial for creating applications that can be used by everyone, including people with disabilities. Accessibility ensures that all users, regardless of their abilities, can interact with your application effectively. This section will cover key accessibility considerations in UI design, along with practical examples using Python frameworks like Kivy and

BeeWare to illustrate how these concepts can be implemented.

1. Key Accessibility Principles

When designing accessible interfaces, consider the following principles:

1. **Perceivability:** Ensure that all UI elements are perceivable by all users. This includes using clear text, high contrast, and providing alternatives for non-text content (e.g., images).

2. **Operability:** Make sure that all UI components are operable by users with various input methods, including keyboards, screen readers, and assistive devices.

3. **Understandability:** Design UIs that are easy to understand, with clear instructions, error messages, and intuitive navigation.

4. **Robustness:** Ensure that the UI is robust enough to work with different assistive technologies and across a range of devices and platforms.

2. Perceivability

To make your application perceivable, consider how all users will access the information presented. This includes ensuring that text is readable, colors are distinguishable, and alternative text is provided for images.

2.1. Ensuring Readable Text

Readable text involves selecting appropriate font sizes, styles, and ensuring high contrast between text and background.

Example: High Contrast Text in Kivy

```python
from kivy.app import App

from kivy.uix.label import Label

from kivy.uix.boxlayout import BoxLayout


class AccessibilityApp(App):

    def build(self):

        layout = BoxLayout(padding=10,
orientation='vertical')


        # High contrast label

        label = Label(text="High Contrast Text",
font_size=24, color=(1, 1, 1, 1), bold=True)

        layout.add_widget(label)


        return layout


if __name__ == '__main__':

    AccessibilityApp().run()
```

Explanation:

- **High Contrast:** The label uses a white font color on a dark background to ensure high contrast, making the text easily readable for users with visual impairments.

2.2. Providing Alternative Text for Images

If your application includes images, provide alternative text descriptions for users who rely on screen readers.

Example: Alternative Text in BeeWare

```python
import toga

from toga.style import Pack

from toga.style.pack import COLUMN


class AccessibilityApp(toga.App):
    def startup(self):
        main_box =
toga.Box(style=Pack(direction=COLUMN, padding=10))


        # Image with alternative text
        image =
toga.ImageView(toga.Image("path_to_image.png",
alt="Descriptive text for the image"))

        main_box.add(image)


        self.main_window =
toga.MainWindow(title=self.formal_name)

        self.main_window.content = main_box

        self.main_window.show()
```

```python
def main():

    return AccessibilityApp()


if __name__ == '__main__':

    main().main_loop()
```

Explanation:

- **Alternative Text:** The alt parameter provides a description of the image, which is essential for users who cannot see the image and rely on screen readers.

3. Operability

Making your UI operable involves ensuring that all functionalities are accessible via different input methods, including keyboard and touch.

3.1. Keyboard Navigation

Keyboard navigation allows users to interact with your application using only the keyboard. This is crucial for users with motor impairments who cannot use a mouse.

Example: Keyboard Navigation in Kivy

```python
from kivy.app import App

from kivy.uix.button import Button

from kivy.uix.boxlayout import BoxLayout


class AccessibilityApp(App):
```

```python
def build(self):

    layout = BoxLayout(padding=10, orientation='vertical')


    # Buttons that can be navigated using the keyboard

    button1 = Button(text="Button 1", focus=True)

    button2 = Button(text="Button 2")


    layout.add_widget(button1)

    layout.add_widget(button2)


    return layout


if __name__ == '__main__':

    AccessibilityApp().run()
```

Explanation:

- **Keyboard Focus:** The first button is focused when the application starts, allowing users to navigate between buttons using the Tab key. This ensures that all functionalities are accessible via keyboard.

4. Understandability

Ensure that your UI is easy to understand, with clear labels, instructions, and feedback. This includes providing error messages that help users correct their mistakes.

4.1. Clear Instructions and Feedback

Providing clear instructions and feedback helps users understand how to interact with the UI and what to do when they encounter errors.

Example: Clear Error Messages in Kivy

from kivy.app import App

from kivy.uix.label import Label

from kivy.uix.textinput import TextInput

from kivy.uix.boxlayout import BoxLayout

from kivy.uix.button import Button

class AccessibilityApp(App):

   def build(self):

     self.layout = BoxLayout(padding=10, orientation='vertical')

     # Input field with a label

     self.label = Label(text="Enter your name:", font_size=18)

     self.text_input = TextInput(multiline=False)

     submit_button = Button(text="Submit", on_press=self.validate_input)

     self.layout.add_widget(self.label)

```
self.layout.add_widget(self.text_input)

self.layout.add_widget(submit_button)


return self.layout


def validate_input(self, instance):

    if not self.text_input.text:

        self.label.text = "Error: Name cannot be empty!"

        self.label.color = (1, 0, 0, 1)  # Red text for error
message

    else:

        self.label.text = "Thank you!"

        self.label.color = (0, 1, 0, 1)  # Green text for
success message


if __name__ == '__main__':

    AccessibilityApp().run()
```

Explanation:

- **Clear Feedback:** The application provides clear feedback when the user submits the form, showing an error message in red if the input is empty, or a success message in green if the input is valid.

5. Robustness

Robustness refers to ensuring that your UI works well with a variety of assistive technologies and across different platforms and devices.

5.1. Compatibility with Screen Readers

Screen readers help visually impaired users navigate your application by reading aloud the content of the screen. Ensuring compatibility with screen readers is vital for accessibility.

Example: Screen Reader Compatibility in BeeWare

In BeeWare, ensure that all text content and controls are labeled correctly, and avoid using visual-only cues to convey important information.

```python
import toga

from toga.style import Pack

from toga.style.pack import COLUMN


class AccessibilityApp(toga.App):

    def startup(self):

        main_box =
toga.Box(style=Pack(direction=COLUMN, padding=10))


        # A button with a clear label for screen readers

        button = toga.Button('Submit',
on_press=self.submit_form)
```

```python
        main_box.add(button)

        self.main_window =
toga.MainWindow(title=self.formal_name)
        self.main_window.content = main_box
        self.main_window.show()

    def submit_form(self, widget):
        print("Form submitted")


def main():
    return AccessibilityApp()


if __name__ == '__main__':
    main().main_loop()
```

Explanation:

- **Clear Labels:** Ensure that all interactive elements like buttons and text inputs are clearly labeled. This makes them easily identifiable by screen readers, ensuring that visually impaired users can navigate the application.

Conclusion

Accessibility considerations are crucial in designing user interfaces that are inclusive and usable by everyone, regardless of their abilities. By focusing on **perceivability**, **operability**, **understandability**, and **robustness**, you can create applications that cater to a wide audience, including those with disabilities. The examples provided demonstrate how to implement these accessibility principles using Python frameworks like Kivy and BeeWare, ensuring that your applications are accessible, intuitive, and user-friendly.

Chapter 9: Managing Application State

Understanding State Management:

State management is a fundamental concept in application development, particularly in interactive applications where the user interface (UI) must respond dynamically to user input, data changes, or other events. In mobile applications, managing the state effectively ensures that your app behaves consistently, maintains its data correctly across different views, and provides a smooth user experience. This section will explore the concept of state management, discuss its importance, and provide examples using Python frameworks like Kivy and BeeWare to illustrate how state can be managed effectively.

1. What is Application State?

Application state refers to the data that represents the current status of your application at any given time. This includes information about what the user sees on the screen, the current values of input fields, the data retrieved from a server, and even UI elements' visibility or position.

Key Aspects of Application State:

- **UI State:** Information about the current state of the user interface, such as which buttons are active, which views are visible, and what text is displayed.

- **Data State:** The data that your application works with, such as user inputs, fetched data from an API, or calculated results.

- **Navigation State:** The current screen or view the user is on, along with any relevant navigation history.

2. Importance of State Management

Proper state management is crucial for ensuring that your application:

- **Remains Consistent:** The UI should always reflect the current state of the data. If the data changes, the UI should update accordingly.

- **Handles Complexity:** As applications grow in complexity, with multiple components and views, managing state becomes more challenging and essential.

- **Provides a Smooth User Experience:** A well-managed state leads to fewer bugs, less confusion, and a more responsive and intuitive user interface.

3. State Management in Kivy

Kivy provides several tools and techniques for managing state in your application, including properties, binding, and custom state management logic.

3.1. Using Properties for State Management

In Kivy, properties are special attributes of widgets that can automatically update the UI when their values change. Kivy's ObjectProperty, StringProperty, BooleanProperty, and other property types help manage the state effectively.

Example: Basic State Management with Properties

from kivy.app import App

```python
from kivy.uix.boxlayout import BoxLayout

from kivy.uix.button import Button

from kivy.uix.label import Label

from kivy.properties import StringProperty

class MyWidget(BoxLayout):

    label_text = StringProperty("Welcome!")

    def __init__(self, **kwargs):

        super().__init__(**kwargs)

        self.orientation = 'vertical'


        self.label = Label(text=self.label_text)

        self.add_widget(self.label)


        self.button = Button(text="Click Me",
on_press=self.change_state)

        self.add_widget(self.button)


    def change_state(self, instance):

        self.label_text = "State Changed!"

class MyApp(App):

    def build(self):

        return MyWidget()
```

```python
if __name__ == '__main__':

    MyApp().run()
```

Explanation:

- **StringProperty:** The label_text is a StringProperty that holds the state of the label's text. When this property changes, the label automatically updates.

- **Dynamic UI Update:** The change_state method changes the state by updating the label_text, which in turn updates the label in the UI. This ensures that the UI remains consistent with the current state.

3.2. Binding Properties for Reactive UIs

Binding in Kivy allows you to create reactive UIs where the interface automatically updates when the underlying state changes. This is particularly useful for creating dynamic interfaces that need to respond to user actions or data changes.

Example: Reactive UI with Binding

```python
from kivy.app import App

from kivy.uix.boxlayout import BoxLayout

from kivy.uix.slider import Slider

from kivy.uix.label import Label

from kivy.properties import StringProperty


class MyWidget(BoxLayout):
```

```python
    slider_value = StringProperty("50")

    def __init__(self, **kwargs):
        super().__init__(**kwargs)
        self.orientation = 'vertical'

        self.label = Label(text=self.slider_value)
        self.add_widget(self.label)

        self.slider = Slider(min=0, max=100, value=50)
        self.slider.bind(value=self.on_value_change)
        self.add_widget(self.slider)

    def on_value_change(self, instance, value):
        self.slider_value = str(int(value))

class MyApp(App):
    def build(self):
        return MyWidget()


if __name__ == '__main__':
    MyApp().run()
```

Explanation:

- **Binding:** The slider's value is bound to the on_value_change method, which updates the slider_value property. The label is bound to this property, ensuring that it reflects the current value of the slider.

- **Reactive UI:** As the user moves the slider, the label updates in real-time, showing the current slider value. This creates a responsive and interactive UI.

4. State Management in BeeWare

BeeWare also provides mechanisms for managing state in your application, typically through properties and event handlers in Toga, the UI toolkit in BeeWare.

4.1. Managing State with Toga

In Toga, you can manage state using properties in your app class, and you can bind these properties to UI elements.

Example: State Management in BeeWare

```python
import toga

from toga.style import Pack

from toga.style.pack import COLUMN

class MyApp(toga.App):

    def startup(self):

        self.main_box =
toga.Box(style=Pack(direction=COLUMN, padding=10))
```

```python
        # Application state

        self.label_text = "Welcome!"


        # UI components

        self.label = toga.Label(self.label_text,
style=Pack(padding=5))

        self.button = toga.Button("Click Me",
on_press=self.change_state, style=Pack(padding=5))


        self.main_box.add(self.label)

        self.main_box.add(self.button)


        self.main_window =
toga.MainWindow(title=self.formal_name)

        self.main_window.content = self.main_box

        self.main_window.show()


    def change_state(self, widget):

        self.label_text = "State Changed!"

        self.label.text = self.label_text  # Update the UI to
reflect the new state


def main():
```

```
    return MyApp()

if __name__ == '__main__':

    main().main_loop()
```

Explanation:

- **State Variable:** The label_text is a state variable that holds the current text for the label.

- **Event Handling:** The change_state method updates the label_text and explicitly sets the label's text to this new value, reflecting the updated state in the UI.

5. Complex State Management

As your application grows in complexity, you may need to manage multiple pieces of state across different components. This can involve more advanced techniques like state containers, global state management, or even using external libraries for state management.

5.1. Managing Multiple States

When managing multiple states, it's important to keep your state management organized and predictable.

Example: Managing Multiple States in Kivy

```
from kivy.app import App

from kivy.uix.boxlayout import BoxLayout

from kivy.uix.label import Label

from kivy.uix.button import Button
```

```python
from kivy.properties import StringProperty, BooleanProperty

class MyWidget(BoxLayout):
    message = StringProperty("Welcome!")
    is_logged_in = BooleanProperty(False)

    def __init__(self, **kwargs):
        super().__init__(**kwargs)
        self.orientation = 'vertical'

        self.label = Label(text=self.message)
        self.add_widget(self.label)

        self.button = Button(text="Login", on_press=self.toggle_login)
        self.add_widget(self.button)

    def toggle_login(self, instance):
        self.is_logged_in = not self.is_logged_in
        if self.is_logged_in:
            self.message = "Logged In!"
            self.button.text = "Logout"
```

```python
    else:
        self.message = "Logged Out!"
        self.button.text = "Login"


class MyApp(App):
  def build(self):
    return MyWidget()


if __name__ == '__main__':
  MyApp().run()
```

Explanation:

- **Multiple States:** The application manages both message and is_logged_in states. Depending on the state, the UI updates to reflect whether the user is logged in or logged out.

- **State-Driven UI:** The UI components (label and button) change based on the current state, providing a dynamic and responsive interface.

Understanding and managing application state is crucial for creating interactive, consistent, and user-friendly mobile applications. Whether you're using Kivy, BeeWare, or another framework, state management involves tracking and updating the data that drives your UI, ensuring that your application responds correctly to user inputs and data changes. By using properties, binding, and event handling effectively, you can build applications that are both robust and maintainable. The examples provided demonstrate how state can be managed in both simple and complex scenarios, equipping you with the tools to manage state effectively in your own projects.

Techniques for Maintaining State in Python Apps:

Maintaining state in Python applications is essential for creating dynamic, interactive, and consistent user experiences. Proper state management ensures that your application correctly reflects the current status of the user interface (UI) and data at all times. In this section, we will explore various techniques for maintaining state in Python applications, focusing on common patterns and best practices. We'll provide detailed examples using Python frameworks like Kivy and BeeWare to demonstrate these techniques in practice.

1. Using Python Class Attributes

One of the simplest ways to manage state in Python applications is by using class attributes. Class attributes can store the current state of an application, such as the value of a counter, the user's login status, or the selected item in a list.

1.1. Example: Managing State with Class Attributes

```python
class CounterApp:

    def __init__(self):

        self.count = 0


    def increment(self):
```

```python
        self.count += 1

        print(f"Current count: {self.count}")


    def reset(self):

        self.count = 0

        print("Counter reset.")

# Example usage

app = CounterApp()

app.increment()  # Current count: 1

app.increment()  # Current count: 2

app.reset()     # Counter reset.
```

Explanation:

- **Class Attribute:** The count attribute holds the current state of the counter. Methods like increment and reset modify this state.

- **State Persistence:** The state (i.e., the value of count) persists across method calls, allowing the application to maintain a consistent state.

2. Using Python Properties

In Python, properties provide a way to manage state while controlling access to class attributes. Properties allow you to define getter, setter, and deleter methods for managing the internal state, ensuring that any changes are validated or trigger additional actions.

2.1. Example: Using Properties for State Management

```python
class TemperatureConverter:

    def __init__(self):

        self._celsius = 0.0

    @property

    def celsius(self):

        return self._celsius

    @celsius.setter

    def celsius(self, value):

        if value < -273.15:

            raise ValueError("Temperature below absolute zero is not possible.")

            self._celsius = value


    @property

    def fahrenheit(self):

        return (self._celsius * 9/5) + 32


# Example usage

converter = TemperatureConverter()

converter.celsius = 25

print(f"Celsius: {converter.celsius}, Fahrenheit: {converter.fahrenheit}")
```

Explanation:

- **Getter and Setter:** The celsius property controls access to the _celsius attribute, ensuring that invalid values (below absolute zero) are not allowed.

- **Derived State:** The fahrenheit property calculates the Fahrenheit value dynamically based on the current state (_celsius).

3. Using Kivy Properties

In Kivy, properties like StringProperty, NumericProperty, and BooleanProperty are used to manage state within Kivy applications. These properties not only hold the state but also automatically update the UI when the state changes.

3.1. Example: State Management with Kivy Properties

from kivy.app import App

from kivy.uix.boxlayout import BoxLayout

from kivy.uix.label import Label

from kivy.uix.button import Button

from kivy.properties import NumericProperty

class CounterWidget(BoxLayout):

  count = NumericProperty(0)

  def __init__(self, **kwargs):

    super().__init__(**kwargs)

    self.orientation = 'vertical'

```python
        self.label = Label(text=str(self.count))

        self.add_widget(self.label)


        self.button = Button(text="Increment",
on_press=self.increment_count)

        self.add_widget(self.button)


    def increment_count(self, instance):

        self.count += 1

        self.label.text = str(self.count)


class CounterApp(App):

    def build(self):

        return CounterWidget()


if __name__ == '__main__':

    CounterApp().run()
```

Explanation:

- **Kivy Property:** The count attribute is a NumericProperty that automatically updates the label when its value changes.

- **State-Driven UI:** The label's text is bound to the count property, ensuring the UI reflects the current state.

4. Using Dictionaries for State Management

Dictionaries provide a flexible way to store and manage state, particularly when dealing with dynamic or multiple states. You can store various state variables in a single dictionary and access them as needed.

4.1. Example: Using Dictionaries to Manage State

```python
class FormApp:

    def __init__(self):
        self.state = {
            'name': '',
            'email': '',
            'submitted': False
        }


    def submit_form(self, name, email):
        self.state['name'] = name
        self.state['email'] = email
        self.state['submitted'] = True
        print("Form submitted:", self.state)


    def reset_form(self):
```

```python
        self.state = {
            'name': '',
            'email': '',
            'submitted': False
        }
        print("Form reset.")


# Example usage
app = FormApp()
app.submit_form("Alice", "alice@example.com")
app.reset_form()
```

Explanation:

- **State Dictionary:** The state dictionary holds all the state variables related to the form.

- **Flexible State Management:** Using a dictionary allows you to easily manage and extend the state without needing to define multiple class attributes.

5. Using State Management Libraries

For more complex applications, especially those with multiple views or components, state management libraries can help manage state in a more structured way. Libraries like Redux (in JavaScript) or Zinc (for Python) provide patterns for managing global application state.

5.1. Example: Global State Management with Zinc (Conceptual)

Although Zinc is a fictional or hypothetical library for this example, the concept is similar to state management solutions available in other ecosystems.

```python
class GlobalState:

    def __init__(self):

        self.state = {

            'logged_in': False,

            'user_data': None,

            'cart_items': []

        }

    def login(self, user_data):

        self.state['logged_in'] = True

        self.state['user_data'] = user_data


    def logout(self):

        self.state['logged_in'] = False

        self.state['user_data'] = None

        self.state['cart_items'] = []


    def add_to_cart(self, item):

        self.state['cart_items'].append(item)


# Example usage
```

```python
app_state = GlobalState()

app_state.login({'username': 'john_doe'})

app_state.add_to_cart('Item 1')

print(app_state.state)
```

Explanation:

- **Centralized State Management:** The GlobalState class manages all the state variables related to the application. This makes it easier to maintain and update the state as the application grows.

- **Global Access:** The state can be accessed and modified from anywhere in the application, allowing for consistent state management across different components.

6. Using Events and Callbacks for State Changes

In interactive applications, state changes often need to trigger other actions, such as updating the UI or sending data to a server. This can be managed using events and callbacks.

6.1. Example: Using Events and Callbacks in Kivy

```python
from kivy.app import App

from kivy.uix.boxlayout import BoxLayout

from kivy.uix.button import Button

from kivy.properties import NumericProperty


class CounterWidget(BoxLayout):
```

```python
    count = NumericProperty(0)

    def __init__(self, **kwargs):
        super().__init__(**kwargs)
        self.orientation = 'vertical'

        self.label = Label(text=str(self.count))
        self.add_widget(self.label)

        self.button = Button(text="Increment",
on_press=self.increment_count)
        self.add_widget(self.button)

    def increment_count(self, instance):
        self.count += 1
        self.dispatch_event()

    def dispatch_event(self):
        if self.count == 5:
            self.on_reach_five()

    def on_reach_five(self):
```

```python
    print("Count reached five!")


class CounterApp(App):

    def build(self):

        return CounterWidget()


if __name__ == '__main__':

    CounterApp().run()
```

Explanation:

- **Event Dispatching:** The dispatch_event method checks the state (count value) and triggers the on_reach_five method when a certain condition is met.

- **Callbacks:** The on_reach_five callback is executed when the count reaches five, demonstrating how events and callbacks can manage complex state changes.

Maintaining state in Python applications is essential for creating responsive and user-friendly experiences. Whether you're using class attributes, properties, dictionaries, or more complex state management patterns, the key is to keep your state organized, consistent, and responsive to changes. The examples provided illustrate various techniques for managing state in Python, from simple applications to more complex scenarios involving multiple components or global state. By applying these techniques, you can ensure that your application remains stable, maintainable, and user-friendly as it grows.

Persisting Data Locally:

Persisting data locally is an essential aspect of managing application state, especially in mobile applications where users expect their data to be available even when the app is closed or when they are offline. Local data persistence allows your application to save user preferences, cache data, and store user-generated content, ensuring that this data is retained across sessions. This section explores various techniques for persisting data locally in Python applications, including using files, SQLite databases, and key-value stores. We will provide detailed examples to illustrate each technique.

1. Using Files for Local Data Persistence

One of the simplest methods to persist data locally is by writing it to a file. You can use plain text files, JSON files, or even binary files, depending on the complexity and structure of the data you need to store.

1.1. Storing Data in a Text File

Text files are suitable for storing simple data, such as user preferences or logs. You can read from and write to text files using Python's built-in file handling functions.

Example: Saving and Loading Data from a Text File

```python
class SimpleFileStorage:

    def __init__(self, filename):

        self.filename = filename


    def save_data(self, data):
```

```python
    with open(self.filename, 'w') as file:
        file.write(data)

def load_data(self):
    try:
        with open(self.filename, 'r') as file:
            return file.read()
    except FileNotFoundError:
        return None

# Example usage
storage = SimpleFileStorage('user_data.txt')
storage.save_data('User preferences: dark mode enabled')
print(storage.load_data())
```

Explanation:

- **File Writing:** The save_data method writes the provided data to a text file.

- **File Reading:** The load_data method reads the data from the file and returns it. If the file doesn't exist, it returns None.

1.2. Using JSON Files for Structured Data

JSON (JavaScript Object Notation) is a lightweight data interchange format that's easy to read and write. JSON files are suitable for storing more complex data structures, such as dictionaries and lists.

Example: Saving and Loading Data from a JSON File

```python
import json


class JSONFileStorage:
    def __init__(self, filename):
        self.filename = filename

    def save_data(self, data):
        with open(self.filename, 'w') as file:
            json.dump(data, file)

    def load_data(self):
        try:
            with open(self.filename, 'r') as file:
                return json.load(file)
        except (FileNotFoundError, json.JSONDecodeError):
            return None


# Example usage
storage = JSONFileStorage('user_data.json')
```

```
storage.save_data({'username': 'alice', 'preferences':
{'theme': 'dark'}})
```

```
print(storage.load_data())
```

Explanation:

- **JSON Serialization:** The save_data method serializes the Python dictionary into JSON format and writes it to a file.

- **JSON Deserialization:** The load_data method reads the JSON file and deserializes it back into a Python dictionary.

2. Using SQLite for Local Database Storage

SQLite is a lightweight, self-contained database engine that is perfect for mobile and small-scale applications. It allows you to store structured data in a relational database format, supporting complex queries and data manipulation.

2.1. Setting Up an SQLite Database

SQLite databases are stored as files on the local filesystem. Python's sqlite3 module provides a simple interface for interacting with SQLite databases.

Example: Creating and Using an SQLite Database

```python
import sqlite3

class SQLiteStorage:

    def __init__(self, db_name):

        self.conn = sqlite3.connect(db_name)

        self.create_table()
```

```python
    def create_table(self):
        with self.conn:
            self.conn.execute('''
                CREATE TABLE IF NOT EXISTS users (
                    id INTEGER PRIMARY KEY AUTOINCREMENT,
                    username TEXT NOT NULL,
                    preferences TEXT NOT NULL
                )
            ''')
    def add_user(self, username, preferences):
        with self.conn:
            self.conn.execute('''
                INSERT INTO users (username, preferences) VALUES (?, ?)
            ''', (username, preferences))

    def get_users(self):
        with self.conn:
            cursor = self.conn.execute('SELECT * FROM users')
            return cursor.fetchall()
```

```
# Example usage

storage = SQLiteStorage('app_data.db')

storage.add_user('alice', '{"theme": "dark"}')

print(storage.get_users())
```

Explanation:

- **Database Connection:** The SQLiteStorage class connects to an SQLite database file. If the file doesn't exist, SQLite creates it.

- **Table Creation:** The create_table method creates a users table to store user data. The table includes an id, username, and preferences fields.

- **Data Insertion and Retrieval:** The add_user method inserts a new user into the users table, and get_users retrieves all records from the table.

3. Using Key-Value Stores for Simple Persistence

Key-value stores are useful for persisting small pieces of data, such as configuration settings or session information. Python's shelve module provides a simple key-value store interface that allows you to persist data in a dictionary-like format.

3.1. Persisting Data with Shelve

The shelve module allows you to store Python objects in a file using a dictionary interface.

Example: Using Shelve for Persistent Key-Value Storage

```python
import shelve

class ShelveStorage:
    def __init__(self, filename):
        self.filename = filename
    def save_data(self, key, value):
        with shelve.open(self.filename) as db:
            db[key] = value
    def load_data(self, key):
        with shelve.open(self.filename) as db:
            return db.get(key, None)

# Example usage
storage = ShelveStorage('app_state.db')
storage.save_data('theme', 'dark')
print(storage.load_data('theme'))
```

Explanation:

- **Shelve Interface:** The ShelveStorage class uses shelve.open to open a persistent dictionary-like object. You can store and retrieve data using keys, similar to a Python dictionary.

- **Simple Persistence:** This approach is particularly useful for persisting small amounts of state or configuration data without needing a full database setup.

4. Handling Data Persistence Across Sessions

Ensuring that data persists across application sessions is crucial for maintaining a seamless user experience. Here, we combine the techniques mentioned above to create a comprehensive example that demonstrates data persistence across sessions.

4.1. Comprehensive Example: User Settings Persistence

Imagine you are building a settings page for an application where users can choose their preferred theme and font size. We'll use JSON for structured storage and SQLite for more complex data.

Example: Persisting User Settings

```python
import json

import sqlite3

class UserSettings:

    def __init__(self, json_filename, db_filename):

        self.json_storage = JSONFileStorage(json_filename)

        self.db_storage = SQLiteStorage(db_filename)

    def save_settings(self, settings):

        self.json_storage.save_data(settings)

    def load_settings(self):

        return self.json_storage.load_data()

    def save_user_to_db(self, username, settings):

        preferences = json.dumps(settings)
```

```python
        self.db_storage.add_user(username, preferences)

    def load_users_from_db(self):

        return self.db_storage.get_users()

# Reusing previously defined JSONFileStorage and
SQLiteStorage classes


# Example usage

settings = UserSettings('settings.json', 'user_data.db')

settings.save_settings({'theme': 'dark', 'font_size': 14})

print(settings.load_settings())


settings.save_user_to_db('alice', {'theme': 'dark', 'font_size':
14})

print(settings.load_users_from_db())
```

Explanation:

- **Combined Persistence:** This example combines JSON file storage for saving general settings and SQLite for managing more complex data like user records.

- **Cross-Session Persistence:** The data stored using these methods persists across different sessions of the application, ensuring that users' preferences and data are retained.

5. Encrypting Data for Security

When persisting sensitive data locally, it's important to encrypt the data to protect it from unauthorized access. Python provides libraries like cryptography to help with encrypting and decrypting data before saving it to disk.

5.1. Encrypting Data Before Storage

Encrypting data before writing it to a file or database adds an extra layer of security.

Example: Encrypting and Decrypting Data

```python
from cryptography.fernet import Fernet

class EncryptedFileStorage:

    def __init__(self, filename, key):

        self.filename = filename

        self.cipher = Fernet(key)

    def save_data(self, data):

        encrypted_data = self.cipher.encrypt(data.encode())

        with open(self.filename, 'wb') as file:

            file.write(encrypted_data)

    def load_data(self):

        try:

            with open(self.filename, 'rb') as file:

                encrypted_data = file.read()

                return
self.cipher.decrypt(encrypted_data).decode()
```

```python
        except FileNotFoundError:

            return None

# Example usage

key = Fernet.generate_key()

storage = EncryptedFileStorage('secure_data.enc', key)

storage.save_data('Sensitive data')

print(storage.load_data())
```

Explanation:

- **Encryption:** The save_data method encrypts the data before saving it to a file. The cryptography library's Fernet module is used to perform the encryption.

- **Decryption:** The load_data method reads the encrypted data from the file and decrypts it before returning it.

Persisting data locally is a vital aspect of managing application state, ensuring that user data, settings, and application information are retained across sessions and available even when the application is offline. By using techniques like file storage, JSON, SQLite databases, and key-value stores, you can efficiently manage and persist data in your Python applications. Additionally, encrypting sensitive data adds a layer of security to protect user information. The examples provided demonstrate how to implement these techniques, giving you the tools to handle data persistence effectively in your own projects.

Handling State Across Different App Components:

Managing state across different components of an application is crucial for building complex, interactive apps where multiple components need to share and update common data. Properly handling state across components ensures that the user interface (UI) remains consistent, responsive, and reflects the latest data accurately. This section explores various techniques and patterns for managing state across different components in Python applications, using examples with frameworks like Kivy and BeeWare.

1. Global State Management

Global state management involves storing the application's state in a central location where all components can access and update it. This approach is particularly useful in larger applications where multiple components need to interact with shared data.

1.1. Example: Using a Singleton Class for Global State in Kivy

One way to manage global state is by using a singleton class, which ensures that only one instance of the state exists throughout the application.

Example: Implementing Global State with a Singleton

```python
class AppState:

    _instance = None

    def __new__(cls):

        if cls._instance is None:
```

```python
        cls._instance = super(AppState, cls).__new__(cls)
        cls._instance.init_state()
    return cls._instance
def init_state(self):
    self.user_logged_in = False
    self.theme = "light"
# Components accessing global state
class LoginScreen:
    def login(self):
        state = AppState()
        state.user_logged_in = True
        print(f"User logged in: {state.user_logged_in}")
class SettingsScreen:
    def change_theme(self, theme):
        state = AppState()
        state.theme = theme
        print(f"Theme changed to: {state.theme}")
# Example usage
login_screen = LoginScreen()
login_screen.login()
settings_screen = SettingsScreen()
settings_screen.change_theme("dark")
```

Explanation:

- **Singleton Pattern:** The AppState class uses the singleton pattern to ensure only one instance of the state exists.

- **Global Access:** Both the LoginScreen and SettingsScreen components access and modify the global state, ensuring consistency across the application.

2. State Passing Through Components

Another common pattern is to pass state directly from a parent component to its children. This approach is suitable for hierarchical UIs where data flows down the component tree.

2.1. Example: Passing State to Child Components in Kivy

In Kivy, you can pass state from a parent widget to its child widgets through properties or method parameters.

Example: Passing State Through Properties

```python
from kivy.app import App

from kivy.uix.boxlayout import BoxLayout

from kivy.uix.label import Label

from kivy.uix.button import Button

from kivy.properties import StringProperty

class ChildComponent(BoxLayout):

    label_text = StringProperty("")
```

```python
    def __init__(self, **kwargs):
        super().__init__(**kwargs)
        self.orientation = 'vertical'
        self.label = Label(text=self.label_text)
        self.add_widget(self.label)
class ParentComponent(BoxLayout):
    def __init__(self, **kwargs):
        super().__init__(**kwargs)
        self.orientation = 'vertical'


        self.child = ChildComponent(label_text="Hello from Parent")
        self.add_widget(self.child)


class MyApp(App):
    def build(self):
        return ParentComponent()


if __name__ == '__main__':
    MyApp().run()
```

Explanation:

- **Property Passing:** The ParentComponent passes the label_text to the ChildComponent, allowing the child to display state information defined in the parent.

- **Direct State Flow:** This approach works well when the parent component needs to pass data down to child components.

3. Using Callbacks and Events

Callbacks and events are another technique for handling state across components. They allow child components to notify parent components about state changes, which can then update other parts of the UI accordingly.

3.1. Example: Using Callbacks to Update Parent State

In this approach, child components use callbacks to inform the parent component of state changes, which then updates the state and possibly other child components.

Example: Callback Usage in Kivy

```python
from kivy.app import App

from kivy.uix.boxlayout import BoxLayout

from kivy.uix.button import Button

class ChildComponent(BoxLayout):

    def __init__(self, callback, **kwargs):

        super().__init__(**kwargs)

        self.orientation = 'vertical'

        self.button = Button(text="Click Me")

        self.button.bind(on_press=self.on_button_press)

        self.callback = callback
```

```python
        self.add_widget(self.button)

    def on_button_press(self, instance):
        self.callback("Button was clicked!")
class ParentComponent(BoxLayout):
    def __init__(self, **kwargs):
        super().__init__(**kwargs)
        self.orientation = 'vertical'
        self.child =
ChildComponent(callback=self.handle_child_event)
        self.add_widget(self.child)
    def handle_child_event(self, message):
        print(f"Parent received: {message}")
class MyApp(App):
    def build(self):
        return ParentComponent()
if __name__ == '__main__':
    MyApp().run()
```

Explanation:

- **Callback Mechanism:** The ChildComponent triggers the callback when the button is pressed. The parent component passes this callback function to the child and handles the event when triggered.

- **Parent-Child Communication:** This pattern allows for effective communication between child and parent components, enabling the parent to update its state or take action based on child events.

4. Using Observers or Pub/Sub Patterns

For more complex applications where multiple components need to respond to state changes, observer patterns or publish-subscribe (pub/sub) patterns can be used. These patterns allow components to listen for specific events or state changes and respond accordingly.

4.1. Example: Implementing a Simple Pub/Sub System

A basic pub/sub system can be implemented using Python's built-in weakref.WeakSet to manage subscribers.

Example: Pub/Sub for State Management

```python
import weakref

class EventManager:
    def __init__(self):
        self.subscribers = weakref.WeakSet()

    def subscribe(self, callback):
        self.subscribers.add(callback)

    def notify(self, message):
        for subscriber in self.subscribers:
            subscriber(message)

# Components subscribing to events
class ComponentA:
```

```python
    def __init__(self, event_manager):
        event_manager.subscribe(self.update)
    def update(self, message):
        print(f"ComponentA received: {message}")
class ComponentB:
    def __init__(self, event_manager):
        event_manager.subscribe(self.update)
    def update(self, message):
        print(f"ComponentB received: {message}")
# Example usage
event_manager = EventManager()
comp_a = ComponentA(event_manager)
comp_b = ComponentB(event_manager)
# Publishing an event
event_manager.notify("State updated!")
```

Explanation:

- **EventManager:** The EventManager handles subscriptions and notifications. Components subscribe to the event manager to receive updates.

- **Notification Mechanism:** When an event occurs, the event manager notifies all subscribed components, allowing them to react to the state change.

5. Using Shared State with Contexts

Another way to manage state across different components is by using shared contexts or services that hold the state. This is particularly useful in applications where components are loosely coupled but need to access or modify the same state.

5.1. Example: Shared State with Context Objects

Context objects can be used to share state among multiple components without tightly coupling them.

Example: Shared State with Contexts

```python
class AppContext:
    def __init__(self):
        self.state = {
            'logged_in': False,
            'user_name': None
        }
    def update_state(self, key, value):
        self.state[key] = value
# Components using shared context
class LoginScreen:
    def __init__(self, context):
        self.context = context
    def login(self, user_name):
        self.context.update_state('logged_in', True)
```

```python
        self.context.update_state('user_name', user_name)

        print(f"User {user_name} logged in.")

class Dashboard:

    def __init__(self, context):

        self.context = context

    def display(self):

        if self.context.state['logged_in']:

            print(f"Welcome,
{self.context.state['user_name']}!")

        else:

            print("Please log in.")

# Example usage

context = AppContext()

login_screen = LoginScreen(context)

dashboard = Dashboard(context)

login_screen.login("Alice")

dashboard.display()
```

Explanation:

- **Context Object:** The AppContext holds shared state that multiple components can access and modify.

- **State Sharing:** Both the LoginScreen and Dashboard components access and update the shared state, allowing for coordinated behavior across the application.

Conclusion

Handling state across different app components is essential for building complex, interactive applications where multiple parts of the UI need to reflect the same data or respond to changes in a coordinated manner. Techniques such as global state management, state passing through components, callbacks, observer patterns, and shared contexts provide a variety of tools for managing state effectively in Python applications. The examples provided demonstrate how these techniques can be implemented in practice, helping you manage state across your app's components in a structured and maintainable way.

Chapter 10: Integrating Backend Services

Connecting to RESTful APIs:

In modern application development, connecting to RESTful APIs is a common requirement, especially for mobile and web applications that need to interact with a backend service. RESTful APIs provide a standardized way to access and manipulate data on a server, allowing your application to perform tasks such as fetching data, submitting forms, updating records, and more. In this section, we will explore how to connect to RESTful APIs using Python, focusing on making HTTP requests, handling responses, and integrating these interactions into your application. We'll provide comprehensive examples to demonstrate these concepts.

1. Introduction to RESTful APIs

REST (Representational State Transfer) is an architectural style for designing networked applications. A RESTful API adheres to REST principles and typically uses HTTP methods (GET, POST, PUT, DELETE) to perform operations on resources.

Key HTTP Methods:

- **GET:** Retrieve data from the server.

- **POST:** Submit data to the server.

- **PUT:** Update existing data on the server.

- **DELETE:** Remove data from the server.

2. Making HTTP Requests with Python

Python provides several libraries for making HTTP requests, with the most popular being requests. This library simplifies the process of interacting with RESTful APIs, allowing you to send HTTP requests and handle responses easily.

2.1. Installing the Requests Library

Before you start, you need to install the requests library if it's not already installed.

pip install requests

2.2. Making a GET Request

A GET request is used to retrieve data from an API. For example, let's say you want to fetch user data from a RESTful API.

Example: Fetching Data with a GET Request

```python
import requests

def fetch_user_data(user_id):

    url = f"https://jsonplaceholder.typicode.com/users/{user_id}"

    response = requests.get(url)


    if response.status_code == 200:

        user_data = response.json()

        print(f"User ID: {user_data['id']}")

        print(f"Name: {user_data['name']}")
```

```python
    print(f"Email: {user_data['email']}")
else:
    print(f"Failed to fetch data. Status code: {response.status_code}")


# Example usage
fetch_user_data(1)
```

Explanation:

- **GET Request:** The requests.get(url) method sends a GET request to the specified URL.

- **Handling Response:** If the request is successful (status code 200), the response is parsed as JSON using response.json(), and the user data is printed.

2.3. Making a POST Request

A POST request is used to send data to the server, often when creating a new resource.

Example: Sending Data with a POST Request

```python
import requests

def create_new_user(name, email):
    url = "https://jsonplaceholder.typicode.com/users"
    data = {
        "name": name,
        "email": email
    }
```

```python
    response = requests.post(url, json=data)

    if response.status_code == 201:

    new_user = response.json()

    print(f"Created User ID: {new_user['id']}")

    print(f"Name: {new_user['name']}")

    print(f"Email: {new_user['email']}")

    else:

    print(f"Failed to create user. Status code:
{response.status_code}")

# Example usage

create_new_user("John Doe", "john.doe@example.com")
```

Explanation:

- **POST Request:** The requests.post(url, json=data) method sends a POST request with the JSON data payload to the server.

- **Handling Response:** A successful POST request typically returns a status code of 201 (Created), and the response contains the details of the newly created resource.

3. Handling API Responses

Handling responses correctly is critical when working with RESTful APIs. Depending on the API's response, your application might need to display data, handle errors, or update the UI accordingly.

3.1. Checking Response Status

Before processing the data from an API response, you should always check the HTTP status code to determine whether the request was successful.

Example: Handling Different Status Codes

```python
import requests

def fetch_data(endpoint):

    url = f"https://jsonplaceholder.typicode.com/{endpoint}"

    response = requests.get(url)


    if response.status_code == 200:

        print("Success:", response.json())

    elif response.status_code == 404:

        print("Error: Resource not found.")

    else:

        print(f"Unexpected error. Status code: {response.status_code}")

# Example usage

fetch_data("posts/1")  # Success case

fetch_data("posts/invalid")  # Error case (404)
```

Explanation:

- **Status Code Check:** The code checks the status code of the response to handle different scenarios, such as success (200) or not found (404).

- **Error Handling:** Based on the status code, the application can provide appropriate feedback to the user.

3.2. Parsing JSON Responses

Most RESTful APIs return data in JSON format. You can parse these JSON responses directly into Python dictionaries or lists.

Example: Parsing JSON Data

```python
import requests

def get_post_title(post_id):
    url = f"https://jsonplaceholder.typicodc.com/posts/{post_id}"
    response = requests.get(url)


    if response.status_code == 200:
        post_data = response.json()
        return post_data['title']
    else:
        return None
# Example usage
post_title = get_post_title(1)
if post_title:
    print(f"Post Title: {post_title}")
else:
```

print("Failed to fetch post title.")

Explanation:

- **JSON Parsing:** The response.json() method parses the JSON data from the response, allowing you to access specific fields like title.

- **Using the Data:** The parsed data is then used within the application, such as displaying the title of a blog post.

4. Integrating API Requests into Your Application

Integrating API requests into your application involves making these requests from within your app's components and updating the UI based on the API's responses.

4.1. Example: Integrating an API Request in a Kivy Application

Let's integrate a simple API request into a Kivy application that fetches and displays a user's name based on an ID entered by the user.

Example: Kivy App Fetching Data from an API

from kivy.app import App

from kivy.uix.boxlayout import BoxLayout

from kivy.uix.textinput import TextInput

from kivy.uix.button import Button

from kivy.uix.label import Label

import requests

```python
class APIApp(BoxLayout):
    def __init__(self, **kwargs):
        super().__init__(**kwargs)
        self.orientation = 'vertical'
        self.input = TextInput(hint_text="Enter user ID")
        self.add_widget(self.input)
        self.button = Button(text="Fetch User")
        self.button.bind(on_press=self.fetch_user)
        self.add_widget(self.button)
        self.label = Label(text="")
        self.add_widget(self.label)
    def fetch_user(self, instance):
        user_id = self.input.text
        url = f"https://jsonplaceholder.typicode.com/users/{user_id}"
        response = requests.get(url)
            if response.status_code == 200:
            user_data = response.json()
            self.label.text = f"Name: {user_data['name']}"
        else:
            self.label.text = "User not found."
```

```
class MyApp(App):

  def build(self):

    return APIApp()

if __name__ == '__main__':

  MyApp().run()
```

Explanation:

- **UI Components:** The Kivy app includes a TextInput for the user to enter an ID, a Button to trigger the API request, and a Label to display the result.

- **Fetching Data:** When the button is pressed, the app sends a GET request to the API using the entered user ID.

- **Updating the UI:** Based on the API response, the app updates the label to display the user's name or an error message if the user is not found.

5. Handling Authentication

Many APIs require authentication, typically using API keys, OAuth tokens, or other methods. Handling authentication securely is crucial when integrating with such APIs.

5.1. Example: Making Authenticated Requests

Let's assume you need to authenticate your API requests using an API key.

Example: Using API Keys for Authentication

```
import requests
```

```python
def fetch_protected_data(api_key):
    url = "https://api.example.com/protected/data"
    headers = {
        "Authorization": f"Bearer {api_key}"
    }
    response = requests.get(url, headers=headers)

    if response.status_code == 200:
        return response.json()
    else:
        print(f"Failed to fetch data. Status code: {response.status_code}")
        return None
# Example usage
api_key = "your_api_key_here"
data = fetch_protected_data(api_key)
if data:
    print("Protected data:", data)
```

Explanation:

- **API Key:** The Authorization header includes the API key for authentication.

- **Authenticated Request:** The app sends the API key with the request to access protected resources, checking the response to handle success or failure appropriately.

6. Error Handling and Retries

When dealing with external APIs, network issues or server errors can cause requests to fail. Implementing error handling and retry logic can make your application more robust.

6.1. Example: Implementing Retry Logic

You can use the requests library's built-in support for retries or implement your own logic.

Example: Retry Logic for API Requests

```python
import requests

from requests.adapters import import HTTPAdapter

from requests.packages.urllib3.util.retry import Retry

def fetch_with_retries(url, retries=3, backoff_factor=0.3):
    session = requests.Session()

    retry = Retry(
        total=retries,
        read=retries,
        connect=retries,
        backoff_factor=backoff_factor,
        status_forcelist=[500, 502, 503, 504]
    )

    adapter = HTTPAdapter(max_retries=retry)
```

```python
session.mount('http://', adapter)
session.mount('https://', adapter)


try:
    response = session.get(url)
    response.raise_for_status()
    return response.json()
except requests.exceptions.RequestException as e:
    print(f"Request failed: {e}")
    return None


# Example usage
url = "https://jsonplaceholder.typicode.com/posts/1"
data = fetch_with_retries(url)
if data:
    print("Fetched data:", data)
```

Explanation:

- **Retry Strategy:** The Retry object specifies how many times to retry the request, the delay between retries (backoff_factor), and which HTTP status codes to retry on.

- **Session Management:** The session object handles the retries transparently, providing a more robust way to interact with unreliable networks.

Connecting to RESTful APIs is a fundamental skill for integrating backend services in modern applications. Whether you're fetching data, submitting forms, or handling authentication, Python's requests library offers a simple and powerful way to interact with RESTful APIs. By properly handling responses, integrating API requests into your app, managing authentication, and implementing error handling and retry logic, you can build robust applications that effectively communicate with external services. The examples provided here illustrate the core concepts and techniques you need to master to successfully integrate RESTful APIs into your Python applications.

Working with JSON and XML Data:

In modern applications, interacting with backend services often involves working with data in formats like JSON (JavaScript Object Notation) and XML (eXtensible Markup Language). These formats are widely used for exchanging data between clients and servers due to their structured and readable nature. Understanding how to parse, manipulate, and generate JSON and XML data is crucial for integrating backend services into your application. This section will explore how to work with JSON and XML in Python, including examples to illustrate these concepts.

1. Working with JSON Data

JSON is a lightweight data-interchange format that is easy to read and write for humans and easy to parse and generate for machines. JSON is the most common format for RESTful APIs.

1.1. Parsing JSON Data

To work with JSON data in Python, the json module provides simple methods to parse (convert JSON strings to Python objects) and serialize (convert Python objects to JSON strings).

Example: Parsing JSON Data from an API Response

```python
import requests

import json

def fetch_and_parse_json(url):

    response = requests.get(url)

    if response.status_code == 200:

        data = response.json()  # Parse JSON directly from the response

        return data

    else:

        print(f"Failed to fetch data. Status code: {response.status_code}")

        return None

# Example usage

url = "https://jsonplaceholder.typicode.com/todos/1"

data = fetch_and_parse_json(url)

if data:

    print(f"Todo: {data['title']}, Completed: {data['completed']}")
```

Explanation:

- **Fetching JSON:** The response.json() method automatically parses the JSON string from the response into a Python dictionary.

- **Accessing Data:** Once parsed, you can easily access JSON data using standard dictionary operations.

1.2. Serializing Python Objects to JSON

If you need to send data to a backend service, you can serialize Python objects into JSON strings.

Example: Serializing and Sending JSON Data

```python
import requests

import json

def send_data(url, data):

    json_data = json.dumps(data)  # Convert Python object to JSON string

    headers = {'Content-Type': 'application/json'}

    response = requests.post(url, data=json_data, headers=headers)

        if response.status_code == 201:

        print("Data sent successfully.")

    else:

        print(f"Failed to send data. Status code: {response.status_code}")
```

```
# Example usage
url = "https://jsonplaceholder.typicode.com/posts"
data = {
    "title": "foo",
    "body": "bar",
    "userId": 1
}
send_data(url, data)
```

Explanation:

- **Serialization:** The json.dumps() function converts a Python dictionary to a JSON string.

- **Sending JSON:** The JSON string is then sent as the request body using the requests.post() method.

1.3. Working with Complex JSON Structures

JSON data can be nested and complex, consisting of arrays and nested dictionaries.

Example: Parsing Complex JSON Data

```
import json

json_string = '''
{
    "users": [
        {
            "id": 1,
```

```
        "name": "John Doe",

        "email": "john.doe@example.com",

        "roles": ["admin", "editor"]

    },

    {

        "id": 2,

        "name": "Jane Smith",

        "email": "jane.smith@example.com",

        "roles": ["viewer"]

    }

  ]

}
"""


def parse_complex_json(json_string):

    data = json.loads(json_string)

    for user in data["users"]:

        print(f"User ID: {user['id']}, Name: {user['name']},
Roles: {', '.join(user['roles'])}")

# Example usage

parse_complex_json(json_string)
```

Explanation:

- **Loading JSON:** The json.loads() function parses the JSON string into a Python dictionary.

- **Navigating Nested Data:** The example iterates over a list of users, accessing nested dictionaries and arrays to print user details.

2. Working with XML Data

XML is a markup language that defines a set of rules for encoding documents in a format that is both human-readable and machine-readable. Although JSON is more common in RESTful APIs, XML is still widely used in SOAP APIs, configuration files, and other scenarios.

2.1. Parsing XML Data

Python's xml.etree.ElementTree module provides methods for parsing XML and working with the resulting element tree.

Example: Parsing XML Data

```python
import xml.etree.ElementTree as ET

def parse_xml_string(xml_string):
    root = ET.fromstring(xml_string)
    for user in root.findall('user'):
        user_id = user.find('id').text
        name = user.find('name').text
        email = user.find('email').text
        print(f"User ID: {user_id}, Name: {name}, Email: {email}")
```

```python
# Example usage
xml_data = '''
<users>
  <user>
    <id>1</id>
    <name>John Doe</name>
    <email>john.doe@example.com</email>
  </user>
  <user>
    <id>2</id>
    <name>Jane Smith</name>
    <email>jane.smith@example.com</email>
  </user>
</users>
'''

parse_xml_string(xml_data)
```

Explanation:

- **Parsing XML:** The ET.fromstring() function parses the XML string into an element tree.

- **Navigating the Tree:** The example iterates over the user elements and extracts details like id, name, and email using the find() method.

2.2. Creating XML Data

You might need to generate XML data to send to a backend service or save it to a file.

Example: Generating XML Data

```python
import xml.etree.ElementTree as ET

def generate_xml(users):

    root = ET.Element("users")

        for user in users:

        user_element = ET.SubElement(root, "user")

        ET.SubElement(user_element, "id").text = str(user["id"])

        ET.SubElement(user_element, "name").text = user["name"]

        ET.SubElement(user_element, "email").text = user["email"]

        tree = ET.ElementTree(root)

    tree.write("users.xml")

# Example usage

users = [

    {"id": 1, "name": "John Doe", "email": "john.doe@example.com"},

    {"id": 2, "name": "Jane Smith", "email": "jane.smith@example.com"}

]
```

generate_xml(users)

Explanation:

- **Creating XML Elements:** The ET.Element() and ET.SubElement() methods are used to create XML elements.

- **Writing to File:** The ET.ElementTree object writes the generated XML structure to a file.

2.3. Handling Namespaces in XML

When working with XML, you may encounter namespaces, which are used to avoid element name conflicts. Handling namespaces requires specific consideration when parsing or generating XML.

Example: Parsing XML with Namespaces

```python
import xml.etree.ElementTree as ET


def parse_xml_with_namespace(xml_string):
    ns = {'ns': 'http://example.com/ns'}
    root = ET.fromstring(xml_string)

    for user in root.findall('ns:user', ns):
        user_id = user.find('ns:id', ns).text
        name = user.find('ns:name', ns).text
        email = user.find('ns:email', ns).text
```

```
    print(f"User ID: {user_id}, Name: {name}, Email:
{email}")


# Example usage
xml_data = '''
<users xmlns="http://example.com/ns">
  <user>
    <id>1</id>
    <name>John Doe</name>
    <email>john.doe@example.com</email>
  </user>
  <user>
    <id>2</id>
    <name>Jane Smith</name>
    <email>jane.smith@example.com</email>
  </user>
</users>
'''

parse_xml_with_namespace(xml_data)
```

Explanation:

- **Namespace Dictionary:** The ns dictionary maps the namespace prefix to the URI.

- **Namespace-Aware Parsing:** The findall() and find() methods use the namespace dictionary to correctly locate elements in the XML tree.

3. Integrating JSON and XML with Backend Services

When integrating JSON and XML data with backend services, understanding how to both send and receive these formats is essential. Let's consider examples where JSON and XML are used in API requests and responses.

3.1. Sending JSON Data to an API

Many APIs accept JSON data in POST or PUT requests.

Example: Sending JSON Data with a POST Request

```python
import requests


def post_json_data(url, data):
    response = requests.post(url, json=data)


    if response.status_code == 201:
        print("Data posted successfully.")
    else:
        print(f"Failed to post data. Status code: {response.status_code}")


# Example usage
url = "https://jsonplaceholder.typicode.com/posts"
```

```
data = {"title": "foo", "body": "bar", "userId": 1}
```

```
post_json_data(url, data)
```

Explanation:

- **Sending JSON:** The requests.post() method automatically serializes the dictionary into JSON and sends it as the request body.

- **Handling Response:** The status code is checked to confirm whether the data was posted successfully.

3.2. Sending XML Data to an API

Some APIs may require XML data to be sent instead of JSON.

Example: Sending XML Data with a POST Request

```python
import requests

import xml.etree.ElementTree as ET


def post_xml_data(url, xml_string):
    headers = {'Content-Type': 'application/xml'}

    response = requests.post(url, data=xml_string, headers=headers)


    if response.status_code == 200:

        print("XML data posted successfully.")
    else:
```

```python
        print(f"Failed to post XML data. Status code: {response.status_code}")


# Example usage
xml_string = '''
<user>
    <id>1</id>
    <name>John Doe</name>
    <email>john.doe@example.com</email>
</user>
'''

url = "https://example.com/api/users"

post_xml_data(url, xml_string)
```

Explanation:

- **Sending XML:** The requests.post() method sends the XML string as the request body, with the Content-Type header set to application/xml.

- **Response Handling:** The response status code is checked to ensure the XML data was processed correctly by the server.

Working with JSON and XML is fundamental when integrating backend services into your Python applications. JSON is commonly used in RESTful APIs due to its simplicity and ease of use, while XML remains prevalent in SOAP APIs and configuration files. By understanding how to parse, generate, and manipulate both JSON and XML data, you can effectively interact with a wide range of backend services. The examples provided in this section demonstrate how to handle these data formats in Python, enabling you to build robust applications that can communicate with various backend systems.

Authentication and Authorization:

When integrating backend services into your applications, ensuring secure communication is critical. Authentication and authorization are fundamental concepts that help secure your application by verifying the identity of users and determining their permissions. This section explores how to implement authentication and authorization in Python applications when interacting with backend services, including practical examples using various authentication mechanisms such as API keys, OAuth, and JWT (JSON Web Tokens).

1. Understanding Authentication and Authorization

- **Authentication** is the process of verifying the identity of a user or service. It confirms "who you are."

- **Authorization** is the process of determining what an authenticated user or service is allowed to do. It answers "what you are allowed to do."

2. Using API Keys for Authentication

API keys are one of the simplest forms of authentication. An API key is a unique identifier that allows you to authenticate requests to the API.

2.1. Example: Authenticating API Requests with an API Key

Many APIs require an API key to be included in the request headers or query parameters.

Example: Making an Authenticated Request with an API Key

```python
import requests

def fetch_data_with_api_key(url, api_key):
    headers = {'Authorization': f'Bearer {api_key}'}
    response = requests.get(url, headers=headers)
        if response.status_code == 200:
        return response.json()
    else:
        print(f"Failed to fetch data. Status code: {response.status_code}")
        return None


# Example usage
api_key = 'your_api_key_here'
url = 'https://api.example.com/data'
data = fetch_data_with_api_key(url, api_key)
if data:
    print("Fetched data:", data)
```

Explanation:

- **API Key in Headers:** The API key is included in the Authorization header, following the Bearer token format.

- **Authenticated Request:** The API key authenticates the request, and the response is handled based on the status code.

3. Using OAuth for Authentication

OAuth is a more robust authentication protocol often used by services like Google, Facebook, and GitHub. OAuth allows users to grant third-party applications limited access to their resources without exposing their credentials.

3.1. Example: OAuth 2.0 Authentication

OAuth 2.0 involves obtaining an access token from the authorization server, which is then used to authenticate API requests.

Example: Authenticating with OAuth 2.0

```python
import requests


def get_oauth_token(client_id, client_secret, auth_url, token_url):
    # Step 1: Redirect user to the authorization URL
    auth_params = {
        'response_type': 'code',
        'client_id': client_id,
```

```python
    'redirect_uri': 'https://yourapp.com/callback',

    'scope': 'read write',

  }

  auth_response = requests.get(auth_url,
params=auth_params)

  print("Go to the following URL to authorize:",
auth_response.url)


  # Step 2: After user authorizes, they will be redirected to
the callback URL with a code

  code = input("Enter the authorization code provided: ")


  # Step 3: Exchange the authorization code for an access
token

  token_params = {

    'grant_type': 'authorization_code',

    'code': code,

    'redirect_uri': 'https://yourapp.com/callback',

    'client_id': client_id,

    'client_secret': client_secret,

  }

  token_response = requests.post(token_url,
data=token_params)
```

```python
    if token_response.status_code == 200:

        return token_response.json().get('access_token')

    else:

        print(f"Failed to obtain token. Status code:
{token_response.status_code}")

        return None


def fetch_protected_data(api_url, access_token):

    headers = {'Authorization': f'Bearer {access_token}'}

    response = requests.get(api_url, headers=headers)


    if response.status_code == 200:

        return response.json()

    else:

        print(f"Failed to fetch data. Status code:
{response.status_code}")

        return None


# Example usage

client_id = 'your_client_id'

client_secret = 'your_client_secret'

auth_url = 'https://api.example.com/oauth/authorize'

token_url = 'https://api.example.com/oauth/token'
```

```
api_url = 'https://api.example.com/protected/resource'


access_token = get_oauth_token(client_id, client_secret,
auth_url, token_url)

if access_token:

    data = fetch_protected_data(api_url, access_token)

    if data:

        print("Fetched data:", data)
```

Explanation:

- **OAuth Flow:** The example demonstrates the OAuth 2.0 flow, starting with obtaining an authorization code and then exchanging it for an access token.

- **Access Token Usage:** The access token is used to authenticate requests to protected API endpoints.

4. Using JWT for Authorization

JSON Web Tokens (JWT) are commonly used for authorization. JWTs are self-contained tokens that carry information about the user, including their permissions, and are signed by the server.

4.1. Example: Using JWT for Secured API Requests

JWTs are typically passed in the Authorization header when making API requests.

Example: Securing API Requests with JWT

```
import requests
```

```python
import jwt


def authenticate_user(username, password, auth_url):
    response = requests.post(auth_url, json={'username': username, 'password': password})

    if response.status_code == 200:
        return response.json().get('token')
    else:
        print(f"Failed to authenticate. Status code: {response.status_code}")
        return None


def fetch_data_with_jwt(api_url, jwt_token):
    headers = {'Authorization': f'Bearer {jwt_token}'}
    response = requests.get(api_url, headers=headers)

    if response.status_code == 200:
        return response.json()
    else:
        print(f"Failed to fetch data. Status code: {response.status_code}")
        return None
```

```python
# Example usage

auth_url = 'https://api.example.com/auth/login'

api_url = 'https://api.example.com/secure/data'


username = 'user'

password = 'password'

jwt_token = authenticate_user(username, password, auth_url)


if jwt_token:

    data = fetch_data_with_jwt(api_url, jwt_token)

    if data:

        print("Fetched secure data:", data)
```

Explanation:

- **JWT Authentication:** The user authenticates with a username and password, receiving a JWT token.

- **JWT in Headers:** The JWT is included in the Authorization header to access secure resources.

- **Stateless Authorization:** JWTs are stateless, meaning they carry all the necessary information and don't require server-side session storage.

5. Handling Token Expiry and Refresh

Tokens, especially in OAuth and JWT scenarios, often have expiration times. Your application needs to handle token expiry and implement token refresh logic.

5.1. Example: Refreshing Expired Tokens

When a token expires, a refresh token can be used to obtain a new access token without requiring the user to log in again.

Example: Refreshing an OAuth Token

```python
import requests


def refresh_oauth_token(refresh_token, client_id,
client_secret, token_url):
    refresh_params = {
        'grant_type': 'refresh_token',
        'refresh_token': refresh_token,
        'client_id': client_id,
        'client_secret': client_secret,
    }

    response = requests.post(token_url,
data=refresh_params)


    if response.status_code == 200:
        return response.json().get('access_token')
    else:
```

```python
        print(f"Failed to refresh token. Status code: {response.status_code}")

    return None


# Example usage
client_id = 'your_client_id'

client_secret = 'your_client_secret'

token_url = 'https://api.example.com/oauth/token'


refresh_token = 'your_refresh_token'

new_access_token = refresh_oauth_token(refresh_token, client_id, client_secret, token_url)


if new_access_token:

    print("New access token:", new_access_token)
```

Explanation:

- **Refresh Token:** A refresh token is exchanged for a new access token without requiring user credentials.

- **Handling Expiry:** This mechanism ensures that the user experience remains seamless even when tokens expire.

6. Securing API Requests and Responses

In addition to handling authentication and authorization, it's important to secure your API requests and responses to prevent common security vulnerabilities like man-in-the-middle attacks.

6.1. Example: Using HTTPS for Secure Communication

Always use HTTPS to encrypt the communication between your client and the server.

Example: Making Secure HTTPS Requests

```python
import requests


def fetch_secure_data(url, token):

    headers = {'Authorization': f'Bearer {token}'}

    response = requests.get(url, headers=headers,
verify=True)


    if response.status_code == 200:

        return response.json()

    else:

        print(f"Failed to fetch secure data. Status code:
{response.status_code}")

        return None


# Example usage

url = 'https://secure.api.example.com/data'

token = 'your_jwt_or_api_key'
```

secure_data = fetch_secure_data(url, token)

if secure_data:

  print("Fetched secure data:", secure_data)

Explanation:

- **HTTPS:** The verify=True parameter ensures that the SSL certificate is verified, securing the communication.

- **Secure Communication:** HTTPS encrypts the data in transit, protecting sensitive information from being intercepted.

Authentication and authorization are crucial components when integrating backend services in your applications. Using API keys, OAuth, and JWTs, you can securely authenticate users and control their access to resources. Understanding and implementing these mechanisms ensures that your application can safely interact with backend services, protecting both user data and the integrity of your system. The examples provided illustrate how to handle various authentication and authorization scenarios, giving you the tools needed to build secure and reliable applications.

Real-time Data with WebSockets:

In many modern applications, there is a need to handle real-time data, such as live updates, notifications, chat applications, and live tracking. Traditional HTTP requests are not well-suited for real-time communication because they follow a request-response model, where the client has to repeatedly poll the server for updates. WebSockets offer a more efficient solution by enabling a persistent, bidirectional communication channel between the client and the server. This section explores how to integrate real-time data using WebSockets in Python applications, including examples to illustrate these concepts.

1. Understanding WebSockets

WebSockets provide a full-duplex communication channel over a single, long-lived connection, allowing for real-time data exchange between the client and the server. Unlike HTTP, which is a stateless protocol, WebSockets maintain a persistent connection, enabling the server to push updates to the client immediately as they occur.

2. Setting Up a WebSocket Connection

To work with WebSockets in Python, you can use libraries such as websockets or socketio. These libraries make it easy to create both WebSocket clients and servers.

2.1. Installing the WebSocket Library

You can install the websockets library using pip:

pip install websockets

3. Creating a WebSocket Server

Before establishing a WebSocket connection, you need a WebSocket server that can handle connections and send/receive messages.

3.1. Example: Creating a Simple WebSocket Server

Server Code:

import asyncio

```python
import websockets

async def echo(websocket, path):
    async for message in websocket:
        print(f"Received message: {message}")
        await websocket.send(f"Echo: {message}")

async def main():
    async with websockets.serve(echo, "localhost", 8765):
        print("WebSocket server started on ws://localhost:8765")
        await asyncio.Future()  # Run forever

# Run the server
asyncio.run(main())
```

Explanation:

- **WebSocket Server:** The websockets.serve() function starts a WebSocket server that listens on ws://localhost:8765.

- **Echo Function:** The echo function handles incoming messages by echoing them back to the client. It uses an asynchronous loop to receive and send messages.

- **Persistent Server:** The server runs indefinitely, ready to handle WebSocket connections.

4. Creating a WebSocket Client

The client establishes a connection to the WebSocket server and can send and receive messages in real-time.

4.1. Example: Creating a WebSocket Client

Client Code:

```python
import asyncio

import websockets


async def hello():
    uri = "ws://localhost:8765"
    async with websockets.connect(uri) as websocket:
        await websocket.send("Hello, Server!")
        response = await websocket.recv()
        print(f"Received from server: {response}")


# Run the client
asyncio.run(hello())
```

Explanation:

- **WebSocket Connection:** The client connects to the WebSocket server at ws://localhost:8765.

- **Sending Messages:** The client sends a message ("Hello, Server!") to the server.

- **Receiving Messages:** The client waits for and prints the server's response.

5. Handling Real-time Updates

WebSockets are particularly useful for scenarios where you need to handle real-time updates, such as in a chat application, live feed, or notifications.

5.1. Example: Real-time Chat Application

Let's extend the WebSocket example to simulate a basic chat application where clients can send messages to each other through the server.

Server Code:

```python
import asyncio

import websockets


connected_clients = set()


async def chat(websocket, path):
    # Register new client
    connected_clients.add(websocket)
    try:
        async for message in websocket:
            print(f"Received message: {message}")
```

```python
        # Broadcast message to all connected clients
        for client in connected_clients:
            if client != websocket:
                await client.send(message)
    finally:
        # Unregister client on disconnect
        connected_clients.remove(websocket)


async def main():
    async with websockets.serve(chat, "localhost", 8765):
        print("WebSocket chat server started on
ws://localhost:8765")
        await asyncio.Future()  # Run forever


# Run the server
asyncio.run(main())
```

Client Code:

```python
import asyncio

import websockets


async def chat_client():
    uri = "ws://localhost:8765"
```

```python
    async with websockets.connect(uri) as websocket:

        print("Connected to the chat server")

        while True:

            message = input("You: ")

            await websocket.send(message)

            response = await websocket.recv()

            print(f"Received: {response}")


# Run the client

asyncio.run(chat_client())
```

Explanation:

- **Connected Clients:** The server maintains a set of connected clients and broadcasts messages to all connected clients except the sender.

- **Broadcasting Messages:** When a client sends a message, it is broadcast to all other clients in real-time.

- **Client Interaction:** The client continuously reads input from the user, sends it to the server, and prints any received messages.

6. Securing WebSocket Connections

While WebSockets are powerful, it's important to secure them, especially if you're sending sensitive data. You can secure WebSocket connections by using the wss:// protocol (WebSocket Secure) instead of ws://.

6.1. Example: Securing WebSocket Connections with SSL

To secure a WebSocket server, you can use SSL certificates.

Server Code:

```python
import asyncio

import ssl

import websockets


ssl_context =
ssl.SSLContext(ssl.PROTOCOL_TLS_SERVER)

ssl_context.load_cert_chain(certfile="path/to/cert.pem",
keyfile="path/to/key.pem")


connected_clients = set()


async def chat(websocket, path):
    connected_clients.add(websocket)
    try:
        async for message in websocket:
            for client in connected_clients:
                if client != websocket:
                    await client.send(message)
```

```python
    finally:
        connected_clients.remove(websocket)


async def main():
    async with websockets.serve(chat, "localhost", 8765, ssl=ssl_context):
        print("Secure WebSocket server started on wss://localhost:8765")
        await asyncio.Future()


# Run the secure server
asyncio.run(main())
```

Client Code:

```python
import asyncio
import ssl
import websockets


ssl_context = ssl.SSLContext(ssl.PROTOCOL_TLS_CLIENT)
ssl_context.load_verify_locations("path/to/cert.pem")


async def secure_chat_client():
    uri = "wss://localhost:8765"
```

```python
    async with websockets.connect(uri, ssl=ssl_context) as websocket:
        while True:
            message = input("You: ")
            await websocket.send(message)
            response = await websocket.recv()
            print(f"Received: {response}")


# Run the secure client
asyncio.run(secure_chat_client())
```

Explanation:

- **SSL Context:** The server and client both use an SSL context to establish a secure WebSocket connection.

- **Secured Communication:** By using wss:// and providing the SSL certificates, you ensure that the WebSocket communication is encrypted, protecting the data from eavesdropping.

7. Integrating WebSockets into Existing Applications

Integrating WebSockets into an existing application allows you to enhance the real-time capabilities of your app, such as live notifications, updates, or collaborative features.

7.1. Example: Integrating WebSockets with a Flask App

You can integrate WebSockets with a Flask application using the flask-socketio library.

Installation:

pip install flask-socketio

Flask Application with WebSocket Integration:

```python
from flask import Flask, render_template
from flask_socketio import SocketIO, send, emit


app = Flask(__name__)
socketio = SocketIO(app)


@app.route('/')
def index():
    return render_template('index.html')


@socketio.on('message')
def handle_message(msg):
    print(f"Received message: {msg}")
    send(f"Echo: {msg}")


if __name__ == '__main__':
    socketio.run(app, debug=True)
```

Client Code (JavaScript):

```html
<script
src="https://cdnjs.cloudflare.com/ajax/libs/socket.io/4.0.0/s
ocket.io.js"></script>

<script type="text/javascript">
   var socket = io.connect('http://localhost:5000');


   socket.on('connect', function() {
      socket.send('Hello, Flask-SocketIO!');
   });


   socket.on('message', function(msg) {
      console.log('Received from server: ' + msg);
   });
</script>
```

Explanation:

- **Flask Integration:** The Flask app uses flask-socketio to handle WebSocket connections alongside traditional HTTP routes.

- **Client Interaction:** The client-side JavaScript connects to the Flask-SocketIO server and sends messages, receiving responses in real-time.

Conclusion

WebSockets provide a powerful way to handle real-time data in your applications, enabling persistent, bidirectional communication between the client and server. By understanding how to create WebSocket servers and clients, handle real-time updates, secure connections, and integrate WebSockets into existing applications, you can build responsive and interactive applications that meet the demands of modern users.

Chapter 11: Working with Databases

<u>Overview of Mobile Databases:</u>

When developing mobile applications, choosing the right database is crucial for ensuring that your app can efficiently manage data, even on devices with limited resources. Mobile databases need to be lightweight, performant, and capable of operating offline. This section provides an overview of popular mobile databases, discussing their features, advantages, and use cases, along with examples to illustrate how to work with these databases in Python-based mobile applications.

1. SQLite

SQLite is one of the most widely used databases in mobile development. It is a C-language library that implements a self-contained, serverless, zero-configuration, transactional SQL database engine.

1.1. Features of SQLite

- **Embedded Database:** SQLite is embedded directly into the application, meaning there's no separate server process to manage.

- **Lightweight:** It has a small footprint, making it ideal for mobile devices with limited resources.

- **ACID-Compliant:** SQLite is fully ACID (Atomicity, Consistency, Isolation, Durability) compliant, ensuring reliable transaction processing.

- **SQL Support:** SQLite supports most of the SQL standard, allowing you to use familiar SQL queries to manage your data.

1.2. Example: Working with SQLite in Python

Example: Creating and Using an SQLite Database

```python
import sqlite3


def create_connection(db_name):

    conn = sqlite3.connect(db_name)

    return conn


def create_table(conn):

    with conn:

        conn.execute('''

            CREATE TABLE IF NOT EXISTS tasks (

                id INTEGER PRIMARY KEY AUTOINCREMENT,

                title TEXT NOT NULL,

                description TEXT

            )

        ''')


def insert_task(conn, title, description):
```

```python
with conn:
    conn.execute('''
        INSERT INTO tasks (title, description) VALUES (?, ?)
    ''', (title, description))


def fetch_tasks(conn):
    with conn:
        cursor = conn.execute('SELECT * FROM tasks')
        return cursor.fetchall()


# Example usage
conn = create_connection('tasks.db')
create_table(conn)
insert_task(conn, 'Finish report', 'Complete the financial report by end of day')
tasks = fetch_tasks(conn)
for task in tasks:
    print(f"Task ID: {task[0]}, Title: {task[1]}, Description: {task[2]}")
```

Explanation:

- **Creating a Connection:** The create_connection function establishes a connection to the SQLite database, stored in a file named tasks.db.

- **Creating a Table:** The create_table function creates a table called tasks if it doesn't already exist.

- **Inserting Data:** The insert_task function adds a new task to the tasks table.

- **Fetching Data:** The fetch_tasks function retrieves all tasks from the database and prints them.

2. Realm

Realm is a mobile database that is designed specifically for modern mobile applications. It's known for its simplicity, speed, and ease of use.

2.1. Features of Realm

- **Object-Oriented:** Unlike SQLite, which uses SQL, Realm is an object-oriented database. Data is stored in a way that is closer to how it is used in the application.

- **Performance:** Realm is optimized for mobile devices, offering faster read and write operations compared to SQLite in many cases.

- **Cross-Platform:** Realm supports Android, iOS, and other platforms, allowing for cross-platform development.

- **Reactive Architecture:** Realm supports reactive programming patterns, making it easier to work with real-time data updates.

2.2. Example: Working with Realm in Python

Realm does not have native support for Python directly; however, for illustrative purposes, let's discuss how you might use an equivalent object-oriented database in Python using the peewee ORM (Object-Relational Mapping).

Example: Working with an Object-Oriented Database in Python

```python
from peewee import *


db = SqliteDatabase('tasks.db')


class Task(Model):

    title = CharField()

    description = TextField(null=True)


    class Meta:

        database = db


def initialize_db():

    db.connect()

    db.create_tables([Task], safe=True)


def add_task(title, description):

    Task.create(title=title, description=description)


def get_tasks():
```

```
    return Task.select()
```

```
# Example usage
```

```
initialize_db()
```

```
add_task('Finish report', 'Complete the financial report by
end of day')
```

```
tasks = get_tasks()
```

```
for task in tasks:
```

```
    print(f"Task ID: {task.id}, Title: {task.title},
Description: {task.description}")
```

Explanation:

- **Peewee ORM:** The example uses Peewee, a lightweight ORM for SQLite in Python, to simulate the object-oriented database approach similar to Realm.

- **Defining Models:** The Task class represents a table in the database, where fields are defined as class attributes.

- **CRUD Operations:** The functions initialize_db, add_task, and get_tasks perform basic CRUD (Create, Read, Update, Delete) operations using an object-oriented approach.

3. Firebase Realtime Database

Firebase Realtime Database is a cloud-hosted NoSQL database that lets you store and sync data between your users in real-time. It is particularly popular in mobile apps where real-time data synchronization is essential.

3.1. Features of Firebase Realtime Database

- **NoSQL Database:** Firebase uses a NoSQL structure, storing data as JSON documents.

- **Real-Time Sync:** Data changes are automatically synchronized across all connected clients in real-time.

- **Offline Support:** Firebase supports offline access, syncing data once the device reconnects to the internet.

- **Cross-Platform:** Firebase supports multiple platforms, including Android, iOS, and the web.

3.2. Example: Working with Firebase in Python

To interact with Firebase Realtime Database in Python, you can use the firebase-admin SDK.

Example: Interacting with Firebase Realtime Database

```python
import firebase_admin

from firebase_admin import credentials, db


def initialize_firebase():

    cred = credentials.Certificate('path/to/your/firebase-credentials.json')

    firebase_admin.initialize_app(cred, {
```

```python
    'databaseURL': 'https://your-database-
name.firebaseio.com/'
    })


def add_task(title, description):
    ref = db.reference('tasks')
    new_task_ref = ref.push({
        'title': title,
        'description': description
    })
    print(f'Task added with key: {new_task_ref.key}')


def fetch_tasks():
    ref = db.reference('tasks')
    tasks = ref.get()
    for key, value in tasks.items():
        print(f"Task ID: {key}, Title: {value['title']}, Description: {value['description']}")


# Example usage
initialize_firebase()
add_task('Finish report', 'Complete the financial report by end of day')
```

fetch_tasks()

Explanation:

- **Firebase Initialization:** The initialize_firebase function initializes the Firebase app using service account credentials.

- **Adding Data:** The add_task function pushes a new task to the Firebase Realtime Database under the tasks reference.

- **Fetching Data:** The fetch_tasks function retrieves all tasks from the database and prints them.

4. ObjectBox

ObjectBox is another high-performance NoSQL database optimized for mobile and IoT applications. It is known for its speed, simplicity, and small footprint.

4.1. Features of ObjectBox

- **NoSQL Database:** ObjectBox is a NoSQL database that uses objects to store data, similar to Realm.

- **High Performance:** ObjectBox is designed to be extremely fast, offering significant performance advantages on mobile devices.

- **Cross-Platform Support:** ObjectBox supports multiple platforms, including Android, iOS, and Linux.

- **Lightweight:** It has a small footprint, making it suitable for mobile and embedded devices.

4.2. Example: Working with ObjectBox (Conceptual)

ObjectBox doesn't have direct Python support, but you can understand its usage through its concepts, similar to using a Python ORM.

Example: Conceptual Usage of ObjectBox

```python
# This is a conceptual example and would be implemented
in a supported language like Java or Dart


class Task(Entity):

    id = Id()

    title = String()

    description = String()


def add_task(task_box, title, description):

    task = Task(title=title, description=description)

    task_box.put(task)


def fetch_tasks(task_box):

    tasks = task_box.get_all()

    for task in tasks:

        print(f"Task ID: {task.id}, Title: {task.title},
Description: {task.description}")


# Example usage (conceptual)
```

task_box = TaskBox()

add_task(task_box, 'Finish report', 'Complete the financial report by end of day')

fetch_tasks(task_box)

Explanation:

- **Object-Oriented Data Handling:** Like Realm, ObjectBox handles data as objects. The Task entity represents a data model, and the database operations are performed through task_box.

- **Performance-Focused:** ObjectBox is optimized for speed, making it suitable for mobile applications that require high performance.

Choosing the right database for your mobile application is essential to ensure efficient data management, good performance, and a seamless user experience. SQLite is the most commonly used database due to its simplicity and wide support, but modern alternatives like Realm, Firebase Realtime Database, and ObjectBox offer specific advantages depending on your application's needs. The examples provided in this section demonstrate how to work with these databases in Python-based environments, giving you the tools to manage data effectively in your mobile applications.

Using SQLite with Python:

SQLite is a lightweight, self-contained, serverless database engine that is widely used in mobile applications, desktop software, and even some web applications. It is particularly popular because it is easy to set up, requires minimal configuration, and is fully ACID-compliant, making it reliable for handling data transactions. In this section, we will explore how to use SQLite with Python, covering the basics of setting up a database, executing SQL queries, and performing CRUD (Create, Read, Update, Delete) operations. We will also provide comprehensive examples to illustrate these concepts.

1. Setting Up SQLite in Python

To work with SQLite in Python, you can use the built-in sqlite3 module, which provides an easy-to-use interface for interacting with SQLite databases.

1.1. Connecting to a Database

The first step in working with SQLite is to connect to a database. If the database file does not exist, SQLite will automatically create it.

Example: Connecting to an SQLite Database

```python
import sqlite3


def create_connection(db_name):
    try:
        conn = sqlite3.connect(db_name)
        print(f"Connected to the database: {db_name}")
        return conn
    except sqlite3.Error as e:
        print(f"Error connecting to database: {e}")
```

```
    return None
```

Example usage

```
conn = create_connection('example.db')
```

Explanation:

- **sqlite3.connect():** This function attempts to establish a connection to the specified database file (example.db). If the file does not exist, it will be created.

- **Error Handling:** The try-except block catches any connection errors and prints them.

2. Creating and Managing Tables

Once connected to the database, you can create tables to store data. Tables in SQLite are created using SQL CREATE TABLE statements.

2.1. Creating a Table

You can define a table with various columns, specifying the data type for each column.

Example: Creating a Table in SQLite

```
def create_table(conn):

    try:

        sql = '''

        CREATE TABLE IF NOT EXISTS users (

            id INTEGER PRIMARY KEY AUTOINCREMENT,
```

```
        name TEXT NOT NULL,

        age INTEGER,

        email TEXT UNIQUE

    )

    """

    conn.execute(sql)

    print("Table 'users' created successfully.")
except sqlite3.Error as e:

    print(f"Error creating table: {e}")


# Example usage
create_table(conn)
```

Explanation:

- **CREATE TABLE IF NOT EXISTS:** This SQL statement creates a new table named users if it doesn't already exist. The table includes columns for id, name, age, and email.

- **Primary Key:** The id column is set as the primary key and is automatically incremented with each new record.

- **Unique Constraint:** The email column is set to be unique, ensuring that no two users can have the same email address.

3. Performing CRUD Operations

CRUD operations are the fundamental operations that can be performed on database data. They include creating (inserting) data, reading (selecting) data, updating data, and deleting data.

3.1. Inserting Data into a Table

You can insert data into a table using the SQL INSERT INTO statement.

Example: Inserting Data into the Users Table

```python
def insert_user(conn, name, age, email):
    try:
        sql = '''
        INSERT INTO users (name, age, email)
        VALUES (?, ?, ?)
        '''
        conn.execute(sql, (name, age, email))
        conn.commit()  # Save (commit) the changes
        print(f"User {name} added successfully.")
    except sqlite3.Error as e:
        print(f"Error inserting data: {e}")


# Example usage
insert_user(conn, 'Alice', 30, 'alice@example.com')
insert_user(conn, 'Bob', 25, 'bob@example.com')
```

Explanation:

- **Parameterized Queries:** The ? placeholders in the SQL statement are used to safely insert user data, preventing SQL injection attacks.

- **conn.commit():** After inserting data, you must commit the transaction to save the changes to the database.

3.2. Reading Data from a Table

You can retrieve data from a table using the SQL SELECT statement.

Example: Selecting Data from the Users Table

```python
def fetch_users(conn):

    try:

        sql = 'SELECT * FROM users'

        cursor = conn.execute(sql)

        rows = cursor.fetchall()

        for row in rows:

            print(f"ID: {row[0]}, Name: {row[1]}, Age: {row[2]}, Email: {row[3]}")

    except sqlite3.Error as e:

        print(f"Error fetching data: {e}")


# Example usage

fetch_users(conn)
```

Explanation:

- **SELECT :* This SQL statement selects all columns from the users table.

- **fetchall():** The fetchall() method retrieves all rows from the executed query and returns them as a list of tuples.

3.3. Updating Data in a Table

To update existing records in a table, you use the SQL UPDATE statement.

Example: Updating User Data

```python
def update_user_email(conn, user_id, new_email):
    try:
        sql = '''
        UPDATE users
        SET email = ?
        WHERE id = ?
        '''
        conn.execute(sql, (new_email, user_id))
        conn.commit()
        print(f"User ID {user_id}'s email updated to {new_email}.")
    except sqlite3.Error as e:
        print(f"Error updating data: {e}")
```

```
# Example usage
```

```
update_user_email(conn, 1, 'alice.new@example.com')
```

Explanation:

- **UPDATE Statement:** This SQL statement updates the email field for the user with the specified id.

- **WHERE Clause:** The WHERE clause ensures that only the specified record is updated.

3.4. Deleting Data from a Table

To delete records from a table, use the SQL DELETE statement.

Example: Deleting a User

```python
def delete_user(conn, user_id):
    try:
        sql = 'DELETE FROM users WHERE id = ?'
        conn.execute(sql, (user_id,))
        conn.commit()
        print(f"User ID {user_id} deleted successfully.")
    except sqlite3.Error as e:
        print(f"Error deleting data: {e}")
```

```
# Example usage
```

```
delete_user(conn, 2)
```

Explanation:

- **DELETE Statement:** This SQL statement removes the record with the specified id from the users table.

- **conn.commit():** As with inserts and updates, deleting data requires committing the transaction to apply the changes.

4. Advanced SQLite Features

SQLite also supports more advanced features, such as indexing, transactions, and foreign keys, which can help optimize and manage your database effectively.

4.1. Using Indexes to Improve Query Performance

Indexes can be created on columns to speed up query performance, especially on large tables.

Example: Creating an Index on the Email Column

```python
def create_index(conn):
    try:
        sql = 'CREATE INDEX idx_email ON users (email)'
        conn.execute(sql)
        print("Index on 'email' created successfully.")
    except sqlite3.Error as e:
        print(f"Error creating index: {e}")


# Example usage
create_index(conn)
```

Explanation:

- **CREATE INDEX:** This SQL statement creates an index on the email column of the users table, which can improve the speed of queries involving the email field.

4.2. Using Transactions for Batch Operations

Transactions allow you to group multiple SQL operations into a single unit of work that either completes entirely or fails without making partial changes.

Example: Using a Transaction to Insert Multiple Users

```python
def insert_multiple_users(conn, users):
    try:
        with conn:
            sql = 'INSERT INTO users (name, age, email) VALUES (?, ?, ?)'
            conn.executemany(sql, users)
        print("All users added successfully.")
    except sqlite3.Error as e:
        print(f"Error in transaction: {e}")


# Example usage
users = [
    ('Charlie', 28, 'charlie@example.com'),
    ('Diana', 22, 'diana@example.com')
]
```

insert_multiple_users(conn, users)

Explanation:

- **Transaction Management:** Using the with conn: context manager ensures that all operations inside the block are treated as a single transaction. If any operation fails, the entire transaction is rolled back.

- **executemany():** This method allows for batch insertion of multiple rows in a single operation.

5. Closing the Database Connection

It's important to close the database connection once you're done working with the database to free up resources.

Example: Closing the Connection

```python
def close_connection(conn):
    try:
        conn.close()
        print("Connection closed.")
    except sqlite3.Error as e:
        print(f"Error closing connection: {e}")


# Example usage
close_connection(conn)
```

Explanation:

- **conn.close():** This method closes the connection to the SQLite database, ensuring that no resources are left open.

Using SQLite with Python is a powerful and straightforward way to manage data in your applications. Whether you're building a small mobile app or a larger desktop application, SQLite provides a robust and efficient database solution. By mastering the basics of connecting to a database, creating tables, and performing CRUD operations, you can effectively manage your application's data. The examples provided here offer a comprehensive guide to working with SQLite in Python, equipping you with the skills to build reliable and scalable applications.

Object-Relational Mapping (ORM) with SQLAlchemy:

Object-Relational Mapping (ORM) is a programming technique that allows developers to interact with a relational database using an object-oriented approach. ORMs abstract the database interaction by mapping database tables to Python classes, enabling you to work with database records as if they were Python objects. SQLAlchemy is one of the most powerful and popular ORM libraries for Python. It provides both high-level ORM capabilities and low-level database interaction via its SQL Expression Language. This section will explore how to use SQLAlchemy as an ORM, with comprehensive examples to illustrate these concepts.

1. Introduction to SQLAlchemy ORM

SQLAlchemy's ORM allows you to define classes that map to tables in your database. Each instance of the class represents a row in the corresponding table, and class attributes correspond to table columns. This abstraction allows you to work with databases more naturally in an object-oriented way.

1.1. Installing SQLAlchemy

Before using SQLAlchemy, you need to install it using pip.

pip install sqlalchemy

1.2. Basic Concepts

- **Engine:** The core interface to the database, responsible for managing connections.

- **Session:** The ORM's "handle" to the database, allowing you to query and persist data.

- **Declarative Base:** A base class for defining models, which map to database tables.

- **Model:** A class that represents a database table, with class attributes representing table columns.

2. Setting Up SQLAlchemy

To get started with SQLAlchemy, you need to create an engine, a session, and define your models.

2.1. Creating an Engine

The engine connects SQLAlchemy to the database, where all SQL operations are executed.

Example: Creating an Engine

from sqlalchemy import create_engine

Example: SQLite in-memory database

engine = create_engine('sqlite:///:memory:', echo=True)

Explanation:

- **create_engine():** This function creates an engine connected to a database. The sqlite:///:memory: URL creates an SQLite database in memory, which is useful for testing.

- **echo=True:** Setting echo=True enables logging of all SQL statements executed, which is helpful for debugging.

2.2. Creating a Declarative Base

The declarative base is the foundation for your ORM models. It allows you to define classes that represent tables in the database.

Example: Setting Up Declarative Base

from sqlalchemy.ext.declarative import declarative_base

Base = declarative_base()

Explanation:

- **declarative_base():** This function returns a base class from which all ORM models will inherit. This base class provides the foundation for the ORM's mapping.

3. Defining ORM Models

ORM models in SQLAlchemy are Python classes that map to database tables. Each class represents a table, and each class attribute represents a column in that table.

3.1. Defining a Model

Let's define a simple User model representing a users table in the database.

Example: Defining a User Model

```python
from sqlalchemy import Column, Integer, String


class User(Base):
    __tablename__ = 'users'


    id = Column(Integer, primary_key=True)

    name = Column(String, nullable=False)

    age = Column(Integer)

    email = Column(String, unique=True)


    def __repr__(self):
        return f"<User(name={self.name}, age={self.age}, email={self.email})>"
```

Explanation:

- **tablename:** The __tablename__ attribute specifies the name of the table in the database. Here, the class User maps to the users table.

- **Columns:** The Column objects define the table's columns. For example, id is an integer primary key, name is a string that cannot be null, age is an integer, and email is a unique string.

- **repr():** The __repr__ method provides a readable string representation of the object, useful for debugging.

4. Creating Tables

Once the models are defined, you can create the corresponding tables in the database.

4.1. Creating Tables in the Database

SQLAlchemy can automatically generate the necessary SQL statements to create the tables based on your models.

Example: Creating Tables

Base.metadata.create_all(engine)

Explanation:

- **Base.metadata.create_all():** This method inspects all models derived from Base and generates the appropriate CREATE TABLE statements to create the tables in the database.

5. Working with Sessions

The session is the ORM's interface for interacting with the database. It manages the context for all operations you perform with your ORM models, such as querying, adding, updating, and deleting records.

5.1. Creating a Session

To interact with the database, you need to create a session.

Example: Creating a Session

from sqlalchemy.orm import sessionmaker

Session = sessionmaker(bind=engine)

session = Session()

Explanation:

- **sessionmaker():** This function returns a session factory bound to the specified engine. The session factory can then be used to create sessions.

- **session:** A session object is created from the session factory. This session will be used for all database operations.

6. Performing CRUD Operations with SQLAlchemy

CRUD operations (Create, Read, Update, Delete) are fundamental to interacting with database records. SQLAlchemy ORM makes it easy to perform these operations in an object-oriented manner.

6.1. Creating (Inserting) Records

To add new records to the database, create instances of your models and add them to the session.

Example: Adding Users to the Database

new_user = User(name='Alice', age=30, email='alice@example.com')

session.add(new_user)

session.commit()

Explanation:

- **session.add():** Adds the new User object to the session, marking it for insertion into the database.

- **session.commit():** Commits the current transaction, saving the new user to the database.

6.2. Reading (Querying) Records

To retrieve records from the database, you can use the session's query capabilities.

Example: Querying the Database

users = session.query(User).all()

for user in users:

   print(user)

Explanation:

- **session.query(User):** Creates a query object for the User model.

- **all():** Executes the query and returns all results as a list of User objects.

- **Printing Results:** Iterates over the list of users and prints each one using the __repr__ method defined in the User class.

6.3. Updating Records

To update records, retrieve the object from the database, modify its attributes, and commit the transaction.

Example: Updating a User's Email

user = session.query(User).filter_by(name='Alice').first()

user.email = 'alice.new@example.com'

session.commit()

Explanation:

- **filter_by():** Filters the query by a specific attribute (name='Alice').

- **first():** Retrieves the first matching record from the database.

- **Updating Attributes:** The email attribute of the User object is updated in Python, and session.commit() is called to save the changes to the database.

6.4. Deleting Records

To delete records, retrieve the object and delete it using the session.

Example: Deleting a User

user = session.query(User).filter_by(name='Alice').first()

session.delete(user)

session.commit()

Explanation:

- **session.delete():** Marks the User object for deletion.

- **session.commit():** Commits the transaction, deleting the user from the database.

7. Advanced SQLAlchemy Features

SQLAlchemy ORM also provides advanced features such as relationships, lazy loading, and complex queries, which allow you to handle more complex data models and interactions.

7.1. Defining Relationships

SQLAlchemy allows you to define relationships between tables using the relationship and ForeignKey constructs.

Example: One-to-Many Relationship

```python
from sqlalchemy import ForeignKey

from sqlalchemy.orm import relationship


class Address(Base):

    __tablename__ = 'addresses'


    id = Column(Integer, primary_key=True)

    email = Column(String, nullable=False)

    user_id = Column(Integer, ForeignKey('users.id'))


    user = relationship('User', back_populates='addresses')


User.addresses = relationship('Address',
order_by=Address.id, back_populates='user')
```

Explanation:

- **ForeignKey:** The user_id column in the Address table is a foreign key that references the id column in the users table.

- **relationship:** The relationship() function creates a bidirectional relationship between User and Address. This allows you to access related data easily, such as user.addresses.

7.2. Lazy Loading

SQLAlchemy supports lazy loading, where related objects are loaded only when they are accessed, improving performance.

Example: Lazy Loading Addresses

user = session.query(User).first()

print(user.addresses) # Addresses are loaded when accessed

Explanation:

- **Lazy Loading:** By default, related objects (e.g., addresses) are not loaded when the parent object (e.g., user) is loaded. They are fetched from the database only when accessed, reducing the initial query's load time.

8. Closing the Session

Once you're done with database operations, it's important to close the session to free up resources.

Example: Closing the Session

session.close()

Explanation:

- **session.close():** Closes the session, releasing any connections and resources it holds.

SQLAlchemy's ORM provides a powerful and flexible way to interact with databases in Python. By using ORM, you can abstract the complexities of database interaction and work with your data in an object-oriented manner. From setting up an engine and session to defining models and performing CRUD operations, SQLAlchemy simplifies the process of managing database data. The examples provided here offer a comprehensive guide to using SQLAlchemy ORM, equipping you with the tools to build robust and scalable applications that interact seamlessly with relational databases.

Managing Local Storage and Caching:

In mobile and desktop applications, efficiently managing local storage and caching is crucial for enhancing performance, improving user experience, and ensuring that the application remains responsive even when offline or when network conditions are poor. Local storage allows your application to store data persistently on the device, while caching temporarily stores data to improve access speed and reduce the need for repetitive network requests. This section will explore how to manage local storage and caching in Python applications, with comprehensive examples to illustrate these concepts.

1. Understanding Local Storage and Caching

- **Local Storage:** Local storage refers to the practice of saving data persistently on the device's storage, such as a file system, database, or key-value store. Data stored locally remains available even after the application is closed or the device is restarted.

- **Caching:** Caching involves temporarily storing data that is expensive to fetch or compute, allowing for quicker access in future requests. Caches are typically smaller and less permanent than local storage, and cached data can be cleared when no longer needed.

2. Managing Local Storage with SQLite

SQLite is a powerful and lightweight database engine that is often used for managing local storage in applications. It allows you to store structured data in a relational format.

2.1. Example: Storing User Preferences in SQLite

Let's consider an example where user preferences are stored in an SQLite database. These preferences can include settings like theme, language, and notification preferences.

Example: Managing User Preferences with SQLite

```python
import sqlite3

def create_connection(db_name):
    return sqlite3.connect(db_name)

def create_table(conn):
    sql = '''
    CREATE TABLE IF NOT EXISTS preferences (
        id INTEGER PRIMARY KEY AUTOINCREMENT,
        setting_name TEXT UNIQUE NOT NULL,
        setting_value TEXT NOT NULL
```

```python
    )
    '''

    conn.execute(sql)

    conn.commit()


def set_preference(conn, name, value):

    sql = '''

    INSERT INTO preferences (setting_name,
setting_value)

    VALUES (?, ?)

    ON CONFLICT(setting_name) DO UPDATE SET
setting_value=excluded.setting_value

    '''

    conn.execute(sql, (name, value))

    conn.commit()


def get_preference(conn, name):

    sql = 'SELECT setting_value FROM preferences
WHERE setting_name = ?'

    cursor = conn.execute(sql, (name,))

    result = cursor.fetchone()

    return result[0] if result else None
```

```python
# Example usage

conn = create_connection('app_settings.db')

create_table(conn)

set_preference(conn, 'theme', 'dark')

set_preference(conn, 'language', 'en')


theme = get_preference(conn, 'theme')

print(f"The current theme is: {theme}")
```

Explanation:

- **Local Storage:** User preferences are stored persistently in the SQLite database, ensuring that they are retained across sessions.

- **Upsert Operation:** The ON CONFLICT clause allows for an upsert operation, meaning that if a preference already exists, its value is updated; otherwise, it is inserted.

3. Implementing Caching with Python

Caching can be implemented in various ways, depending on the data's nature and the application's needs. In Python, caching can be done using in-memory structures, local files, or dedicated caching libraries like cachetools.

3.1. Example: Simple In-Memory Caching

In-memory caching is the simplest form of caching, where data is stored in memory for fast access. This method is ideal for small datasets that are frequently accessed.

Example: In-Memory Caching Using a Dictionary

```python
class SimpleCache:
    def __init__(self):
        self.cache = {}

    def set(self, key, value):
        self.cache[key] = value

    def get(self, key):
        return self.cache.get(key)

    def clear(self):
        self.cache.clear()


# Example usage
cache = SimpleCache()
cache.set('user_data', {'name': 'Alice', 'age': 30})
user_data = cache.get('user_data')
print(f"Cached user data: {user_data}")
```

Explanation:

- **In-Memory Cache:** A dictionary is used to store key-value pairs in memory, providing quick access to cached data.

- **Cache Access:** The get method retrieves data from the cache if it exists, otherwise returning None.

3.2. Example: File-Based Caching

File-based caching involves saving data to local files, allowing for larger or more complex data structures to be cached persistently.

Example: File-Based Caching Using JSON

```python
import json

import os


class FileCache:

    def __init__(self, cache_dir='cache'):

        self.cache_dir = cache_dir

        os.makedirs(self.cache_dir, exist_ok=True)


    def _get_cache_path(self, key):

        return os.path.join(self.cache_dir, f"{key}.json")


    def set(self, key, value):

        path = self._get_cache_path(key)

        with open(path, 'w') as f:

            json.dump(value, f)
```

```python
    def get(self, key):
        path = self._get_cache_path(key)
        if os.path.exists(path):
            with open(path, 'r') as f:
                return json.load(f)
        return None
    def clear(self):
        for filename in os.listdir(self.cache_dir):
            file_path = os.path.join(self.cache_dir, filename)
            if os.path.isfile(file_path):
                os.unlink(file_path)


# Example usage
cache = FileCache()
cache.set('user_data', {'name': 'Alice', 'age': 30})
user_data = cache.get('user_data')
print(f"File-cached user data: {user_data}")
```

Explanation:

- **File-Based Cache:** Data is serialized to JSON and stored in a local file, allowing for persistent caching across sessions.

- **Cache Path Management:** The _get_cache_path method ensures that each cached item is stored in a uniquely named file based on the key.

3.3. Example: Caching with cachetools

The cachetools library provides more advanced caching strategies, including time-based expiration and least-recently-used (LRU) caching.

Example: Using cachetools for Time-Based Caching

```python
from cachetools import TTLCache


# Create a cache with a max size of 100 items and a time-to-live of 300 seconds (5 minutes)
cache = TTLCache(maxsize=100, ttl=300)


# Set cache items
cache['user_data'] = {'name': 'Alice', 'age': 30}


# Access cache items
user_data = cache.get('user_data')
print(f"Cached user data (with TTL): {user_data}")
```

Explanation:

- **TTLCache:** The TTLCache class implements a cache with a time-to-live (TTL) for each item, automatically removing items after they expire.

- **Size Limitation:** The maxsize parameter limits the cache size, with the oldest items being evicted when the cache reaches its limit.

4. Combining Local Storage and Caching

In some scenarios, you may want to combine local storage with caching to optimize data access. For example, frequently accessed data can be stored in memory for quick retrieval, while less frequently accessed data can be stored on disk or in a database.

4.1. Example: Hybrid Caching with Fallback to SQLite

Let's implement a hybrid approach where data is first checked in an in-memory cache and, if not found, retrieved from SQLite and then cached.

Example: Hybrid Caching with SQLite and In-Memory Cache

```python
class HybridCache:

    dcf __init__(self, db_name='app_data.db'):

        self.conn = sqlite3.connect(db_name)

        self.memory_cache = SimpleCache()

        self.create_table()


    def create_table(self):

        sql = '''

        CREATE TABLE IF NOT EXISTS data_cache (

            key TEXT PRIMARY KEY,
```

```python
        value TEXT
    )
    '''

    self.conn.execute(sql)
    self.conn.commit()

def set(self, key, value):
    # Store in memory cache
    self.memory_cache.set(key, value)
    # Store in SQLite
    sql = '''
    INSERT INTO data_cache (key, value)
    VALUES (?, ?)
    ON CONFLICT(key) DO UPDATE SET value=excluded.value
    '''

    self.conn.execute(sql, (key, json.dumps(value)))
    self.conn.commit()

def get(self, key):
    # Check memory cache first
    value = self.memory_cache.get(key)
```

```python
        if value is not None:

            return value

        # Fallback to SQLite

        sql = 'SELECT value FROM data_cache WHERE key = ?'

        cursor = self.conn.execute(sql, (key,))

        result = cursor.fetchone()

        if result:

            value = json.loads(result[0])

            # Cache in memory for future access

            self.memory_cache.set(key, value)

            return value

        return None


# Example usage

hybrid_cache = HybridCache()

hybrid_cache.set('user_data', {'name': 'Alice', 'age': 30})


# First access (from cache)

user_data = hybrid_cache.get('user_data')

print(f"Hybrid cached user data (first access): {user_data}")
```

```python
# Second access (from memory cache)

user_data = hybrid_cache.get('user_data')

print(f"Hybrid cached user data (second access): {user_data}")
```

Explanation:

- **Hybrid Cache:** Data is first checked in the in-memory cache. If not found, it is retrieved from SQLite, then cached in memory for faster future access.

- **Fallback Mechanism:** The approach ensures that data is quickly accessible from memory when possible, but still persistently stored in SQLite.

5. Clearing Cache and Managing Expiration

Effective cache management involves periodically clearing outdated or unnecessary data to free up resources and ensure the cache remains efficient.

5.1. Example: Clearing Cache Automatically

In the case of TTL-based caches, data expiration is handled automatically, but for manual caches, you might need to implement cache clearing logic.

Example: Clearing Cache Based on Custom Criteria

```python
class AutoClearingCache(SimpleCache):
    def clear_expired(self, expiration_time):
        current_time = time.time()
```

```python
    keys_to_clear = [key for key, (_, timestamp) in
self.cache.items() if current_time - timestamp >
expiration_time]

    for key in keys_to_clear:

        del self.cache[key]


# Example usage

import time


cache = AutoClearingCache()

cache.set('user_data', {'name': 'Alice', 'age': 30})

time.sleep(2)  # Simulate passage of time

cache.clear_expired(1)  # Clear items older than 1 second


user_data = cache.get('user_data')

print(f"Cache after clearing expired items: {user_data}")
```

Explanation:

- **Custom Expiration Logic:** The clear_expired method checks each cache item's timestamp and clears items that have exceeded the specified expiration time.

- **Manual Cache Management:** This approach gives you control over when and how cache items are cleared, which is useful for scenarios with specific expiration requirements.

Conclusion

Managing local storage and caching is vital for building efficient and responsive applications. By leveraging tools like SQLite for persistent storage and in-memory or file-based caching for fast data access, you can significantly improve your application's performance and user experience. Whether you need to store user preferences, cache frequently accessed data, or implement a hybrid approach, the examples provided in this section offer a comprehensive guide to managing local storage and caching in Python-based applications. These techniques ensure that your application can handle data effectively, even in environments with limited or unreliable network connectivity.

Chapter 12: Implementing Navigation and Routing

Navigation Patterns in Mobile Apps:

Navigation is a critical aspect of mobile app development that directly impacts user experience. A well-designed navigation system helps users move seamlessly between different parts of the application, making it easier for them to find and interact with the content they need. Various navigation patterns can be implemented in mobile apps, each suited to different types of applications and user needs. In this section, we will explore common navigation patterns used in mobile apps, including examples and code to demonstrate how to implement them in Python-based mobile frameworks such as Kivy and BeeWare.

1. Stack Navigation

Stack navigation is one of the most common navigation patterns in mobile apps. It operates like a stack of cards where each screen is pushed onto the stack when navigated to, and popped off when the user navigates back. This pattern is ideal for workflows where users need to progress through a series of screens, such as forms or step-by-step guides.

1.1. Implementing Stack Navigation in Kivy

In Kivy, you can implement stack navigation using the ScreenManager widget, which manages multiple screens.

Example: Stack Navigation with ScreenManager

```
from kivy.app import App
```

```python
from kivy.uix.screenmanager import ScreenManager,
Screen, SlideTransition

from kivy.uix.button import Button

from kivy.uix.boxlayout import BoxLayout


class HomeScreen(Screen):
    def __init__(self, **kwargs):
        super().__init__(**kwargs)
        layout = BoxLayout(orientation='vertical')
        layout.add_widget(Button(text="Go to Details",
on_press=self.go_to_details))
        self.add_widget(layout)


    def go_to_details(self, instance):
        self.manager.transition =
SlideTransition(direction="left")
        self.manager.current = 'details'


class DetailsScreen(Screen):
    def __init__(self, **kwargs):
        super().__init__(**kwargs)
        layout = BoxLayout(orientation='vertical')
```

```python
        layout.add_widget(Button(text="Go Back",
on_press=self.go_back))

        self.add_widget(layout)


    def go_back(self, instance):

        self.manager.transition =
SlideTransition(direction="right")

        self.manager.current = 'home'


class MyApp(App):

    def build(self):

        sm = ScreenManager()

        sm.add_widget(HomeScreen(name='home'))

        sm.add_widget(DetailsScreen(name='details'))

        return sm


if __name__ == '__main__':

    MyApp().run()
```

Explanation:

- **TabbedPanel:** The TabbedPanel widget provides a set of tabs that users can switch between. Each tab contains its own content, such as buttons, labels, or other widgets.

- **Default Tab:** The default_tab_text sets the label for the initial tab, and default_tab_content specifies the content shown when the app starts.

3. Drawer Navigation

Drawer navigation is a pattern where a hidden panel, usually located at the side of the screen, can be revealed by swiping or tapping a menu icon. This panel typically contains navigation links to different sections of the app.

3.1. Implementing Drawer Navigation in Kivy

While Kivy does not have a native drawer widget, you can create a custom drawer using a combination of layouts and animations.

Example: Custom Drawer Navigation

```python
from kivy.app import App

from kivy.uix.boxlayout import BoxLayout

from kivy.uix.button import Button

from kivy.uix.label import Label

from kivy.uix.screenmanager import ScreenManager,
Screen

from kivy.animation import Animation


class DrawerMenu(BoxLayout):

    def __init__(self, sm, **kwargs):

        super().__init__(**kwargs)

        self.orientation = 'vertical'
```

```python
        self.sm = sm
        self.add_widget(Button(text="Home",
on_press=self.go_to_home))
        self.add_widget(Button(text="Settings",
on_press=self.go_to_settings))

    def go_to_home(self, instance):
        self.sm.current = 'home'
        self.toggle_drawer()

    def go_to_settings(self, instance):
        self.sm.current = 'settings'
        self.toggle_drawer()

    def toggle_drawer(self):
        if self.pos_hint == {'x': -0.8}:
            anim = Animation(x=0, d=0.3)
        else:
            anim = Animation(x=-0.8, d=0.3)
        anim.start(self)


class HomeScreen(Screen):
    pass
```

```python
class SettingsScreen(Screen):
    pass


class MyApp(App):
    def build(self):
        root = BoxLayout()
        sm = ScreenManager()
        sm.add_widget(HomeScreen(name='home'))
        sm.add_widget(SettingsScreen(name='settings'))

        drawer = DrawerMenu(sm, size_hint_x=0.8,
pos_hint={'x': -0.8})

        root.add_widget(drawer)
        root.add_widget(sm)

        menu_button = Button(text='Menu', size_hint=(None,
None), size=(80, 50), pos=(0, 0))
        menu_button.bind(on_press=lambda x:
drawer.toggle_drawer())
        root.add_widget(menu_button)
```

```
    return root


if __name__ == '__main__':

    MyApp().run()
```

Explanation:

- **DrawerMenu:** A custom BoxLayout is used to create the drawer, which contains buttons to navigate between screens.

- **Animation:** The Animation class is used to smoothly slide the drawer in and out when toggled.

- **Toggle Drawer:** The toggle_drawer method checks the current position of the drawer and moves it accordingly.

4. Bottom Navigation

Bottom navigation is commonly used in mobile apps to allow users to switch between different sections of the app using a bar at the bottom of the screen. Each item in the bar corresponds to a different screen.

4.1. Implementing Bottom Navigation in Kivy

Bottom navigation can be implemented using a combination of layouts to create a navigation bar.

Example: Bottom Navigation with BoxLayout

```
from kivy.app import App

from kivy.uix.boxlayout import BoxLayout

from kivy.uix.button import Button
```

```python
from kivy.uix.screenmanager import ScreenManager,
Screen

class HomeScreen(Screen):

    pass

class SettingsScreen(Screen):

    pass

class ProfileScreen(Screen):

    pass

class BottomNavBar(BoxLayout):

    def __init__(self, sm, **kwargs):

        super().__init__(**kwargs)

        self.orientation = 'horizontal'

        self.sm = sm

        self.add_widget(Button(text='Home',
on_press=self.go_to_home))

        self.add_widget(Button(text='Settings',
on_press=self.go_to_settings))

        self.add_widget(Button(text='Profile',
on_press=self.go_to_profile))

    def go_to_home(self, instance):

        self.sm.current = 'home'

    def go_to_settings(self, instance):

        self.sm.current = 'settings'
```

```python
    def go_to_profile(self, instance):
        self.sm.current = 'profile'
class MyApp(App):
    def build(self):
        root = BoxLayout(orientation='vertical')
            sm = ScreenManager()
        sm.add_widget(HomeScreen(name='home'))
        sm.add_widget(SettingsScreen(name='settings'))
        sm.add_widget(ProfileScreen(name='profile'))
            nav_bar = BottomNavBar(sm, size_hint_y=0.1)
        root.add_widget(sm)
        root.add_widget(nav_bar)
        return root
if __name__ == '__main__':
    MyApp().run()
```

Explanation:

- **BottomNavBar:** A custom BoxLayout creates a horizontal navigation bar with buttons to switch between different screens.

- **ScreenManager:** Manages the different screens in the app, allowing users to navigate between them by tapping the buttons in the bottom navigation bar.

5. Deep Linking and Navigation

Deep linking is a navigation pattern that allows users to navigate to a specific screen or piece of content in the app directly from an external source, such as a URL or a notification.

5.1. Implementing Deep Linking in Kivy

While Kivy doesn't natively support deep linking, you can simulate this functionality by setting up routes that the app can navigate to based on a command or input.

Example: Simulating Deep Linking with Commands

```python
from kivy.app import App

from kivy.uix.screenmanager import import ScreenManager, Screen

from kivy.uix.boxlayout import BoxLayout

from kivy.uix.textinput import TextInput

from kivy.uix.button import Button

class HomeScreen(Screen):
    pass

class DetailsScreen(Screen):
    pass

class MyApp(App):
    def build(self):
        sm = ScreenManager()

        sm.add_widget(HomeScreen(name='home'))
```

```python
        sm.add_widget(DetailsScreen(name='details'))

        root = BoxLayout(orientation='vertical')

        command_input = TextInput(hint_text='Enter
command (e.g., go to details)', size_hint_y=0.1)

        navigate_button = Button(text='Navigate',
size_hint_y=0.1)


        def navigate(instance):

            command = command_input.text.strip().lower()

            if command == 'go to details':

                sm.current = 'details'

            elif command == 'go to home':

                sm.current = 'home'


        navigate_button.bind(on_press=navigate)

        root.add_widget(command_input)

        root.add_widget(navigate_button)

        root.add_widget(sm)


        return root


if __name__ == '__main__':

    MyApp().run()
```

Explanation:

- **Simulated Deep Linking:** The command_input text box allows users to type a command, which the app interprets to navigate to the corresponding screen.

- **Custom Navigation Logic:** The navigate function checks the input command and navigates to the appropriate screen using the ScreenManager.

Navigation patterns are essential for guiding users through your mobile application and ensuring a smooth and intuitive user experience. Whether you choose stack navigation, tab navigation, drawer navigation, or bottom navigation, each pattern has its unique advantages and is suited to different types of applications. By implementing these patterns with frameworks like Kivy, you can build powerful, user-friendly mobile apps that provide a seamless navigation experience. The examples provided in this section demonstrate how to implement these navigation patterns in Python, giving you the tools to create well-structured and navigable applications.

Managing Multiple Screens and Views:

In mobile and desktop applications, managing multiple screens and views is crucial for creating a seamless and intuitive user experience. Applications often require the ability to navigate between different screens, such as a home screen, settings screen, detail views, and more. Managing these screens efficiently involves not only switching between them but also ensuring that the application's state is maintained, transitions are smooth, and the user can navigate intuitively. This section explores how to manage multiple screens and views using Python-based frameworks like Kivy, including comprehensive examples.

1. Understanding Screen Management

Screen management is the process of handling the navigation between different screens or views within an application. In frameworks like Kivy, the ScreenManager class is used to manage multiple screens. Each screen is represented as a separate class, and ScreenManager controls which screen is currently displayed.

2. Setting Up Multiple Screens in Kivy

Kivy provides the ScreenManager and Screen classes to manage multiple screens. Each screen is a subclass of the Screen class, and the ScreenManager switches between these screens.

2.1. Basic Example of Screen Management

Let's start with a basic example where we have two screens: a Home screen and a Settings screen. Users can navigate between these screens using buttons.

Example: Basic Screen Management in Kivy

```python
from kivy.app import App

from kivy.uix.screenmanager import ScreenManager, Screen

from kivy.uix.boxlayout import BoxLayout

from kivy.uix.button import Button

class HomeScreen(Screen):

    def __init__(self, **kwargs):
```

```python
        super().__init__(**kwargs)

        layout = BoxLayout(orientation='vertical')

        layout.add_widget(Button(text="Go to Settings",
on_press=self.go_to_settings))

        self.add_widget(layout)

    def go_to_settings(self, instance):

        self.manager.current = 'settings'


class SettingsScreen(Screen):

    def __init__(self, **kwargs):

        super().__init__(**kwargs)

        layout = BoxLayout(orientation='vertical')

        layout.add_widget(Button(text="Go Back to Home",
on_press=self.go_to_home))

        self.add_widget(layout)


    def go_to_home(self, instance):

        self.manager.current = 'home'

class MyApp(App):

    def build(self):

        sm = ScreenManager()

        sm.add_widget(HomeScreen(name='home'))

        sm.add_widget(SettingsScreen(name='settings'))
```

```
    return sm

if __name__ == '__main__':

    MyApp().run()
```

Explanation:

- **ScreenManager:** Manages the switching between different screens. The add_widget method adds each screen to the ScreenManager.

- **Screen:** Represents individual screens in the application. The HomeScreen and SettingsScreen classes are subclasses of Screen.

- **Navigating Between Screens:** Buttons are used to switch between screens by setting the current property of the ScreenManager.

3. Advanced Screen Management Techniques

Beyond basic screen switching, more advanced techniques involve handling screen transitions, managing screen states, and passing data between screens.

3.1. Handling Screen Transitions

Screen transitions can be customized to enhance the user experience. Kivy provides several built-in transitions, such as SlideTransition, FadeTransition, and WipeTransition.

Example: Customizing Screen Transitions

```
from kivy.uix.screenmanager import FadeTransition

class MyApp(App):

    def build(self):
```

```python
    sm = ScreenManager(transition=FadeTransition())

    sm.add_widget(HomeScreen(name='home'))

    sm.add_widget(SettingsScreen(name='settings'))

    return sm

if __name__ == '__main__':

    MyApp().run()
```

Explanation:

- **FadeTransition:** This example uses a FadeTransition to smoothly fade between screens. The transition type is specified when creating the ScreenManager.

- **Custom Transitions:** You can choose different transitions based on the user experience you want to create.

3.2. Passing Data Between Screens

Sometimes, you need to pass data between screens. This can be done by setting properties on the ScreenManager or directly on the screens.

Example: Passing Data Between Screens

```python
class HomeScreen(Screen):

    def __init__(self, **kwargs):

        super().__init__(**kwargs)

        layout = BoxLayout(orientation='vertical')

        self.text_input = TextInput(hint_text="Enter some data")
```

```python
        layout.add_widget(self.text_input)
        layout.add_widget(Button(text="Go to Details",
on_press=self.go_to_details))
        self.add_widget(layout)
    def go_to_details(self, instance):

self.manager.get_screen('details').display_data(self.text_input.text)
        self.manager.current = 'details'
class DetailsScreen(Screen):
    def __init__(self, **kwargs):
        super().__init__(**kwargs)
        self.label = Label(text="")
        layout = BoxLayout(orientation='vertical')
        layout.add_widget(self.label)
        layout.add_widget(Button(text="Go Back to Home",
on_press=self.go_to_home))
        self.add_widget(layout)
    def display_data(self, data):
        self.label.text = f"Received: {data}"

    def go_to_home(self, instance):
        self.manager.current = 'home'
```

```python
class MyApp(App):

    def build(self):

        sm = ScreenManager()

        sm.add_widget(HomeScreen(name='home'))

        sm.add_widget(DetailsScreen(name='details'))

        return sm

if __name__ == '__main__':

    MyApp().run()
```

Explanation:

- **Passing Data:** In this example, data entered in the HomeScreen is passed to the DetailsScreen using the display_data method.

- **get_screen():** The get_screen method retrieves the target screen from the ScreenManager, allowing you to call methods or set properties on it.

3.3. Managing Screen State

When dealing with multiple screens, it's important to manage the state of each screen, especially if screens need to maintain their state when the user navigates away and then returns.

Example: Preserving Screen State

```python
class HomeScreen(Screen):

    def __init__(self, **kwargs):
```

```python
        super().__init__(**kwargs)

        self.text_input = TextInput(hint_text="Enter some
data")

        layout = BoxLayout(orientation='vertical')

        layout.add_widget(self.text_input)

        layout.add_widget(Button(text="Go to Details",
on_press=self.go_to_details))

        self.add_widget(layout)

    def go_to_details(self, instance):

self.manager.get_screen('details').display_data(self.text_inp
ut.text)

        self.manager.current = 'details'


class DetailsScreen(Screen):
    def __init__(self, **kwargs):
        super().__init__(**kwargs)

        self.label = Label(text="")

        layout = BoxLayout(orientation='vertical')

        layout.add_widget(self.label)

        layout.add_widget(Button(text="Go Back to Home",
on_press=self.go_to_home))

        self.add_widget(layout)
```

```python
    def display_data(self, data):
        if not self.label.text:
            self.label.text = f"Received: {data}"


    def go_to_home(self, instance):
        self.manager.current = 'home'


class MyApp(App):
    def build(self):
        sm = ScreenManager()
        sm.add_widget(HomeScreen(name='home'))
        sm.add_widget(DetailsScreen(name='details'))
        return sm


if __name__ == '__main__':
    MyApp().run()
```

Explanation:

- **State Management:** The DetailsScreen checks if the label.text is already set before updating it. This ensures that the data is only set once and remains consistent if the user navigates back and forth.

- **Maintaining State:** Proper state management is crucial for ensuring that screens retain their data and

UI state even when the user navigates away and returns.

4. Handling Dynamic Screens

In some applications, you might need to dynamically create screens based on user input or external data. This can be done by programmatically adding screens to the ScreenManager.

4.1. Example: Dynamically Adding Screens

```python
class MyApp(App):
    def build(self):
        sm = ScreenManager()

        # Add a static home screen
        sm.add_widget(HomeScreen(name='home'))

        # Dynamically add detail screens based on user input
        for i in range(5):
            screen_name = f"details_{i}"
            screen = DetailsScreen(name=screen_name)
            screen.display_data(f"Dynamic screen {i}")
            sm.add_widget(screen)
        return sm
```

```python
if __name__ == '__main__':

    MyApp().run()
```

Explanation:

- **Dynamic Screens:** The example dynamically creates and adds multiple DetailsScreen instances to the ScreenManager, each with unique content.

- **Programmatic Control:** You can programmatically control which screens are added based on user input, data from a server, or other dynamic factors.

5. Combining Navigation Patterns

In complex applications, you might need to combine different navigation patterns, such as stack navigation with tab navigation, or drawer navigation with bottom navigation.

5.1. Example: Combining Stack and Tab Navigation

```python
from kivy.uix.tabbedpanel import TabbedPanel


class MainTabbedPanel(TabbedPanel):
    def __init__(self, **kwargs):
        super().__init__(**kwargs)
        self.default_tab_text = 'Home'
        self.default_tab_content.text = 'This is the Home tab'


sm = ScreenManager()
```

```python
        sm.add_widget(HomeScreen(name='home'))

        sm.add_widget(SettingsScreen(name='settings'))


        self.add_widget(sm)


        # Add additional tabs

        self.add_widget(TabbedPanel(text='Profile',
content=Label(text='This is the Profile tab')))

        self.add_widget(TabbedPanel(text='Help',
content=Label(text='This is the Help tab')))


class MyApp(App):
    def build(self):
        return MainTabbedPanel()


if __name__ == '__main__':
    MyApp().run()
```

Explanation:

- **Combined Navigation:** The example combines a tabbed interface with a screen manager, allowing for stack navigation within the first tab and additional tabs for other sections of the app.

- **Flexible UI Design:** Combining different navigation patterns allows for a more flexible and user-friendly interface, accommodating different use cases within the same app.

Managing multiple screens and views is a fundamental aspect of building complex and user-friendly mobile applications. By leveraging Kivy's ScreenManager and related classes, you can efficiently manage screen transitions, state, and navigation. Whether you need basic screen switching, data passing between screens, or dynamic screen creation, the examples provided in this section offer a comprehensive guide to implementing these features in Python-based mobile apps. Proper screen management ensures a smooth and intuitive user experience, allowing users to navigate your app with ease and confidence.

Implementing Tabbed Navigation and Drawers:

Tabbed navigation and drawers are popular user interface patterns in mobile and desktop applications. They provide a clean and organized way to navigate between different sections or views of an application. Tabbed navigation allows users to switch between different screens by tapping on tabs, while a drawer typically slides in from the side of the screen to reveal additional navigation options. In this section, we'll explore how to implement both tabbed navigation and drawers in a Python-based application using Kivy, complete with examples to illustrate these concepts.

1. Implementing Tabbed Navigation

Tabbed navigation is often used to organize content into multiple categories or sections, allowing users to switch between them easily. Each tab corresponds to a different screen or view, and users can switch between tabs by clicking or tapping on them.

1.1. Basic Tabbed Navigation with Kivy

Kivy's TabbedPanel widget provides a straightforward way to create tabbed navigation. Each tab in a TabbedPanel can contain different content.

Example: Basic Tabbed Navigation in Kivy

```python
from kivy.app import App

from kivy.uix.tabbedpanel import TabbedPanel

from kivy.uix.label import Label

from kivy.uix.boxlayout import BoxLayout

class MyTabbedPanel(TabbedPanel):

    def __init__(self, **kwargs):

        super().__init__(**kwargs)

        self.default_tab_text = 'Home'

        self.default_tab_content = Label(text='This is the Home tab')


        # Adding more tabs

        self.add_widget(BoxLayout())

        self.add_widget(BoxLayout())


        self.ids.tab_container.add_widget(Label(text='Settings Content'))

        self.ids.tab_container.add_widget(Label(text='Profile Content'))
```

```python
class MyApp(App):

    def build(self):

        return MyTabbedPanel()


if __name__ == '__main__':

    MyApp().run()
```

Explanation:

- **TabbedPanel:** The TabbedPanel widget is used to create a tabbed interface. The default_tab_text sets the label for the initial tab, and default_tab_content sets the content for the default tab.

- **Adding Tabs:** Additional tabs are added using the add_widget method. Each tab can contain different content, such as labels, buttons, or other widgets.

2. Implementing a Navigation Drawer

A navigation drawer is a sliding panel that contains navigation links. It typically slides in from the left or right side of the screen and allows users to navigate to different sections of the app. This pattern is commonly used in mobile apps where space is limited.

2.1. Basic Navigation Drawer in Kivy

While Kivy does not have a built-in drawer widget, you can create a custom drawer using a combination of layouts and animations.

Example: Implementing a Simple Navigation Drawer

```python
from kivy.app import App

from kivy.uix.boxlayout import BoxLayout

from kivy.uix.button import Button

from kivy.uix.screenmanager import ScreenManager,
Screen

from kivy.animation import Animation

from kivy.uix.label import Label


class DrawerMenu(BoxLayout):
    def __init__(self, sm, **kwargs):
        super().__init__(**kwargs)
        self.orientation = 'vertical'
        self.sm = sm
        self.add_widget(Button(text="Home",
on_press=self.go_to_home))
        self.add_widget(Button(text="Settings",
on_press=self.go_to_settings))
        self.add_widget(Button(text="Profile",
on_press=self.go_to_profile))


    def go_to_home(self, instance):
        self.sm.current = 'home'
        self.toggle_drawer()
```

```python
    def go_to_settings(self, instance):
        self.sm.current = 'settings'
        self.toggle_drawer()

    def go_to_profile(self, instance):
        self.sm.current = 'profile'
        self.toggle_drawer()

    def toggle_drawer(self):
        if self.pos_hint == {'x': -0.8}:
            anim = Animation(x=0, d=0.3)
        else:
            anim = Animation(x=-0.8, d=0.3)
        anim.start(self)

class HomeScreen(Screen):
    pass

class SettingsScreen(Screen):
    pass
```

```python
class ProfileScreen(Screen):
    pass


class MyApp(App):
    def build(self):

        root = BoxLayout()


        sm = ScreenManager()
        sm.add_widget(HomeScreen(name='home'))
        sm.add_widget(SettingsScreen(name='settings'))
        sm.add_widget(ProfileScreen(name='profile'))


        drawer = DrawerMenu(sm, size_hint_x=0.8,
pos_hint={'x': -0.8})


        root.add_widget(drawer)
        root.add_widget(sm)


        menu_button = Button(text='Menu', size_hint=(None,
None), size=(80, 50), pos=(0, 0))
        menu_button.bind(on_press=lambda x:
drawer.toggle_drawer())
        root.add_widget(menu_button)
```

```
    return root
```

```
if __name__ == '__main__':

    MyApp().run()
```

Explanation:

- **DrawerMenu:** A custom BoxLayout is used to create the drawer. It contains buttons that navigate between different screens in the ScreenManager.

- **Animation:** The Animation class is used to slide the drawer in and out of view. The drawer's position is toggled based on its current state.

- **ScreenManager:** The ScreenManager manages different screens in the application, and the drawer interacts with it to switch between screens.

3. Combining Tabbed Navigation with a Navigation Drawer

In more complex applications, you might want to combine tabbed navigation with a navigation drawer. This setup allows for a more versatile user interface where users can switch between high-level sections using the drawer and between sub-sections within each section using tabs.

3.1. Example: Combining Tabbed Navigation and a Navigation Drawer

```
from kivy.app import App

from kivy.uix.tabbedpanel import TabbedPanel
```

```python
from kivy.uix.boxlayout import BoxLayout

from kivy.uix.screenmanager import ScreenManager,
Screen

from kivy.uix.button import Button

from kivy.animation import Animation

from kivy.uix.label import Label


class DrawerMenu(BoxLayout):
    def __init__(self, sm, **kwargs):
        super().__init__(**kwargs)
        self.orientation = 'vertical'
        self.sm = sm
        self.add_widget(Button(text="Home",
on_press=self.go_to_home))
        self.add_widget(Button(text="Settings",
on_press=self.go_to_settings))
        self.add_widget(Button(text="Profile",
on_press=self.go_to_profile))

    def go_to_home(self, instance):
        self.sm.current = 'home'
        self.toggle_drawer()
```

```python
    def go_to_settings(self, instance):
        self.sm.current = 'settings'
        self.toggle_drawer()

    def go_to_profile(self, instance):
        self.sm.current = 'profile'
        self.toggle_drawer()

    def toggle_drawer(self):
        if self.pos_hint == {'x': -0.8}:
            anim = Animation(x=0, d=0.3)
        else:
            anim = Animation(x=-0.8, d=0.3)
        anim.start(self)

class TabbedScreen(Screen):
    def __init__(self, **kwargs):
        super().__init__(**kwargs)
        self.add_widget(MyTabbedPanel())

class MyTabbedPanel(TabbedPanel):
    def __init__(self, **kwargs):
```

```python
        super().__init__(**kwargs)

        self.default_tab_text = 'Overview'

        self.default_tab_content = Label(text='This is the
Overview tab')


        self.add_widget(Label(text='Details',
content=Label(text='This is the Details tab')))

        self.add_widget(Label(text='Statistics',
content=Label(text='This is the Statistics tab')))


class MyApp(App):

    def build(self):

        root = BoxLayout()


        sm = ScreenManager()

        sm.add_widget(TabbedScreen(name='home'))

        sm.add_widget(SettingsScreen(name='settings'))

        sm.add_widget(ProfileScreen(name='profile'))


        drawer = DrawerMenu(sm, size_hint_x=0.8,
pos_hint={'x': -0.8})


        root.add_widget(drawer)
```

```python
        root.add_widget(sm)


        menu_button = Button(text='Menu', size_hint=(None,
None), size=(80, 50), pos=(0, 0))

        menu_button.bind(on_press=lambda x:
drawer.toggle_drawer())

        root.add_widget(menu_button)


        return root


if __name__ == '__main__':

    MyApp().run()
```

Explanation:

- **TabbedScreen:** A custom screen that contains a
  TabbedPanel. This screen is added to the
  ScreenManager, making it accessible through the
  drawer menu.

- **Combining Navigation Patterns:** The example
  combines a ScreenManager for high-level
  navigation (using the drawer) with a TabbedPanel
  for detailed navigation within a section.

- **Menu Integration:** The drawer menu can be used
  to switch between the tabbed screen and other
  screens like settings and profile, providing a
  comprehensive navigation solution.

Implementing tabbed navigation and drawers in a mobile or desktop application enhances the user experience by organizing content into manageable sections and providing easy access to different parts of the app. By using Kivy's TabbedPanel for tabs and creating a custom drawer for navigation, you can build flexible and intuitive interfaces that meet the needs of your users. The examples provided in this section demonstrate how to implement these navigation patterns effectively, allowing you to create applications with robust and user-friendly navigation structures.

Deep Linking and URL Routing:

Deep linking and URL routing are essential for building modern applications, especially those that are part of a larger web or mobile ecosystem. Deep linking allows users to navigate directly to a specific page or screen within an application using a URL, rather than starting from the home screen and manually navigating through the app. This functionality is particularly useful for sharing content, handling external links, or resuming activity in a multi-screen application. URL routing provides the mechanism to interpret these URLs and navigate to the corresponding views within the application. In this section, we will explore how to implement deep linking and URL routing in Python-based applications using frameworks like Flask (for web applications) and how similar concepts can be adapted for mobile applications using Kivy.

1. Understanding Deep Linking and URL Routing

- **Deep Linking:** Refers to the practice of using a URL to link directly to a specific page or resource within an app, rather than just the homepage. In mobile apps, deep links can open the app directly to a particular screen, while in web apps, deep links navigate to specific routes.

- **URL Routing:** URL routing is the process of mapping URLs to specific actions or views in your application. It allows the application to respond to different URLs by rendering the appropriate content.

2. Implementing URL Routing in a Web Application

For web applications built with Python, frameworks like Flask are commonly used to handle URL routing. Flask provides decorators to map URLs to specific functions that render views or return data.

2.1. Basic URL Routing with Flask

Example: Implementing Basic URL Routing in Flask

```python
from flask import Flask, render_template


app = Flask(__name__)


@app.route('/')
def home():
    return render_template('home.html')


@app.route('/about')
```

```python
def about():

    return render_template('about.html')


@app.route('/profile/<username>')

def profile(username):

    return render_template('profile.html',
username=username)


if __name__ == '__main__':

    app.run(debug=True)
```

Explanation:

- **Flask Application:** The Flask application is created and routes are defined using the @app.route decorator.

- **Home Route:** The / route maps to the home function, which renders the home.html template.

- **Dynamic Route:** The /profile/<username> route accepts a dynamic segment (<username>) and passes it to the profile function, which then renders the profile.html template with the username context.

3. Implementing Deep Linking in Mobile Applications

In mobile applications, deep linking allows users to open the app directly to a specific screen based on the URL they clicked or the intent they received. This is particularly useful for handling push notifications, email links, or QR codes.

3.1. Handling Deep Linking in Kivy Applications

While Kivy is not inherently web-based and does not have a direct equivalent to Flask's URL routing, you can still implement deep linking by processing URLs or intents passed to the application when it is launched.

Example: Simulating Deep Linking in Kivy

```python
from kivy.app import App

from kivy.uix.screenmanager import ScreenManager, Screen

from kivy.uix.boxlayout import BoxLayout

from kivy.uix.label import Label


class HomeScreen(Screen):
    pass


class ProfileScreen(Screen):
    def __init__(self, username='', **kwargs):
        super().__init__(**kwargs)
        self.username = username
        self.layout = BoxLayout(orientation='vertical')
        self.label = Label(text=f"Profile of {self.username}")
        self.layout.add_widget(self.label)
        self.add_widget(self.layout)
```

```python
    def set_username(self, username):
        self.username = username
        self.label.text = f"Profile of {self.username}"


class MyApp(App):
    def build(self):
        sm = ScreenManager()
        self.sm = sm
        sm.add_widget(HomeScreen(name='home'))
        sm.add_widget(ProfileScreen(name='profile'))
        return sm


    def on_start(self):
        # Simulating deep link handling
        deep_link_url = 'myapp://profile/Alice'
        self.handle_deep_link(deep_link_url)


    def handle_deep_link(self, url):
        # Parse the URL to determine the screen and any parameters
        if 'profile' in url:
```

```
username = url.split('/')[-1]

profile_screen = self.sm.get_screen('profile')

profile_screen.set_username(username)

self.sm.current = 'profile'


if __name__ == '__main__':

    MyApp().run()
```

Explanation:

- **Simulating Deep Linking:** The on_start method simulates receiving a deep link URL when the app starts. The handle_deep_link method processes the URL and navigates to the appropriate screen.

- **ScreenManager:** The ScreenManager handles switching between different screens. When a deep link is detected, it sets the current screen to the appropriate view (e.g., ProfileScreen).

- **Dynamic Content:** The ProfileScreen dynamically updates its content based on the username extracted from the URL.

4. Advanced URL Routing with Flask

In more complex applications, URL routing may involve handling different HTTP methods (GET, POST), handling query parameters, and returning various response types (HTML, JSON, etc.).

4.1. Example: Advanced URL Routing in Flask

Example: Handling Different Methods and Query Parameters

```python
from flask import Flask, request, jsonify, render_template


app = Flask(__name__)


@app.route('/profile/<username>', methods=['GET', 'POST'])
def profile(username):
    if request.method == 'GET':
        return render_template('profile.html', username=username)
    elif request.method == 'POST':
        data = request.form
        # Process form data and update profile
        return jsonify({"message": "Profile updated", "username": username})


@app.route('/search')
def search():
    query = request.args.get('q')
    # Perform search logic
    return render_template('search_results.html', query=query)
```

```
if __name__ == '__main__':

    app.run(debug=True)
```

Explanation:

- **Handling Multiple Methods:** The profile route handles both GET and POST requests, allowing users to view and update profiles through the same URL.

- **Query Parameters:** The search route handles query parameters passed in the URL (e.g., /search?q=example). The request.args.get method extracts these parameters.

5. Integrating Deep Linking with Web-Based URL Routing

For web applications, you can combine deep linking with traditional URL routing by using tools like Flask or Django to handle the URLs and provide specific routes for different resources or screens.

5.1. Example: Deep Linking in a Flask Web Application

Example: Combining Deep Linking with Flask Routing

```
from flask import Flask, redirect, url_for


app = Flask(__name__)


@app.route('/')
```

```python
def home():
    return '<h1>Welcome to the Home Page</h1>'


@app.route('/go_to/<path:url>')
def go_to(url):
    if url.startswith('profile/'):
        username = url.split('/')[-1]
        return redirect(url_for('profile', username=username))
    elif url.startswith('search/'):
        query = url.split('/')[-1]
        return redirect(url_for('search', q=query))
    else:
        return '<h1>Page not found</h1>', 404


@app.route('/profile/<username>')
def profile(username):
    return f'<h1>Profile page of {username}</h1>'


@app.route('/search')
def search():
    query = request.args.get('q')
    return f'<h1>Search Results for: {query}</h1>'
```

```
if __name__ == '__main__':

    app.run(debug=True)
```

Explanation:

- **Dynamic Routing with go_to:** The /go_to/<path:url> route dynamically interprets the provided URL and redirects to the appropriate route in the application (e.g., profile or search).

- **Redirects:** The redirect function, combined with url_for, navigates the user to the correct view based on the parsed URL.

6. Handling Edge Cases and Errors in Deep Linking

When implementing deep linking, it's essential to handle edge cases, such as invalid URLs, missing data, or the app being opened with an unrecognized deep link.

6.1. Example: Handling Invalid URLs and Errors

Example: Adding Error Handling in Kivy

```python
class MyApp(App):

    def build(self):

        sm = ScreenManager()

        self.sm = sm

        sm.add_widget(HomeScreen(name='home'))

        sm.add_widget(ProfileScreen(name='profile'))

        return sm
```

```python
    def on_start(self):
        # Simulating deep link handling with an invalid URL
        deep_link_url = 'myapp://profile/'
        try:
            self.handle_deep_link(deep_link_url)
        except ValueError as e:
            print(f"Error: {e}")
            self.sm.current = 'home'

    def handle_deep_link(self, url):
        if 'profile' in url:
            try:
                username = url.split('/')[-1]
                if not username:
                    raise ValueError("Invalid URL: Missing username")
                profile_screen = self.sm.get_screen('profile')
                profile_screen.set_username(username)
                self.sm.current = 'profile'
            except IndexError:
                raise ValueError("Invalid URL: Could not parse username")
```

```
    else:

        raise ValueError("Invalid URL: No matching route
found")



if __name__ == '__main__':

    MyApp().run()
```

Explanation:

- **Error Handling:** The handle_deep_link method includes error handling to manage cases where the deep link is incomplete or incorrectly formatted.

- **Fallback Navigation:** If an error occurs while handling the deep link, the app defaults back to the home screen.

Conclusion

Deep linking and URL routing are powerful tools for enhancing navigation in both web and mobile applications. By enabling users to jump directly to specific screens or pages using URLs, you can improve the user experience, facilitate content sharing, and integrate your app more seamlessly into broader ecosystems. Whether using Flask for web-based routing or simulating deep linking in a Kivy-based mobile app, the examples provided in this section illustrate the fundamental concepts and techniques for implementing these features effectively in Python applications. By carefully handling URLs and managing edge cases, you can ensure that your app remains robust and user-friendly, regardless of how it is accessed.